# American Glass Bottles

by
Marian Klamkin
with
Charles B. Gardner

Photography by Charles Klamkin

AF530904

Copyright © 1977
Marian Klamkin

ISBN 0-87069-149X
Library of Congress # 76-41433

Wallace-Homestead Book Co.
1912 Grand
Des Moines, Iowa 50305

For Nina

# Contents

## Chapter One

# The Collector

This is the story of one man's collection of American glass bottles, how the collection was started and what it contained after 45 years of unrelenting pursuit of a hobby that now involves thousands of Americans and hundreds of bottle collecting clubs all over the country. Charles B. Gardner was known to all those who find old glass bottles a constant source of interest and fascination as the "dean of bottle collectors." He had never made a claim that his collection was the largest or the best, only that it gave him 45 years of pleasure and purpose that he insisted no other hobby could have done.

**Charles B. Gardner with flask made in his honor by the Somers (Connecticut) Bottle (collecting) Club. Flask, made by the Pairpoint Glass Company, Sagamore, Massachusetts, is white opalescent glass. Obverse had portrait of collector and his signature with "Conn's Dean of Antique Bottles" in ribbon above. Below signature is date, "1973." Reverse has seal of Somers Bottle Club.**

For any story it is best to start at the beginning and the Gardner collection does have a definite beginning. Since it included over 3,000 bottles of every type used in American trade since the seventeenth, to the end of the nineteenth century, the obvious question asked Mr. Gardner by the beginning collector was, "How did you start? When did you buy your first bottle?"

In 1934 Charley, as he was known by friends everywhere, was invited to give a talk, the first of many, on bottle collecting and specifically, his own interests in collecting, to a convention of the Early American Glass Club held at Plymouth, Massachusetts. He described the purchase of his first bottle on that occasion:

> At one time I collected guns and later, living up to my name, became an amateur gardener. My attention was first attracted to bottles by a display of colored bottles, arranged in the window of a friend's summer cottage, with a few of the large demijohns scattered about the house. This was in August, 1929. Within a week I had purchased my first bottle, a large bubble of olive green glass holding about five gallons. I then began to attend the nearby auctions and to comb the shops within a radius of 50 miles, buying practically all the bottles bearing a pontil mark that came within the range of my pocket-book. My first flask was a Horn of Plenty for which I paid $3.

That first cornucopia flask was really the beginning of one of the most important collections of American historical flasks ever gathered under one roof. Charley, who disliked pretentiousness, later said that the couple at whose house he had seen his first antique bottle were "early American buffs" who served their meals and drinks in old pewter. They had "too many spinning wheels" and other antiques crowding their house for his taste, but the early, pontilled bottles really appealed to him. The gun collection and the gardening were forgotten and bottles and the study of their origins took their place.

Charley Gardener was in a good position in his working life to add to his rapidly growing collection and to justify long hours spent at glass and bottle auctions throughout New England. He was in the moving and storage business and his frequent attendance at auctions made him known to auctioneers and their clients who had need of his services for careful packing and handling as well as storage of antiques. He acquired a lot of knowledge of antiques of all kinds and this became very helpful to him in his work. Eventually the Gardner Moving and Storage Company became known for its careful handling of fine antiques and auction attendees often asked for its services when they had to have newly acquired antiques moved long distances. In this manner Charles Gardner could combine his vocation and his avocation.

One of the many advantages enjoyed by Charley in connection with his hobby in the early days was the necessity for research and study of American history that is mandatory for any serious collector of antiques. Shortly after he had acquired his first historical flask he realized that he knew little about the history of glass-making in this country and decided to try to find out all that he could:

> Having read all the books in the local library on the subject of early American glass, I began to collect a library of my own. Naturally, the first book I purchased was Stephen Van Rensselaer's so-called "Bottle Bible" which contains some thousands of illustrations of bottles and flasks. This book will invariably fill the new collector with enthusiasm to match every illustration therein. Edwin A. Barber's *American Glassware* is the first book published on old bottles and is most interesting. Perhaps the glass collectors in general still appreciate more than any other book on the subject, Rhea Mansfield Knittle's *Early American Glass,* which is very easy to understand and covers the subject very thoroughly. Laura Woodside Watkins devotes a chapter of her *Cambridge Glass* to bottles.
>
> *Old Glass, European and American* by N. Hudson Moore also contains a world of information on the subject. Mary Harrod Northend devotes part of her book *American Glass* to the bottle manufacturing phase of glassmaking. The *Saturday Evening Post* of October 19, 1929, contains one of the most interesting articles I have ever read. The title is "Why I Collect Empty Bottles," and the author Edwin LeFevre. I have a number of older books dealing with the compounding and manufacture of glass. My scrap book in which I have arranged all the articles I could possibly collect on the subject of bottles as obtained from *Antiques, Antiquarian, American Collector, Hobbies* and a host of newspaper articles and pamphlets as well as pictures and photographs is helpful.

This then, was the only source material available to the serious bottle collector in the early 1930s. The hobby was relatively new at the time and to collectors of American antique glass, bottles were considered the orphans of the hobby. Most glass collectors preferred to search for tableware and decorative glass and saw no beauty or value in empty bottles. "Cup plates!" said Charley. "Imagine spending all your spare time looking for those silly things."

In those days the bottle collector was pretty much on his own and depended upon the expertise of the few bottle collectors and early glass dealers for advice and guidance. The two most important dealers and collectors in the country at that time were, fortunately for Charley Gardner, in the East. They were Stephen Van Rensselaer and George McKearin. Later, McKearin, with his daughter, Helen, would write the definitive work on American glass, a book which has become the major source of information on all early American glass, including historical flasks and bottles. It was a source of pride to Charley Gardner that some of his bottles were used as illustrations for the McKearin book and that he eventually purchased many other bottles from the McKearin collection to add to his own.

When Charley Gardner began his bottle collection in 1929 the hobby was considered very esoteric and it was limited to the East Coast since that is where most of the early historical flasks were made. Specialized collecting was still in its infancy and the bottle collectors and dealers enjoyed a camaraderie that involved the search for more information than had been previously published and collectors and dealers traded among themselves. Charley, an eager buyer and a man who easily fitted in with the company of other men with whom he had so much in common, found himself with many new friends and his buying trips for bottles became more frequent and successful.

Early in his bottle collecting history Charley became friendly with Stephen Van Rensselaer. "He told me," said Charley, "he was going to make me the biggest bottle collector in the country." This didn't seem to be too much of a challenge, because by that time Charley was hooked. He had the bottle bug and even had there been a cure for it, he wouldn't have taken it. The timing was just right to purchase old historical flasks in some quantity at advantageous prices. During the Depression anyone who owned a few old bottles because they looked pretty on a windowsill was willing to part with them for a dollar or two. There were few people during those years who could afford a hobby of any kind and the handful of expert dealer-collectors that there were were getting on in years. Charley Gardner had the time, the interest and eventually the knowledge that made it possible for him to buy what he wanted with very little competition. His collection continued to grow rapidly and it began to fill the rooms in his New London house.

There isn't any truly dedicated collector who does not buy more than he intends to keep. Although he never considered himself a dealer in the true sense of the word, Charley purchased all worthwhile early bottles and when he found that he had duplicates he eventually began to sell as well as buy. Throughout most of his years of collecting he ran advertisements in collecting magazines offering to purchase all historical flasks and other early bottles. He also wanted and bought all printed material relating to the early glass industry in America. These related materials, called "go-withs" by Charley, became an important part of his collection. There were old billheads and envelopes from glassmakers, lithographs and engravings of the early glasshouses, advertisements, scrip that was printed to pay the workers and tax stamps. Anything related to the manufacture of early glass in America was always of interest to Charley and this educational material was a special part of his collection.

By the mid-1930s it was clear that bottle collecting had become an all-consuming passion to Charley. He named his house "The Empty Bottle" and by this time had turned an entire room in his house into a "bottle room." It wasn't big enough for the ever-growing collection and bottles overflowed onto shelves, windowsills and closets in other rooms of the house. His earlier interest in antique guns was abandoned and eventually that collection was sold with the exception of a few favorite examples. Charley needed the space for his bottles. By this time his collection had grown to about 2,000 examples of historical flasks and it was beginning to receive some attention in local newspapers. Bottles were still thought to be so unusual as collectors' items that reporters became fascinated with the collection and the man who had gathered it.

Reporters sought Charley out for interviews and material for copy during the thirties and forties. The intense enthusiasm for bottles and their history seemed to be contagious and these early articles on the Gardner collection helped spread interest in bottle collecting as a hobby. In a 1936 interview Charley stated that his collection was then worth around $9,000. At the time he chose as his most valuable bottle an amethyst "General Taylor" portrait flask which he stated was worth "about $150." Present-day collectors found it to have increased in value when it was finally auctioned.

By this time, also, Charley's collection had grown so large that he realized the necessity for some kind of cataloging system. As his collection started to become known to other collectors through the publicity he had received and the advertisements he placed in antiques magazines, other glass and bottle collectors began to correspond with him and he used this mailing list to send lists of his surplus bottles, duplicates and "go-withs" that he didn't want. As time went on this list became longer and longer. The duplicate old flasks and bitters bottles, especially, were in short supply in the West and Midwest and bottle collectors began to trade with and buy from Charley Gardner.

From his first collecting days as a member of the Early American Glass Club, which was based in Boston, Charley studied and learned all he could about the early manufacture of bottles and he became chairman of the research committee, a post he held for many years. He prepared some slide lectures which he willingly gave to interested organizations and arranged loan exhibitions for his local museum. His expertise grew and with it his reputation for having a lot of knowledge about old glass and bottles. Collectors with whom he was in touch looked to him for advice in their purchases. Meanwhile, Charley's search for old bottles continued. "I went after bottles and I just bought them," he said.

By the 1950s the Gardner trucking and storage business had prospered in the Navy town of New London and Charley's collection had grown to around 3,000 bottles. It was clear that some move had to be made to display and store the bottles that were crowding the Gardners out of their house. By this time two upstairs rooms had been taken over and the basement overflowed with bottles as well. The collection had expanded to include all available old Connecticut bottles made in glassworks in New London, Manchester, Coventry, West Wilmington and Westwood. This special area of collecting always remained close to Charley's heart and his group of Connecticut bottles was undoubtedly the best that existed. In addition, Charley was astute enough in his wanderings, to purchase all early bitters, soda and medicinal bottles, all early ink and scent bottles, and was beginning to invest in pottery bottles as well.

The answer to the display and storage problem was for Charley to add a large room to the back of his house in 1956 which would serve as a private museum, office and library. The room was designed expressly for the collection and involved a one-story structure with finished basement below. It was enclosed on three sides by glass walls with movable glass shelving and sliding doors. In this way the bottles could be seen to their best advantage with natural light behind them.

In the upstairs room were displayed the best of the Gardner bottles. One wall held the earliest bottles used in America, the demijohns, carboys, seal bottles, case gin bottles of all sizes and other older bottles dating from the late seventeenth century. The two long walls were used mainly for the display of the Connecticut collection and other nineteenth century historical flasks, the cream of the Gardner collection. The flasks were arranged according to the historical significance of the embossments with each type of flask being grouped with all known variants.

One section of a long wall was given over to the late eighteenth century and early nineteenth century pocket flasks. There was also a group of Nailsea glass which was included in the collection to show the prototypes for American glassware. Other early bottles made elsewhere were in this grouping and this included some jade snuff bottles from China. There were also examples of unusual pottery figural bottles displayed here.

By the 1950s the Gardner library of books on glass and glassmaking had grown large enough to require special shelf space, and provision was made in the main room for books, magazines and records of purchase and sales.

The basement room, surrounded by windows on three sides, and accessible from the main display room by a circular iron staircase, was reserved for the remainder of the Gardner collection. It had always been this room that was of special interest to collectors of bitters and medicine bottles, soda bottles, ink bottles, perfurmes and colognes, and figural bottles of both pottery and glass. During the years that Charley was amassing this collection there were relatively few collectors of these bottles from the second half of the nineteenth century and there had been little written about them. They could be purchased for very little money and many of the old bottles Charley found still bore their original labels. Charley was astute enough not to remove labels or, when the bottles still held their original contents, not to wash them out.

**Authors at work in bottle room of Gardner home in New London, Connecticut. On table in foreground (under bell jar) is small collection of ancient glass bottles. Glass bottles from the Gardner collection lined walls of this room.**

Therefore, the large collection of bitters and medicine bottles was an excellent study collection for the identification of many of the bottles and the Gardner collection was used frequently by collectors and writers. The presence of the labels made it possible to identify otherwise anonymous bottles that were made with no embossments.

Since the major medicinal "cure" in nineteenth century America was alcohol, usually mixed with exotic herbs or syrup, Charley arranged for his own room for the American "cure" in another part of his basement during his remodeling. He built a replica of a turn-of-the-century barroom in the older part of his basement. The room has dark paneling, an old mahogany bar, and one wall is decorated with a stained glass panel that has the word "cafe" in it. His other decorations are also authentic. Probably as a rejection of his teetotaling upbringing he collected early temperance prints. Early bitters advertisements and other nineteenth century liquor advertising items also decorated the room. For further authenticity he added a couple of old slot machines and lined the shelves with rows of cobalt blob-top soda bottles. Most of Charley's visitors ended their visit in the bar where the only son of a teetotaling mother played genial host. It was there that the guests were usually joined by Nina Gardner, who, although she did not share Charley's all-consuming passion for bottles, certainly delighted in the increasing number of collectors who came from everywhere to see the Gardner museum and collection.

Homer Eaton Keyes, at one time editor of the magazine *Antiques,* found himself in the Gardner barroom after having spent some long hours examining the famous collection. Once settled on a stool in front of the mahogany bar he said, "Gardner, I am glad to find one of these damn fool collectors who appreciates a full bottle as well as an empty one." This is a story that Charley had always been fond of repeating. Many overly dedicated collectors place the objects for which they search above everything else. Charley was always able to keep his hobby in enough perspective to enjoy, even more than the purchase of a rare flask or bottle, the hundreds of friends he had made throughout the years who shared his interest in American glass. His happiest moments were when he could discuss his favorite topic in his own basement with others who shared his interest.

## Chapter Two

# The History of Bottle Collecting

Through the 1950s interest in the collecting of American bottles grew slowly. Although more and more collectors were added to the Gardner mailing lists as time went on, there was still no indication in the 1950s that bottle collecting would grow to the proportions it was destined to do in the next two decades. Interest was beginning to develop in all parts of the country and those people who had heard of Charles Gardner and shared his enthusiasm for American glass corresponded with Charley. Often they were looking for information and there were few other such knowledgeable sources from whom they could find out what they wanted to know. They were always assured of a prompt and carefully documented answer. By this time the older bottle collector-dealers were gone and only Charley Gardner remained as the last of the old-time collectors.

By 1960 there were some serious collectors scattered across the country and many of them began to specialize in various classifications of bottles. They looked to the only expert they knew of to get help in identifying and finding old ink bottles, soda bottles, historical flasks, bitters and medicine bottles. Some collectors searched

**Window of flasks and bottles. Four rows on bottom, right, include Gardner collection of Connecticut glass.**

only for bottles made or used in their home locations and others began to search for bottles in dumps or sites of old mining towns in the West. A few of the more serious collectors wrote short monographs or books that they published and sold privately which were lists of their own collections. It was obvious by this time that what had been a somewhat esoteric collectible was beginning to become more and more popular.

Where Charley Gardner in his early collecting days had had the advice and guidance of experts such as George McKearin, Edwin LeFevre, James M. Thompson and Stephen Van Rensselaer, the new collectors had Charles B. Gardner. Unlike some of his predecessors, Charley hadn't written anything about the hobby but had used his collection as a basis for articles written by others and he had given many interviews and lectures which received attention in the ever-growing bottle collecting world. He had gained many friends through his massive correspondence. Fortunately, a book on bitters bottles, written by James H. Thompson in 1947, gave Charley enough impetus and interest to expand that portion of his collection. The book also inspired many new bottle collectors to look for these more accessible bottles. By this time the historical flasks were becoming increasingly expensive, but anyone could find and afford the later bitters bottles. This early attempt at classifying and identifying many of the bitters bottles also interested many Midwestern and Western hobbyists who had little chance of finding the historical flasks in their areas.

Bitters bottles could be dug or found in old dumps anywhere in the country. They were (and are) interesting for their associations with the settling of the West and their involvement with early medical and business history. They recalled the romance of frontier towns, traveling peddlers and medicine men. They had great appeal both to historian-collectors and outdoor types who loved the idea of prospecting in abandoned ghost towns and mining areas in search of the bottles and other relics. Charley Gardner never prospected for bottles, but the rapid growth of this segment of his hobby fascinated him and he did his best to try to identify drawings and illustrations sent him from Western bottle diggers.

The bottle collecting hobby grew rapidly through the 1950s and on October 15, 1959, a small group of people interested in the collecting and preservation of old bottles formed a club called the Sacramento Antique Bottle Collectors Association of California. From a nucleus of 17 original members the club grew to 100 members within just a few months and by 1962 there were over 250 family memberships in 23 states. Somewhere along the way the "of California" was dropped from the club's name. Organized bottle collecting was on its way to becoming one of America's most important hobbies.

For Charley Gardner this intense interest in organized bottle collecting was a wonderful thing; it was just poorly located. Early in the organization of the California club, Charley began to have some correspondence with the club's first president, John C. Tibbetts, and the minutes of most subsequent meetings of the club show that Charles Gardner was a guiding influence in those early days. He sent information correcting misconceptions about certain bottles listed by members, answered many questions for the group, and was made an honorary member. It was he who first suggested that the club expand to include members in other areas of the country who might not be able to attend meetings but who would benefit from receiving the published bulletins issued monthly by the club. He sent slides and material for programs to the group and constantly made it clear that he would be happy to play host to any of the members who might be able to come East. "Invite your group to stop in if they come East and I can assure them of a real treat," he wrote. He described his collection to Tibbetts and asked him to come to see it. "This may appeal to visiting bottle collectors as I have an old bar for the purpose of entertaining." He offered to include applications to join the club in his correspondence. He said it would be worthwhile for any collector to join. "Even if they are not in California, the *Pontil* [the club's newsletter] will repay them."

Charley felt left out of the action, but he kept in constant touch with the members of the group and some of them purchased duplicate bottles from him. He wrote them, "You are a very enthusiastic group and seem to function smoothly. Believe me, if I was nearer I would be in the thick of it." He continually guided the club's activities from across the continent and yearned for an opportunity to show his collection to the members. "Does seem as if some of your members might make a trip East and get a chance to see my collection. After all, there is a lot of pleasure in owning these treasures but it is really more fun to show them off to an understanding audience."

For years the Gardner collection had been available to anyone who wanted to see it and hundreds of people had visited the Gardner home to look at Charley's bottles. Most of these were people interested, generally, in anything antique and who were not especially enamoured of bottles. Within a short time, however, the Gardner collection would have a much more appreciative audience.

The Antique Bottle Collectors Association rapidly became national in scope and associated clubs began to form across the country. By the end of the 1960s there were well over 100 bottle-collecting clubs and the hobby had grown to proportions never dreamed of by Charles Gardner or any of the earlier lonely bottle collectors. As interest in the hobby grew, so, of course, did the literature on the subject. More and more research was done by club members and they identified regional and national bottles. Lists of collections were made and published and price guides began to appear that would give the novice collector some guidance as to what they should pay for additions to their collections. Bottles were sold, swapped and traded within the clubs and more dealers began to appear on the scene. As always happens when demand begins to exceed supply, prices for the rare bottles began to rise rapidly. The Gardner collection that its owner had modestly appraised in 1956 as being "worth a few thousand dollars" became increasingly valuable. Charley had never thought of his collection as an investment. It was a hobby that he loved. He began to realize that his bottles had become "treasures" to others besides himself.

During the great expansion of the bottle-collecting clubs Charley was a guiding light for many of the organizers. Several clubs were started in his own state and he was called upon frequently to give talks. He was host to many groups and by the mid-1960s the hobby had grown to such proportions that busloads of visitors did come, many from great distances, to see the Gardner collection, to ask questions and advice, and less frequently, someone would show him a bottle that he might not already have. He still indulged in a little buying and trading, but by this time his collection was, as far as he was concerned, almost complete. There was only one historical flask he wanted, a pint version of a Lafayette/Liberty Cap flask with no stars over the cap. The bottle was made in Coventry, Connecticut, by Stebbins and Stebbins and was unlisted in the pint size in any book. Charley knew where one existed but was never able to purchase it. This, he felt, left his Connecticut collection incomplete.

All of the important early collectors of American historical flasks, including Stephen Van Rensselaer and George McKearin, were into selling and trading in a much larger way than Charles Gardner. Both had written books which were undoubtedly helpful to their businesses. From this point of view, there was never any burning necessity for Charley to write a book on his own collection, but he always felt that in his final years he would tackle such a project. However, when he finally retired from his business and had the time to devote to writing, he found that he was more enthusiastic about traveling across the country and visiting many of the enthusiastic collectors to whom he had been an inspiration for many years. His time at home was taken up with the ever-increasing number of bottle collectors who flocked to see the collection and friendships with other important collectors across the country became a pleasurable, although time-consuming, preoccupation. He was in heavy demand by bottle club program chairmen and he gave many slide lectures in the sixties. In addition, the bottle collectors clubs had started having annual or semiannual shows and exhibits and Charley was invited frequently to judge the educational exhibits of bottles prepared by the members. He and his wife, Nina, made many trips to the West and Southwest and met hundreds of friends Charley had only known previously through active correspondence. As the Gardners saw more and more collections of old bottles, they began to realize that Charley's collection was unique and gaining value all the time.

Back in 1932 Charley began to keep diary notes of his bottle wanderings and transactions. He attended auctions every Saturday night over a period of many years and added some desirable bottles to his own collection from both the Van Rensselaer and McKearin collections when his old friends died. The prices Charley paid for bottles in the early days of collecting would make any of today's collectors wince in envy. In one month in 1932 he purchased a Bininger gin bottle for 50 cents, a saddle flask for $4, and a Coventry, Connecticut, Lafayette and DeWitt Clinton flask for $9. He paid $3 for two chestnut flasks, $6.50 for a Kentucky violin flask and $4 for a Lowell (Massachusetts) "Success to the Railroad" flask.

Only once in his bottle-purchasing days did Charley ever get stuck with an inferior or fake bottle. He bought a New England sunburst flask for $20 that turned out, upon close inspection, to be a recent reproduction. "It was a Saturday night auction, and we had been partying a lot before that." He did, however, purchase all bottles that he knew of that were new reproductions of the early flasks. These reproductions have always been instructive to new collectors and when a known reproduction was of especially good quality Charley respected the work that had gone into it. He felt that the manufacture of mouth-blown reproductions kept bottle-blowing from becoming a lost art. Most of the new bottles went on a separate shelf, but a few that were especially good were placed on the shelves with his antique bottles and, because they were in the Gardner collection, few visitors ever questioned their authenticity.

Because Charley had always felt that the manufacture of respectable and easily identifiable reproductions should be made, he offered a few of his early bottles to a glass company for use in making new molds. His Booz cabin bottle and an early concentric eagle flask were used for this purpose by a large glass company to make a limited edition of each bottle. Charley was firm in his insistence, however, that a mark be placed on the base of each reproduction so that it could be easily distinguished from the original bottles by future collectors. The marks on the new bottles were designed in such a way that they cannot be removed without the bottle shattering.

There are still several other private collections of American historical bottles that probably are equal in quality and number to the Gardner collection. Because they were started much later, they undoubtedly represent a much larger monetary investment than the Gardner collection. What made Charley's collection unique was not so much the bottles themselves, but their collector. He was the connecting link between the legendary early collector-dealers and writers and the new breed of bottle diggers and collectors. He devoted thousands of hours to instruct and guide the newer collectors and to help them in indentification and research.

Although he was always hospitable and polite to collectors of new figural bottles, he held these bottles in some contempt. He clearly felt that the purchase of new Jim Beam figural bottles and other new collectibles was a waste of time and money and that the market for them was purposely inflated and would soon go down, leaving the collectors with machine-made bottles that would have little value. "There is," he said, "nothing to be learned from them and that is the excitement in collecting old historical bottles and flasks. My bottles are wrapped in history. You learn a lot about America when you go to find out why the Pikes Peak bottles were made, where the early glass houses were located and how they operated. If you own some Lafayette flasks you want to read all you can about his visit to America in 1824. You can't learn a thing from owning a hundred Avon and Jim Beam bottles, except that you wasted your time and money."

Enthusiasm for a collecting hobby from which there is always something more to learn and love for the hand-made are two qualities that Charles Gardner brought to the bottle collecting field and he was always delighted to pass on his knowledge and passion for collecting to others. Over the years the Gardner collection became the unattainable ideal for most of the younger collectors. As new books were written during the past 10 years many of the bottles in the Gardner collection were studied and photographed. Charley was never really happy with the quality of the photography that was done and often he was not even given credit for his help with many projects. Yet he hated to see a new book about bottle collecting appear without illustrations of at least a few of his bottles in it. He happily endorsed any project that had to do with bottle collecting and urged every collector he knew to buy each new book as it appeared on the market.

Until now, with the exception of the Gardner auction catalog, no single book based just on the Gardner collection had been written, although it always would have been useful for both new and advanced collectors. Charley just couldn't find the time or would not take time from what he considered the more enjoyable work of studying glass and visiting with other collectors across the country. What he didn't realize is that he had already written the book that was needed; the catalog that he had been keeping for 40 years. It is this catalog, written by Charles B. Gardner, with some editorial comments, which will be presented on the following pages.

## Chapter Three

# The Charles B. Gardner Bottle Collection

Those who do not have hobbies are always amazed at the amount of energy, time and study the dedicated collector is willing to give to his favorite pastime. With many collectors the hobby often becomes all-consuming and continual acquisition their only purpose in life. This was not true of Charles Gardner. As much as he loved his collection, he had other interests and preferred spending his spare time with interesting people. If they shared his interest in American glass, so much the better, but he did not impose his knowledge and enthusiasm on anyone who had other things to talk about.

Many of the world's great museum collections were originally gathered by collectors as enthusiastic and knowledgeable as Charles Gardner. The availability of money for purchases is, of course, necessary for the building of any purposeful collection, but large sums are not always necessary to build meaningful collections. Energy, knowledge and an inquiring mind are also extremely helpful. It could easily be argued by today's collectors of antique American bottles that Charley Gardner was fortunate in that he got there first. This is, of course, every collector's fantasy; to buy something that only he realizes will have more value than is currently being asked and that has little competition.

Although it has already been stated that Charley never bought additions to his collection with the idea that he was investing, he could not help but be aware during the 1960s that his collection was becoming very valuable. He simply loved pontilled bottles and bought them when he could find and afford them. That he did invest in a collectible that has recently become so popular is simply good fortune. In any case, he thought he would never

**One section of Gardner collection includes many sunbursts, calabashes and Jenny Lind flasks.**

be able to part with a single bottle from his cataloged collection during his lifetime. He always understood that the desire of many of today's collectors was to own, someday, certain bottles that he had in his collection, but he was more intent on keeping the collection intact so that it would be available for future collectors and historians for study and enjoyment. He was always forgiving about certain collectors who seemed all too eager for the day when his collection might be placed on the auction block and simply felt that they didn't have enough of a grasp on the necessity for keeping a unique collection intact.

The cataloging of a private collection as large as the Gardner bottle collection is an arduous task and for someone without museum training it has to be a labor of love. Charley kept his catalog up-to-date throughout the years, although all the bottles he owned were not entered. As prices of bottles began to rise the code prices were updated and the entire catalog would be retyped. Charley's values on his own bottles were never realistic since he had bought most of them for relatively little money in the early days. Additions to the collection were entered periodically and each bottle was carefully researched so that it could be easily identified from the catalog description. The numerical system Charley used was a simple one, starting with the number one, but it became more complicated as the collection grew. As every museum curator knows, the variants of many of the early flasks can make cataloging bottles very complicated.

Because his catalog was kept solely for his own use, Charley kept it as brief as possible. He refrained from classifying his flasks as "rare" or "very rare," even though in some cases he owned the only known flask of a certain design, size or color. Rarity was only shown in the value he placed in code next to every bottle listed. Since the Gardner collection has now been sold, new owners might like to know that the Gardner code was B R I C K M A S O N.<br>1 2 3 4 5 6 7 8 9 0 It was only natural that the code would have something to do with the process of early glassmaking.

Where many collectors with a strong affection for the objects they collect often tend to put unrealistically high prices on their collections, the opposite was true of the Gardner catalog. Charley loved his bottles too much to consider selling any from his collection during his lifetime, although this was its eventual fate. Often, other collectors and some museum people put him under heavy pressure to sell certain rarities that he owned, but he was always able to resist the pressure without alienating the persistent collectors. Duplicates and less important bottles were for selling and trading; once a bottle was cataloged into the collection it would only be removed if a more perfect example of the same specimen became available. In all his years of collecting and handling the fragile bottles, neither Charley nor anyone else who handled them ever broke a single bottle.

Charles Gardner knew well each bottle in his collection and, once he had built his room, every bottle had its own place on the glass shelves. If a bottle had been moved a few inches or was put back in the wrong place he spotted it immediately and corrected the error. He was always generous about letting any other knowledgeable collector or writer handle any of his flasks or bottles and, through days of photographing for this book, he appeared to be unconcerned for the safety of the hundreds of bottles that were handled.

The catalog of the Gardner collection is presented here just as it was kept by Charley. He felt that this listing included the information that would be most valuable to future collectors. The catalog and values were last revised in 1972 and the values certainly turned out to be obsolete. Charley felt that including uncoded prices would tend to make the catalog appear to be some sort of a price guide and he had little use for price guides. However, the coded values have been transposed to a scale of rarity. Those who purchased the Gardner bottles will be able to decipher from the code the price paid for the bottle if the original Gardner label is still attached. Those prices obviously have little relationship to what was paid at the auction. The reader should bear in mind that the bottles that seemed "common" to Charley Gardner, who started collecting in 1929, may now be considered "very rare" to today's more recent collectors who have so much competition in their hobby.

In most cases, but certainly not all, the bottles Charley considered the most rare and valuable were those chosen for illustration. Since the photographs were taken well before the auction, and, indeed, at a time when an auction was not even considered, there will be some bottles that brought extremely high prices at the auction that were not photographed.

Since the Gardner catalog was arranged for the convenience of its compiler, it might appear to be somewhat confusing to the reader. The historical flasks, Charles Gardner's first love, were listed first by category of decoration with that convenient heading, "Miscellaneous," taking in many types of flasks that perhaps should have been listed in separate groups. All portrait flasks except for Washingtons, eagles, cornucopias and Masonics were listed under "Miscellaneous." The Pitkin flasks in a variety of colors and sizes were an important part of the Gardner collection and are in a special section. Pikes Peak flasks, violin flasks, square face gin bottles, sunburst flasks, ink bottles, handled jugs, pickles and peppersauce bottles, bitters bottles, mineral water bottles, early soda and mineral water bottles, scent bottles and snuff and blacking bottles were all listed separately. The collection of bitters bottles was an especially long entry. Figurals and other bottles that did not fit into any of the above categories went conveniently into "Miscellaneous."

Charles Gardner kept a record of the comparative

values that he placed on the bottles in his collection and this was updated periodically, presumably for insurance purposes. However, the prices that he attributed to most of his bottles turned out to be unrealistically low in today's competitive market. It is now a matter of history, but it may be of some interest for collectors to know that Charley's estimate in 1972 (the last time the collection was cataloged) was $170,941 in total value. This figure included china and glass that was not included in the auction.

It seemed a helpful tool for collectors, for us to transcribe the coded monetary values in each category of bottles to a scale of comparative rarity. Therefore, in parantheses, we have placed a number on a scale of one to six that is the Gardner assessment of each bottle **within its own category.** Each bottle was rated, well before the Gardner auction, according to the following scale:

(1) Extremely rare
(2) Very rare
(3) Rare
(4) Comparatively scarce
(5) Scarce
(6) Common

This rating was accomplished by taking the bottles with the highest value in each category and working down from that point. This means that even though a flask might be rated a (1) it might not be worth the same amount of money as an ink or bitters bottle with the same rating. In any case, the question is now moot. The bottles have been sold at auction and the auction prices have been included. The Gardner ratings are left in so that the new owners can compare what was paid for each bottle to the assessment of value by the original owner.

An important factor to be kept in mind when reading the prices paid at the Gardner auction is that provenance **does** matter and the collection was, without doubt, the best-known in the country. Following each Gardner rating number is the number that each bottle was given at the auction. Since the bottles were not sold in categories, the following catalog will put the collection back together again in an orderly fashion. The final entry in each listing is the price each bottle brought at auction. There were a few bottles for which no listing could be found in the auction catalog and there were some discrepancies in descriptions. For the difficult work in matching prices and numbers to the right bottles, credit and gratitude should be given to Noel Tomas, former publisher of the *Down-East Glassman* and a knowledgeable student of glass and bottles.

## Chapter Four

# Historical and Pictorial Flasks

The historical and pictorial flasks in the Gardner collection are unquestionably the most important part of the collection and one that is of special interest to American glass historians. Although by the end of the first quarter of the nineteenth century, hundreds of thousands of these flasks had been made, relatively few have survived and it was not until the publication of *AMERICAN GLASS* by George S. and Helen McKearin in 1941 that all known flasks and their variants were properly cataloged and identified. However, Charles Gardner had been collecting the flasks for years before this and the flasks that represent America's early history were always his favorite part of the collection.

Of all American historical or pictorial flasks the oldest and, to Charley, the most interesting are the Connecticut flasks made at the Pitkin Glass Works. This company started in business around 1773 and its founders were William Pitkin, Elisha Pitkin and Samuel Biship. The Pitkin firm made many kinds and types of glass bottles, the most famous of which bears the name of the firm. The Pitkin flasks were made by the German half-post method where the gather is patterned in a mold and then expanded and twisted. This resulted in a swirled design. The method by which the glass was gathered for the bottles, in which they are dipped twice in the gather, identifies the bottles as "Pitkin" or "Pitkin-type." Certainly, not all the flasks that appear to have been double dipped were made at the Pitkin Glass Works. Many were made in other early glasshouses, but the name has become generic for all flasks made by this method. Although Pitkin flasks of this type are not pictorial, they are included in this grouping of glass bottles.

There were historical flasks produced at the Pitkin Glass Works and these molded glass bottles are considered to be among the earliest flasks made with patriotic symbols or portraits of patriots as decoration. The Jared Spencer flasks in the Gardner collection are thought to be early Pitkin bottles. Very little is known about Jared Spencer or why his name appears on the flasks. The Glastonbury, Connecticut, firm is a mystery to all bottle collectors and glass historians. It is known that the company stayed in business until 1830, so that all flasks and bottles attributed to the firm were made previous to that time.

Another group of Connecticut flasks that is to be found in the Gardner collection was made in the town of Coventry. Little is known about the Coventry Glass Works except that it was started around 1813 and operated until around 1848. Some of their best-known flasks were marked with the initials "T.S" for Thomas Stebbins who ran the operation for some years after 1820. Some flasks are marked "S&C" for Stebbins and Chamberlin. There are two flasks which bear the initials "S&S" and it is not known who might have been in partnership with Stebbins. Some of the Coventry flasks are marked with the identification of the glass firm. It is thought that all Coventry historical and pictorial flasks were made before 1830.

While the Gardner collection was especially rich in Connecticut flasks it was certainly not lacking in examples of the historical and pictorial flasks made by other glass firms throughout the country. There were many American eagle flasks, flasks that were made with Masonic decoration, portrait flasks of George Washington, Benjamin Franklin, General Lafayette, DeWitt Clinton, Major Samuel Ringgold, Louis Kossuth, Henry Clay, John Adams, Andrew Jackson, Fanny Ellsler (a famous European dancer who toured the country in the 1840s) and Jenny Lind. Miss Lind was brought to this country by P. T. Barnum in 1851 and her successful tour led the glassmakers to commemorate the singer on calabash and violin flasks.

Flasks commemorating the beginning of the railroad expansion in America are also represented in some number in the collection as are many other flasks with patriotic or political motifs. A large group of flasks is decorated with the symbol of plenty, the cornucopia.

The Gardner collection included almost every known historical and pictorial flask in a great variety of colors. The embossments represent all of the glass houses in existence that produced the flasks in the nineteenth century and many of the flasks can be identified as to their makers by the embossments derived from the molds used.

Note: All numbers in parentheses beginning with "G" are McKearin numbers that have become standard for identifying all known pictorial and historical flasks.

## Chapter Five

# American Eagle Flasks

1 Large eagle with raised wings, head turned to left, shield on breast, two arrows in left talons, branch on right. Ribbon held in beak flies to right and contains 5 stars. Below the eagle is an ornate medallion. Quart. Olive green. (GII-26 (3).

1A Same, brilliant amber. (3) (#593) $1,300

1B Same, blue green. (3) (#2652) $600

1C Same, yellow green. (3) (#2401) $1,200

1D Same, yellow green. (3) (#1097) $850

1E Same, yellow green. (3) (#724) $550

2A 14 star eagle over stellar motif. Corrugated edges. Pint. Blue. (GII-24). (2) (#449) $2,900

2B Same, green. (3) (#2940) $1,050

2C Same, amber. (3) (#2724) $800

2D Same, honey amber. (3) (#1897) $900

2F Same, olive yellow. (3) (#1937) $675

2V Similar, but no "U" on banner. (3) (#2355) $280

3 14 star eagle over stellar motif. Corrugated sides. Reverse: 12-branched floral motif over star. Pint. Aqua. (GII-23). (2) (#292) $1,175

**Fourteen star eagle over stellar motif. Corrugated sides. Reverse: twelve-branched floral motif over star. Aqua. (3)**

4 Same. Reverse: 14 stars over lyre. Pint. Aqua. (GII-22). (2) (#1676) $800

5 5 stars on banner over eagle to left over stellar motif. Corrugated edges. Reverse (Farley & Taylor Richmond, Ky). 2½ quarts. Aqua (GII-27). (1) (#657) $3,250

6 10 stars over right on eagle on beaded oval. Diagonal ribbing to left and right below. Corrugated edges. Pint. Pale yellow green. (GII-2). (4) (#2219) $750

6A Similar to above with variations. Pint. Aqua. (GII-4). (4) (#491) $460

7 9 stars over eagle over heavily beaded oval. Ribbing to right and left below. Dot in oval. Pint. Aqua. (GII-3). (4) (#1115) $225

8 10 stars. Beaded oval. Ribbing right and left. Pint. Aqua. (GII-1). (4) (#3) $160

9 Double eagle, marked (Granite Glass Co.) in oval. Reverse (Stod (d) ard N. H.) 1 quart. Deep amber. (2) (#1529) $500

10 Similar, but marked (Stoddard N. H.). Pint. (#2306) $150
Deep amber. Made by Granite Glass Co. (5)
Same. Light olive amber. (#2906) $130

11 Similar, but 1 side, only, marked (Stoddard N. H.). Pint. Amber. (3) (#82) $110

12 Similar, but no marks in ovals. ½ pint. Amber. (3) (#1866) $55

13 Similar, but no marks in ovals. Pint. Amber. (3)

14 Similar, no marks in ovals. Quart. Amber. (3) (#290) $250

15 Similar but marked (X) in one oval only. ½ pint. Amber. (3) (#930) $220

16 Similar but with dot in oval. (3) (#2835) $70

17 Spread eagle on grass plot. ½ pint. Amber. (5)

18 Double eagle with star at right of eagle on side only. Pint. Aqua. (5) (#2410) $35

19 Rayed eagle over beaded oval. Reverse: Same. Pint. Emerald green. (2) (#1609) $500

19A Same, yellow green. (GII-40). (#1081) $850

20 Double eagle. Pittsburgh type. Pint. Olive green. (4) (#2482) $40

21 Similar to above. Pint. Yellow green. (GII-40) (#642) $190

21A Similar, pint, yellow green. (#2649) $250

22 Double eagle. Pittsburgh type. Pint. Aqua. (5) (#434) $50

23 Similar to above. Pint. Aqua. (5) (#1642) $25

24 Similar to #20. Pint. Aqua. (5) (#1722) $40

25 Similar. Quart. Aqua. (5) (#2770) $55
Similar. Quart. Aqua. (5) (#706) $50
Similar. Quart. Aqua. (5) (#1723) $110

25V Similar to #5. Corrugations on wings coarser than on #25. Quart. Aqua. (5) (1586) $40

26 Crude eagle, blocked banner overhead. Shield forms lower part of body. ½ pint. Aqua. (5) (#1130) $45

27 Eagle with head to right, banner overhead. Corrugated on wings. 5 bars on shield over irregular oval. ½ pint. Aqua. (5) (#1746) $40

28 Eagle left, wide banner overhead. Corrugated on wings. 5 bars on shield over irregular oval. ½ pint. Aqua. (5)

29 Eagle looking to right with banner overhead. Arrows and plain oval. ½ pint. Deep amber. (5) (#306) $70

30 6 stars over eagle over small oval. Reverse: eagle with snake in beak curling over back. Bull's eyes around edges. ½ pint. Amethystine. (GII-9). (1) (#2305) $12,500

31 Eagle to left over panel marked (Zanesville Ohio). Reverse: eagle over plain oval. Pint. Aqua. (4) (#1681) $210

**Flask in aqua with plain reverse side. (33)**

32 Eagle to left over panel marked (Louisville Ky). Reverse: eagle over oval marked (Glass Works). Quart. Aqua. (4) (#1386) $70

32V Similar. Pint. Aqua. (4) (#2850) $840

33 Marked (D. Kirkpatrick & Co.) over eagle right. (Chattanooga Tenn.) below. Reverse: plain. Quart. Aqua. (3) (#2275) $2,100

33V Same. Pint. Aqua. (4) (#1899) $260

34 Vertically ribbed. Eagle in oval panel. Reverse: same. Quart. Emerald green, heavy glass. (GII-31). (3) (#801) $800

34V Same. Vertically ribbed, small eagle. (GII-32). (#227) $425

35 Vertically ribbed. Eagle in oval over panel marked (Louisville Ky Glass Works). Reverse: plain. Quart. Aqua. (GII-35) (4) (#1451) $100

36 Similar to 35. Pint. Aqua. (GII-36) (4) (#963) $110

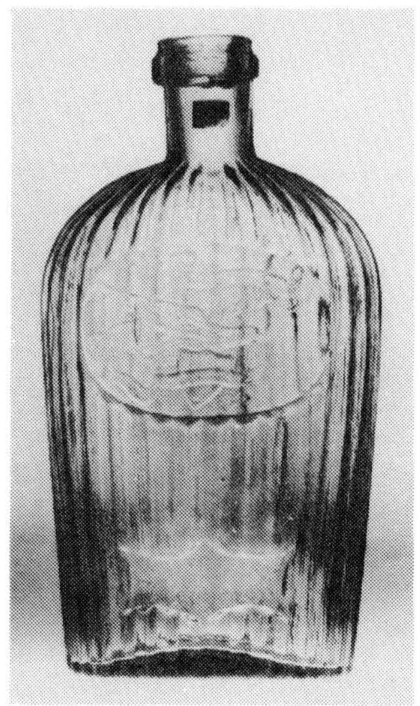

**Vertically ribbed flask with eagle in oval over panel marked "Louisville Ky Glass Works." Aqua. (36).**

37 Vertically ribbed. Eagle in oval. Reverse (Louisville, Ky Glass Works) in oval. ½ pint. Deep amber brown. (GII-33). (1) (#2908) $1,300

37A Same. Green. (GII-33). (4) (#852) $825

38 Eagle head to left, standing on narrow base in circular panel. Vertically ribbed. ½ pint. Aqua. (GII-30). (5) (#1916) $250

38V Same. Pint. Aqua. (GII-29). (5) (#2761) $800

39 Canteen shape. Concentric rings surrounding eagle in circular panel on each side. ¾ quart. Green. (GII-76). **Very rare.** (1) (#2049) $4,500

**Canteen-shaped concentric ring eagle flask. Green. (39).**

40 Eagle over oval marked (Pittsburgh). Reverse: 13 stars over (Union) and (A & DHC). Pint. Amber. (5) (2962) $180

41 Eagle over oval marked (Geo. A. Berry & Co) Reverse: eagle over plain oval. Pint. Aqua. (5) (#2258) $40

42 Eagle over oval marked (C&I). Reverse: same. ½ pint. Aqua. (5) (#1393) $45

42A Eagle over panel marked (C&I). Reverse: same. Pint. Aqua. (5) (#1393) $30

43 Eagle over oval marked (Cunningham & Co Pittsburgh). Reverse (Glass Manufacturers). Pint. Aqua. (5) (#1850) $55

44 Similar markings to above but better formed eagles and different ovals. Pint. Light olive green. (4) (#402) $200

44V Same as above. Quart. Golden amber. (4) (771) $150

45 Eagle over oval marked: (H&S). Reverse: 13 stars (Union), clasped hands, square and compasses. Pint. Amber. (GIV-40). (4) (#2002) $250

45A Same. ½ pint. Aqua. (GIV-41). (5)

45B Similar to above, but no initials. Quart. Light green. (5) (#2418) $85

45V Similar to #45. Quart. Aqua. (5) (#210) $65
Similar. Quart. Aqua. (#2330) $80

46 Eagle over plain oval. Reverse: 13 stars, clasped hands and oval. On border (L&W). (L&W). Pint. Amber. (5)

47 Small eagle over oval marked (Pittsburgh Pa). Reverse: same except oval plain. ½ pint. Aqua. (5) (#2194) $50

47A Same. Light amber. (5) (#2498) $250 (Called "citron" in auction catalog.)

48 Eagle over oval marked (Pittsburgh Pa). Reverse: same except plain oval. Pint. Yellow green. (5) (#1313) $160

48A Same. Emerald green. (4) (#1563) $160

48B Same. Olive green. (4) (#1194) $150

48C Same. Dark amber. (4) (#299) $65

48D Same. Black olive green. (#2658) $140

49 Eagle over oval marked (Pittsburgh Pa). Reverse: eagle over plain oval. Quart. Emerald green. (5)

49A Same. Dark amber. (4) (#514) $90

49B Same. Deep olive green. (4) (#2179) $140

50 Eagle over oval marked (Pittsburgh) (A&DHC) on ribbon. Reverse: marked (Union) (Old Rye). Pint. Aqua. (5) (#1986) $50

51 Eagle with (A&Co) on ribbon over irregular panel. Reverse (Union), clasped hands, 5 bars on shield. Pint. Yellow amber. (4) (#2322) $360
Same.(#490) $15

51A Similar. Quart. 7 bars on shield. Greenish amber. (4) (#2514) $190

51B Similar to #51 except plain oval. Pint. Dark amber. (4) (#170) $80

52 Eagle to right over panel. Reverse: 13 stars over shield with clasped hands and panel. Pint. Amber. (4) (#90) $85

53 Eagle to right over oval. Reverse: 13 stars over shield with clasped hands and oval. Quart. Aqua. (5) (#2946) $45

54 Practically the same as above but with (Union) over shield. Quart. Aqua. (5) (#2082) $40

55 Smaller eagle over irregular panel. Reverse: 13 stars over (Union), shield and clasped hands. Oval below. Quart. Aqua. (5) (#1146) $40

56 Eagle to right on shield marked (ANDHC), on ribbon (Pittsburgh). Reverse: 13 stars, (Union), clasped hands and (Old Rye) in oval. Quart. Vaseline. (4) (#2938) $150

57 Eagle left over oval marked (Pittsburgh Pa Mc & Co). Reverse: same, but no inscription. Pint. Amber. (4) (#426) $60

58 Eagle to right over panel marked (E. Wormser

& Co Pittsburgh Pa). Reverse: 13 stars around (Union) and clasped hands. Quart. Aqua. (5) (#2490) $60

59 Eagle right on shield with ribbon. Reverse: 13 stars over (Union) and clasped hands. Marked over oval (No2). Quart. Dark amber. (4) (#905) $150

60 Eagle right over oval. Reverse: 13 stars and clasped hands. No (Union). Pint. Aqua. (5) (#802) $45

61 Eagle right on shield over plain oval. Reverse: 11 stars over shield over plain oval. ½ pint. Aqua. (5) (#1594) $30

61A Similar. ½ pint. Deep amber. (#1754) $55

62 Eagle to right on shield over panel. Reverse: 13 stars, (Union), and clasped hands. ½ pint. Aqua. (4) (#2858) $65

63 Eagle to right on shield over oval. Reverse: 13 stars, (Union), and clasped hands. ½ pint. Aqua. (5) (#530) $30

64 Eagle to right on shield over oval. Reverse: 13 stars, (Union), and clasped hands. ½ pint. Aqua. (5) (#562) $40
Same. (5) (1473) $45

65 Eagle to right on shield. Banner marked (C.I. & Sons). Reverse: 13 stars, (Union), and clasped hands. Pint. Dense amber. (4) (#1178) $50

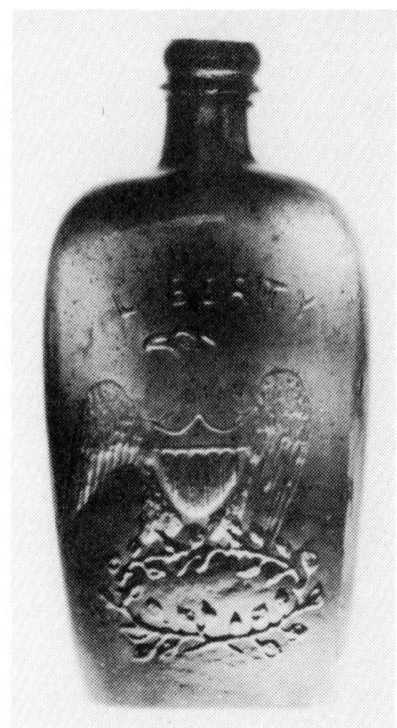

**Eagle flask made in Connecticut.**

68 6 stars over eagle over small, beaded oval. Reverse: large round sunburst. Bull's-eyes around edge. Pint. Green. (GII-7). (1) (#673) $2,600

69 13 stars over eagle over small oval. Reverse: scrolled medallion. Bull's-eyes around edge. Pint. Pale olive yellow. (GII-8). (1) (#1705) $5,600

69A Same. Clear with violet tinge. (1) (273) $6,400

70 Eagle perched on flags. Reverse: morning glory. Pint. Blue aqua. (GII-19) (2) (#1817) $825

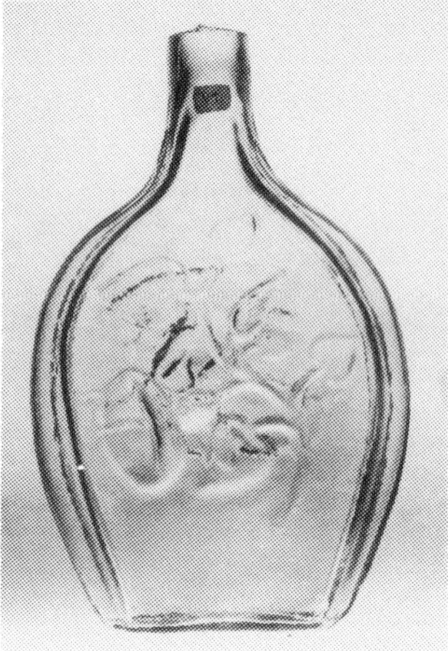

**Eagle perched on flags. Reverse is morning glory. Blue aqua. (70)**

70A Same in brown, mottled pottery. (2) (#1201) $325

72 Small eagle, shield on breast, perched on arrows. Reverse: plain. Short neck. ½ pint. Deep amber. (5) (#1706) $170

72B Same. Light amber. (5)

73 Eagle right over oval marked (Pittsburgh Pa). Reverse: 13 stars over (Union), and clasped hands over oval marked (L. F. & Co). Pint. Aqua. (5) (#1794) $45

73V Same. Quart. Aqua. (5) (#2562) $75

74 Eagle to left. Ball between feet. Reverse: same. Pint. Amber. (5) (#492) $190

74A Same. Blue. (3) (#2740) $1,550

74B Same. Dark amber. (5) (#2354) $70

74V Same. ½ pint. Aqua. (5) (#898) $45

75 Small eagle to left over wreath. Reverse: same. ½ pint. Amethyst. (3) (#180) $450

76 Eagle to right with banner marked (E Pluribus Unum). Reverse (Dyottville Glass Works Philada). Pint. Aqua. (GII-38) (5) (#19) $120

76V Similar. No inscription on banner. Reverse: plain. Pint. Aqua. (GII-39) (5) (#970) $50

77 Eagle lengthwise. Reverse: same. Pint. Olive amber. (GII-70). (4) (#2227) $175

78 Same. ½ pint. Olive green. (GII-71). (4) (#147) $200

79 Eagle to right on shield marked (RB). Reverse (Rheinstrom Bros Cincinnati USA). Globular. ¾ quart. Emerald green. (5) (#3012) $118

79A Same. Light amber. (5) (#760) $17.50
Similar. Yellow. (#1910) $5

79B Same. ½ pint. Emerald green. (5) (#330) $25

79C Same. Dark amber. (5)

79V Same as above. Olive green. (5) (#1076) $30

80 Eagle to right on rock in 2″ medallion. Reverse: plain. Flat broad rib. Pint. Clear. (6) (#370) $12.50

80V Similar, but clear quart. (6) (#130) $225

80A Similar. ½ pint. Marked on base (LS & R Co). (6) (#370) $12.50

81A Calabash. Eagle to right over shield. Reverse: plain. Quart. Bright green. (5) (#931) $140

82 Eagle to left on panel. Beaded edges. Reverse (Liberty) above pine tree. ½ pint. Dark amber. (GII-60). (2) (#289) $1,100

83 Same. Green. (2) (#2913) $1,700

84 Eagle with raised wings in circular medallion. Marked on base (116). (3)

85 Eagle to right over plain oval. Reverse: 13 stars over shield, clasped hands, 14 bars on shield, branches on either side. (Union). Pint. Aqua. (5)

86 Eagle to right over plain oval. Reverse: 13 stars over (Union), clasped hands, 5 solid bars on shield. Branches on either side. Pint. Aqua. (5) (#1226) $30

87 13 stars over ribbed shield with clasped hands and (Union). Reverse: eagle, banner above and below through shield. Calabash. Quart. Dense amber. (4) (#1083) $190

87A Same. Yellow green. (4) (#691) $425

87B Similar, yellow green. Quart.
A•R•S• on banner. (GIV-42). (#2435) $400

# Chapter Six
# Cornucopia Flasks

90 Cornucopia on panel, tail to left. Reverse: 5 bar basket of fruit. Heavy central rib. Depressed dot in middle rib of basket. Pint. Amber. (GIII-5). (4) (#228) $50

90B Similar, but no dot. Pint. Apple green. (4) (#2978) $260

90C Same. Aqua. (4) (1546) $230

90D Same. Olive amber. (4) (#2819) $65

90E Same. Olive green. (4) (#2226) $50

91 Cornucopia on panel, tail to left. Reverse: 6 bar basket of fruit. Heavy central rib. ½ pint. Olive green. (GIII-7). (4) (#1210) $90

91A Same. Light green. (4) (#883) $250

91D Same. Dark green. (4) (#2450) $65

91E Aqua. Same. (4) (#1786) $110

91B Same with dot in basket. Olive amber. (GIII-11). (4) (#2930) $65

91V Same with (SCM). Olive green. (3) (#171) $130

92 Similar, but large dot at left of cornucopia. ½ pint. Aqua. (GIII-9). (4) (#2786) $95

92A Same. Olive green. (4) (#1585) $80

93 Same, but leaf design at left of cornucopia. ½ pint. Amber. (GIII-14). (4) (#1370) $95

94 Cornucopia on panel, tail to right. Reverse: 7 bar basket. ½ pint. Dark amber. (GIII-12). (4) (#2) $80

95 Cornucopia on panel to right. Reverse: 5 bar basket. Marked (Lancaster Glass Works N. Y.). Pint. Greenish blue. (GIII-16). (3) (#563) $600

95A Same. Light green. (3) (#2722) $300

95B Same. Olive green. (3) (#2579) $275

96 Same, but lettering omitted. Pint. Green. (GIII-17). (4) (#553) $300

96A Chocolate amber. (4) (#1515) $50

96B Same, blue green. (4) (#1179) $400

96E Same, medium amber. (4) (#1314) $260

97 Very crude cornucopia, tail to right on panel. Reverse: 7 bar basket. ½ pint. Aqua. (GIII-15). (5) (#146) $80

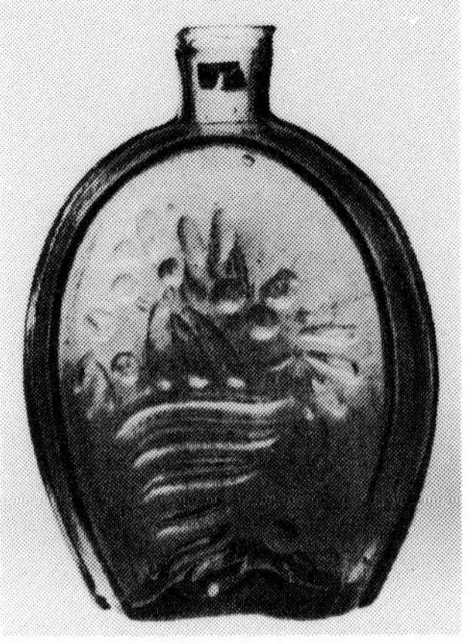

**Cornucopia flask made by the Lancaster Glass Works, New York. (95).**

97A Cornucopia more distinct than above. ½ pint. Emerald green. (GIII-14). (4) (#980) $425

97B Same, yellow green. (4) (#1100) $375

98 Cornucopia to left on panel. Reverse: eagle perched on rocks. Pint. Olive green. (GII-72). (4)

98A Same. Shaded green and amber. (3) (#2883) $850

99 Similar to #97 except cornucopia is broader, center bar shorter. Right handle on basket does not touch and extra short bar in center of base. ½ pint. Amber. (GIII-13). (4) (#763) $275

99A Same, green. (4) (#2994) $340

100 Cornucopia with tail to left on panel. Cross at left. Reverse: eagle. Single line around panel. Pint. Sea green. (GII-74). (4) (#2706) $575

100C Similar, but cross forms a plus sign. Eagle with 4 bars on shield. High central rib. Pint. Aqua. (GII-73). (4) (#859) $90

100D Same, olive green. (4) (#298) $75
Same. (#722) $70
Same. (GII-73). (#2282) $100

100E Same as #100. (GII-74). (4) (#50) $110

101 Cornucopia with tail to left on panel. Reverse: 9 stars over eagle over beaded oval. Diagonal ribbing at base. Corrugated sides. Pint. Aqua. (GII-6). (3) (#851) $560

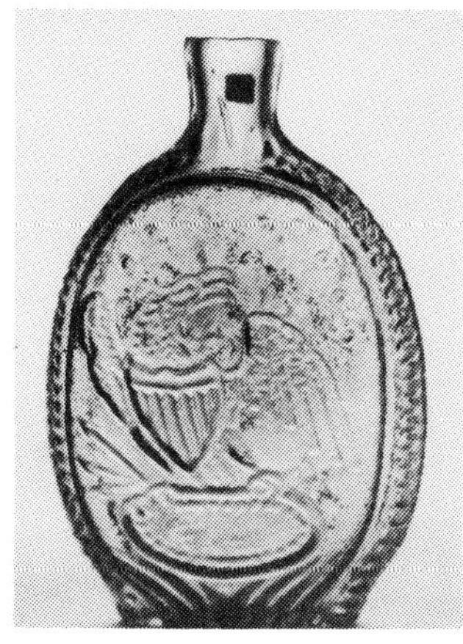

**Cornucopia flask in aqua glass. (101)**

102 Cornucopia with tail to left. Rayed eagle looking to right over beaded oval. ½ pint. Aqua. (GII-43). (4) (#995) $220

103 Cornucopia with tail to left on panel. Marked (Kensington Glass Works Philadelphia) around edge. Reverse: rayed eagle over beaded oval marked (TWD). (E Pluribus Unum One of Many) around edge. ½ pint. Aqua. (GII-43). (4) (#2939) $350

**Aqua Cornucopia flask made and marked by T. W. D(yott), Philadelphia. (103).**

104 Cornucopia to left on panel. Reverse: eagle over plain oval. Heavy central rib. ½ pint. Aqua. (GII-45). (4) (#339) $150

105 Slender cornucopia with tail to left on panel. Eagle over beaded oval. ½ pint. Aqua. (GII-17). (4) (#1019) $200

106 Inverted cornucopia on panel with beaded edges. Reverse: early type eagle looking to left. Diagonal ribbing below. Corrugated edges. ½ pint. Green. (GII-69) (4) (#2851) $1,000

106A Same. Amethystine. (2) (#1435) $900

107 Large inverted cornucopia. Reverse: eagle under 11 stars over beaded oval. Beaded edges. ½ pint. Blue aqua. (GII-11). (3) (#1426) $450

108 Slender cornucopia to left on panel. Reverse: rayed eagle to right, 17 beads in oval. Diagonal ribbing below. ½ pint. Deep aqua. (GII-16). (3) (#2035) $175

109 Large inverted cornucopia. Reverse: eagle under 11 stars over beaded oval. Marked (W. C.). Corrugated edges. ½ pint. Aqua. (GII-12). (2) (#2995) $525

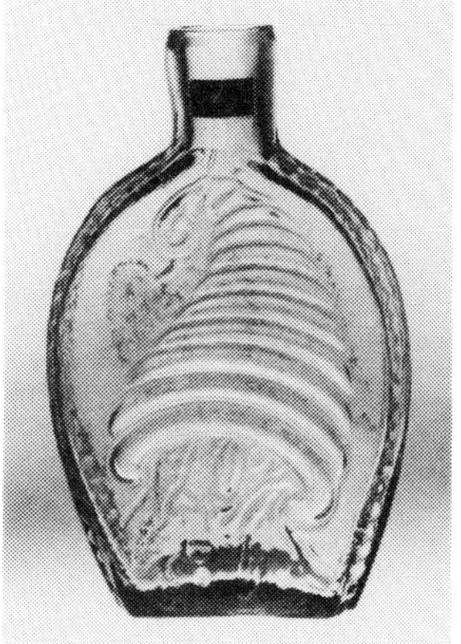

**Large inverted cornucopia flask. Aqua. (109).**

110 Cornucopia on oval panel. Reverse: basket of produce. Pint. Reddish amber. Reproduction flask. Maker unknown. (GII-6) (5) (#300) $40

111 Inverted cornucopia. Reverse: circular medallion with 6-pointed star in center. Palm design below. ½ pint. Aqua. (GIII-1). (3) (#1355) $725

**Reverse of cornucopia flask made in Connecticut and marked "J.P.F." (115).**

112 Slender cornucopia to left on panel. Reverse: same. ½ pint. Aqua. (GIII-2) (3) (#2147) $130

112V Same, except has collared mouth. (3) (#2618) $65

113 Slender cornucopia to left on panel. Reverse: rayed eagle, right, over beaded oval. Marked (FL). (2) (#1243) $425

114 Cornucopia to left on panel. Reverse: rayed eagle to right over beaded oval marked (Zanesville). ½ pint. Red amber. (2) (#2017) $1,300

115 Slender cornucopia with tail to left. Reverse: 13 stars over crude eagle. 3 bars around base. Corrugated edges. ½ pint. Olive green. (GII-58). (1) (#417) $4,100

116 Broad cornucopia with tail to left. Crude and thick flask. Reverse: eagle head, left, with pantaloon-like legs perched on semi-spherical rock. Pint. Olive amber. (GII-75). (1) (#2129) $2,200

117 Slender cornucopia with tail to left on panel. Reverse: small eagle high up on side. ½ pint. Aqua. (GII-46). (3) (#659) $85
Reproduction of above, amethyst. (#1464) $20

## Chapter Seven

# Miscellaneous Flasks

118 Marked (John Q. Adams) over bust. Beaded edges. Reverse: 12 stars over eagle looking to right. Marked (J. T. & Co). Pint. Aqua. (GI-62). (1) (#1369) $5,800

119 Marked (The American System) around early steamboat. Reverse (Use Me But Do Not Abuse Me) around large sheaf of rye. Herringbone edges. Pint. Aqua. (GX-21). (1) (#2545) $10,500

120 6-pointed star, eye and marked (AD). Reverse: star, arm, emblem and (GRJA). Pint. Amber. (4) (#1588) $120

120A Same, sloping, collared mouth. (4) (#579) $100

120B Same, clear olive green. (4) (#2691) $150

121 Anchor near top of side. Reverse: plain. ½ pint. Aqua. (6) (#1274) $40
Same, amber.
Same, clear.

121A Anchor with rope. Reverse: plain, flat rib. ½ pint. Aqua. (6) (#34) $32.50

121B Similar, anchor tipped to left. Amber. (6) (#626) $30

121C Simlar. Reverse marked (John F. Horne Knoxville Tenn). (6) (#338) $60

121D Similar. Marked (AG Co) on base. (6)

121E Similar. Marked (Registered Full Quart), (Made by E. Packham Jr & Co). (Baltimore Md) on base. Quart. Amber. (6)

121V Similar, but (S) on base. ½ pint. Amber. (6)

121J Similar. Amber. (6)

122 Marked (Agriculture) over sheaf of rye and farming implements. Reverse: (W. Ihmsen's) over eagle on oval. Marked (Glass). Pint. Aqua. (GII-10) (2) (#1433) $1,050

123 Apostle bottle. Round with 6 monks on sides in arches. Quart. Golden amber. (4) (#637) $75

124 (Baltimore Glass Works) around anchor. Reverse: sheaf of rye, rake and fork. ½ pint. Aqua. (5) (#2331) $80

124A Same. Olive amber. (5) (#1132) $450

124B Same. Puce. (4) (#1708) $700

125 (Baltimore Glass Works) around anchor. Reverse (Resurgam) with phoenix above. Pint. Amber. (4) (#971) $170

**Flask made by Baltimore Glass Works. (125).**

125A Variant of above (Resurgam) on narrower panel. Olive green. (3) (#2387) $250

125B Same, greenish amber. (3) (#668) $450

126 Monument. Marked (Baltimore Glass Works Est 1790 Baker Bros. & Co). Reverse (The Monumental City 1880 Sesquicentennial). Deep red amber. (4)

127 Calabash. Marked (Baltimore Glass Works) around anchor. Reverse: sheaf, rake and fork. Quart. Dark red amber. (3) (#129) $3,000

128 Same, blue green. (4) (#1041) $700

128A Marked (Baltimore Glass Works) around anchor. Reverse: sheaf, rake and fork. Quart. Dark red amber. (4) (#2756) $700

128E Same, golden amber. (4) (#338) $525

129 Woman riding early bicycle with large wheel. Reverse: eagle over oval marked (A & DHC). Pint. Aqua. (4) (#427) $120

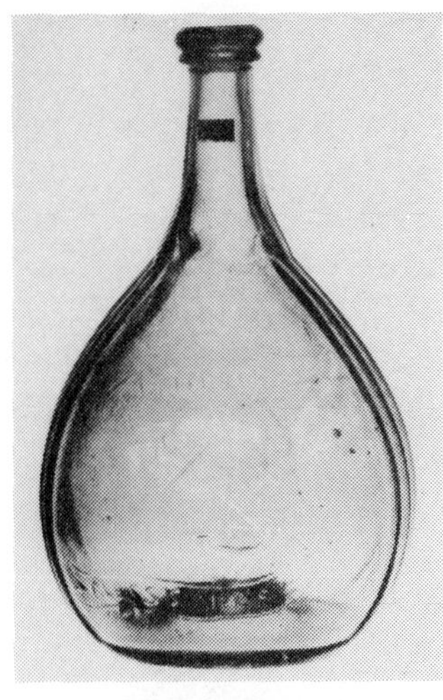

Calabash flask in blue made by the Baltimore Glass Works. (127).

130 Woman riding bicycle with large wheel. Banner with (Not for Joe). Reverse: plain. Pint. Deep amber. (3) (1420) $600

131 Log cabin. Marked (E. G. Booz's Old Cabin Whiskey. 1840) on roof. On one end (E. G. Booz's Old Cabin Whiskey). On other (120 Chestnut St Philadelphia). Quart. Amber. (GIII-3). (2) (#1305) $750

Two Booz bottles, both in amber color. (132, 131)

132 Same, except ends of gables clipped. Quart. Amber. (GIII-4). (2) (#1577) $900

133 Bust of Byron. Reverse: bust of Scott. ½ pint. Amber. (4) (#2485) Not sold because of crack in neck.

134 Rectangular with oval base. Shoulders paneled. Marked (Belle of Anderson Old Fashioned Hand Made Sour Mash) in 6-pointed star. Pint. Milk glass. (3) (#1079) $85

135 Decanter-shaped. 8 panels around sides. Marked with hollow 5-pointed star (E & B Bevan Pittston Pa), on shoulder (I. X. L. Valley Whiskey). ¾ quart. Deep amber. (4) (#1121) $1,150

136 Cylindrical. Marked (Casper's Whiskey Made by Honest North Carolina People). Quart. Blue. (3) (#86) $160

137 Cylindrical, very similar to above. Marked (C. I. Co East Rindge N. H.). Quart. Blue (4)

138 Plain flask marked (Cycle Glass Works) in semicircle above (N. Y.). Reverse: plain. Pint. Amber. (5) (#2124) $65

138A Quart. Dark amber. Same as above. (5) (#2386) $40

138E Same. ½ pint. Dark amber. (5) (2066) $60

138V Same. Quart. Aqua. (5) (#738) $35

139 Barrel. Marked (Chapin & Gore Chicago) (Sour Mash 1867). On base (E. Frank's Pat'd August 1872). ¾ quart. Light amber. (4) (#93) $140

139F Similar to above but no inscription on base. (4) (#2605) $55

140 Similar markings, but marked (Hawley Glass Co Hawley, Pa) on base. (4) (#3012) $11

140V Cylindrical. Paneled. Marked (Chapin & Gore). On base (Hawley Class Co Hawley, Pa). Inside threaded mouth. (6) (#1813) $80

141 (Baltimore) under monument. Reverse (Corn For the World) over ear of corn. ½ pint. Deep red. (GIII-7). (2) (#1785) $1,100

142 Baltimore monument. Reverse: border of grapes and vine around. Marked (A Little More Grape Capt. Bragg). ½ pint. Green. (GVI-6). (4) (#20) $1,000

143 (Baltimore) under monument. Reverse (Corn For The World) over ear of corn. Pint. Shaded amber. (GVI-6). (3) (#225) $1,050

144 (Baltimore) over monument. Reverse (Liberty & Union) on panel. Pint. Olive amber. (GVI-3). (2) (#1125) $2,800

145 (Baltimore) under monument. Reverse (Corn For The World), steps to the left. Quart. Blue green. (GVI-4). (3) (#2708) $1,550

145A Same, brownish amber. (3) (#1196) $650
Same, orange amber. (#769) $1,000

145B Same, olive green. (3)

145C Same, cornflower blue. (3) (#1673) $1,700

145D Same, puce. (3) (#2689) $1,150

145F Same, red amber. (3) (#2916) $525

145E Similar, but steps to right. Slight difference in design. Quart. Amber. (2) (#276) $850

146 Cannon. Marked (J. T. Gayen) above (Altoona). ¾ quart. Amber. (4) (#2521) $1,050

147 Cannon and 15 balls. Marked (Gen Taylor Never Surrenders). Reverse (A Little More Grape Capt. Bragg) surrounded by grapes and vines. No rib on edges. Pint. Green. (GX-5). (3) (#2801) $1,100

147V Similar, but has high central rib. Pint. Aqua. (GX-4). (3) (#2372) $250

148 Similar markings. ½ pint. Green. (3) (#1857) $925

148A Same, deep puce. (3) (#2097) $975

149 Cannon to right, flag, cannon balls and powder can. Reverse: 13 stars, (Union) (FA & Co). ½ pint. Dark amber. (4) (#2563) $130

149V Similar. Pint. Amber. (4) (#2929) $200

150A Cannon to right, flag and cannon balls. Reverse (Union), 13 stars, etc. Pint. Dark amber. (4) (#1259) $225

151 Cannon to left. Smaller flag. Reverse (Union), 13 stars, etc. and (W. Frank & Sons Pitts). Aqua. (4) (#78) $275
(#2947) $250

152 Similar to above with variations. Marked W. Frank & Sons Pitts). Pint. Aqua. (4) (#882) $60

153 Similar to #151. Quart. Amber. (4)

154 Shape of cannon. Marked (Buchanan Distillery Hand Made Sour Mash Whiskey). ¾ quart. Amber. Height: 9″. (3) (#1447) $2,500

155 Log cabin with square chimney. Marked on both sides of roof (Cottage Brand). ¾ quart. Aqua. (4) (#2093) $190

156 Columbia facing left under 13 stars. Reverse: eagle over (B&W). Pint. Aqua. (GI-121). (3) (#1771) $400

157 Square. Columnar corners. Marked (Old Continental Whiskey). Reverse: soldier in uniform over (1776). ¾ quart. Golden amber. (3) (#957) $1,300

157V Flask with high central rib. Marked (Continental) above (1776-1876). Star on base. ½ pint. Aqua. (5) (#1690) $37.50

158 Columbia facing left under 13 stars over (Kensington). Reverse: eagle marked (Union Co.). Vertical ribs at base. Pint. Aqua. (GI-118). (3) (#516) $675

159 Columbia facing left under 13 stars over (Kensington). Reverse: eagle marked (Union Co). Vertical ribs at base. ½ pint. Yellow tinge. (GI-118) (2) (#2412) $3,600

160 5-pointed star over crossed keys. Reverse: square and compasses around reversed (G). Corrugated edges. ½ pint. Olive amber. (GIV-30). (1) (#2865) $7,300

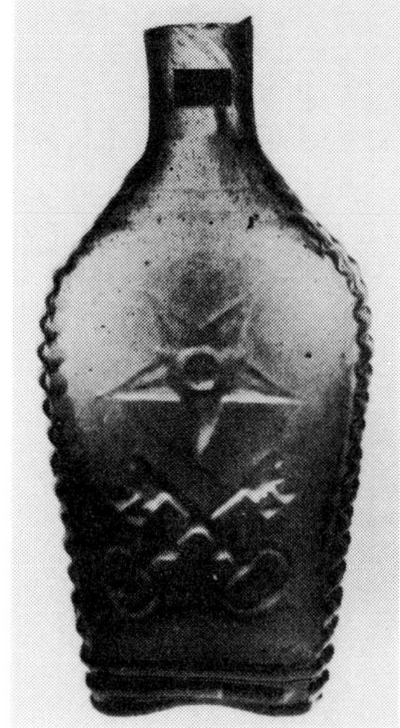
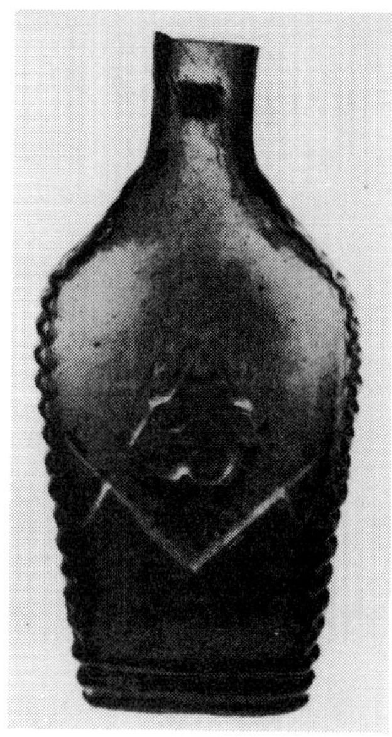

**Rare flask with Masonic symbols. (160).**

161 Marked (Cunningham and Ihmsen Glassmakers Pittsburgh Pa.) Reverse: plain. Pint. Aqua. (5) (#1882) $45

162 Man walking to left, hat off, bag in hand, going towards gun. (Drafted) coming from mouth. Reverse: eagle over irregular panel. Pint. Aqua. (3) (451) $550

163 Flag. Marked (Coffin & Hay Hammonton). Reverse: rayed eagle over oval. Quart. Green. (GII-48) (3) (#2929) $1,850

164 Columbia to left under 13 stars. Plain panel. Reverse: eagle to right, plain panel. 10 ribs at base. Pint. Blue. (GI-119). (1) (#1065) $21,000

165 Flag, marked (Hard Cider) over barrel, plow and stalks of grain. Reverse: 9 stars, log cabin and fence. Corrugated edges. Pint. Cornflower blue. (1) (#513) $5,600

166 Flag to right, 13 stars, 9 bars. Reverse (New Granite Glass Works Stoddard N. H.). Pint. Golden amber. (GI-27). (1) (#369) $2,800

Columbia flask in blue glass. (164).

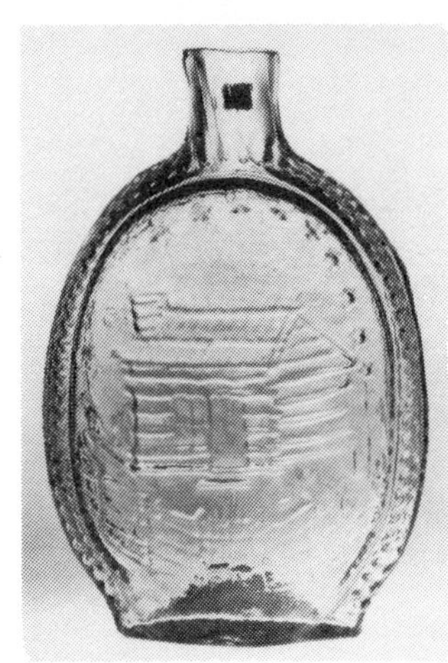

"Hard Cider" flask in cornflower blue. (165).

167 Similar to above. ½ pint. Olive amber. (GI-28). (1) (#2753) $3,700

168 Flag, 20 stars and marked. (For Our Country). Reverse: rayed eagle on shield to right. Pint. Aqua. (GII-53). (3) (#795) $110

169 Flag, 20 stars, (For Our Country). Reverse: rayed eagle left on shield. Pint. Aqua. (GII-54). (3) (#1995) $210

Reproduction, pint, green. (#1620) $15

170 Flag, 13 stars, (For Our Country). Reverse: 13 stars over eagle. Pint. Aqua. (3) (#131) $130

171 Draped female figure. Round base. 8 7/8" high. Amber. (3) (#527) $170

173 (Flora Temple) above horse. Also marked (Harness Trot 219 ¾). Handle on shoulder. Reverse: plain. Pint. Dense amber. (3) (#556) $350

173A Same, lighter amber. (3) (#1580) $350

Flask made in Stoddard, New Hampshire. (167).

174 Same, but 2 dots in place of handle. Puce. (3) (#2628) $525

175A Same. Deep green. (3) (#2619) $575

176 (Flora Temple) above horse. Also (Harness Trot 219 ¾ Oct 15. 1859). Applied handle. Reverse: plain. Quart. Dense amber. (3) (#4) $350

176A Same, amber. Original label. (3)

176C Same, copper color. (3) (#660) $275

177 Same, except dots replace handle. Quart. Green. (3) (#145) $4,700

177V Same, amber quart. (3) (#1020) $275

178 (Benjamin Franklin) over bust. Reverse (T. W. Dyott MD) over bust. On edges (Kensington Glass Works, Philadelphia) and (Eripuit Coelo Fulmen Sceptrumpque Tyrranis). Quart. Yellow green. (GI-96). (1) (#644) $1,300

179 Bust of Franklin on both sides. No in-

Franklin flask, yellow green, made at Kensington Glass Works, Philadelphia. (178).

scription. Quart. Amber. (GI-97). (1) (#2065) $3,800

180 (Benjamin Franklin) over bust. Reverse (T. W. Dyott MD) over bust. On edges (Where Liberty Dwells There is my Country) and (Kensington Glass Works Philadelphia). Pint. Red amber. (GI-94). (1) (#2561) $1,500

**Flask with Franklin on obverse and glassmaker, T. W. Dyott on reverse. (180).**

181 Same as above but with no inscription around edges. Pint. Aqua. (GI-95. (3) (#1372) $240

182 (Benjamin Franklin) over bust varying from above in arrangement of clothes. Letters are larger. Reverse (Wheeling Glass Works) over bust that looks like Dyott but also with different arrangement of clothes. Tiny beads surround panels on each side. Pint. Green. (GI-98). (1) (#833) $4,800

**Franklin flask made at Wheeling Glass Works. (182).**

183 Grapes on panel. Reverse: sheaf of rye. ½ pint. Aqua. (GX-3). (4) (#1228) $200

184 Narrow bunch of grapes on panel. Reverse: 13 stars over eagle with shield on breast. ½ pint. Green. (GII-56). (3) (#804) $1,100

185 Flask with flat rib. Bust of Cleveland in circular medallion. On base (A. C. & Co). Reverse: plain. Pint. Aqua. (4) (#1562) $120

186A Grapes on panel. Reverse: 13 stars over eagle. Quart. Deep blue. Bottle crude and heavy. (GII-55). (3)

186B Similar to above. Amber. (3) (#2977) $950
Reproduction, quart. Light green. (#2140) $125
Reproduction, amber. (#10) $5

187 Grapes in depressed panel. Reverse: plain. Pint. Amber. Threaded mouth. (6) (#1050) $25

188 Squat, chestnut shape. Marked (Gentry Slote & Co) over (New York). Reverse: horse. Quart. Olive green. (4) (#1767) $300

188V Similar, but marked (Good Samaritan Brandy) on reverse. Quart. Olive green. (4)

189 Bust of Grant on panel inside wreath tied with bow. Reverse: eagle over irregular oval marked (Union). Pint. Light yellow green. (4) (#1291) $350

189V Same, but with no inscription in oval. Pint. Aqua. (GX-30). (4)

190 Marked (The Great Western) over figure of hunter. Reverse: deer and (C) on base. Pint. Aqua. (GX-30). (3) (#761) $550

191 Canteen, applied loops on shoulder. Marked (H. A. Graef's Son N. Y. Canteen). ¾ quart. Dark olive green. (4) (#918) $300

192 Marked (Granite Glass Co.). Reverse (Stoddard N. H.). Pint. Amber. (4) (#1450) $100

192A Same, light amber. (4)

193 Same. Quart. Amber. (4)

194 Small barrel. Marked (Hard Cider). Reverse (Tippecanoe Extract). Height: 2″. Clear. (5)

195 Heart-shaped flask. Marked (John Hart & Co) on either edge. Pint. Amber. (4) (#1057) $210

196 Horizontal rows of hobnails either side. Corrugated edges. ½ pint. Green. (4) (#2707) $225

196X Same, cobalt blue. (URG22D1). (#2292) $350

196A Similar, but marked (Frederick). Reverse

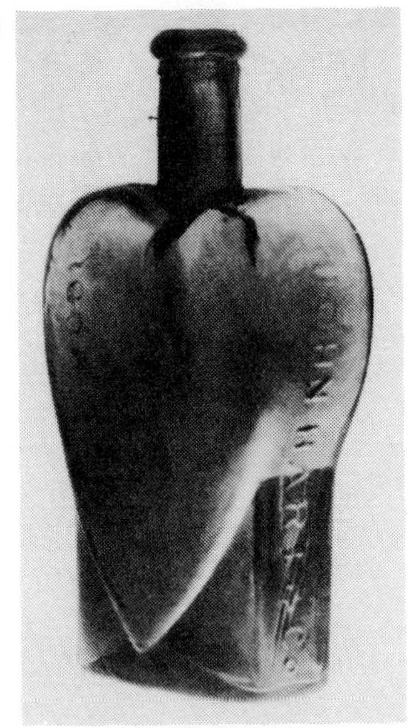

Heart-shaped flask in amber. (195).

(Idsted). ½ pint. Olive amber. (3) (#2724) $100

196B Similar to #196. Pint. Green (4)

196C Same. Pint. Deep Amethyst. (4)

196D Same. Pint. Deep blue. (4)

197 Horseman galloping to right. Reverse: hound. Pint. Light amber. (4) (#2115) $375

197A Same. Puce. (3) (#2113) $900

197B Same. Deep puce. (3) (#2332) $550

198A Horseman in uniform to right. Reverse: hound. Quart. Red Amber. (3) (#35) $160

198B Same. Light amber. (3) (#2433) $1,800

199 Horseman to right, hat flying off. Reverse: hound. ½ pint. Aqua. (3) (#35) $160

200 Same as #197 except has applied handle on neck. Pint. Amber. Spout mouth. (2) (#2433) $1,800

202 Masonic pillars either side with 5 stars, moon, large star and hourglass between. Reverse: same. Corrugated edges. ½ pint. Olive green. (GIV-29). (1) (#481) $6,000

203 Hunter to left. Reverse: vine with berries. Pint. Deep blue. (5) (#666) $280

204 Hunter shooting at rabbit. Dog at feet. Reverse: dog, tree, 2 birds and sun. Ribbed. Pint. Aqua. (5) (#2782) $150

205 Hunter standing near skiff. Reverse: 2 dogs running to left. Pint. Amber. (3) (#969) $375

206 Hunter holding rabbit. Reverse: wreath of oak leaves. Pint. Blue. (5) (#2625) $180

"Horse and hound" flask. Unusual in that it has applied handle. (200).

Masonic flask has same decoration on both sides. (202).

207 Calabash. Hunter to left, 2 birds, 2 dogs. Reverse: fisherman, mill to left. Quart. Deep red amber. (4) (#211) $475

207B Same. Green. (5) (#275) $450

208 Calabash. Hunter left, 2 birds, 1 dog. Reverse: fisherman, mill and tree to right. Quart. Aqua. (5) (#1914) $65

209 Hunter to right, 2 birds, 1 dog. Reverse: fisherman to left. No tree or mill. Quart. Aqua. **This is scarce variant.** (4) (#610) $65

210 Indian, bird, tree and dog. Marked (Cunninghams & Co Pittsburgh Pa). Reverse: eagle

on monument and (Continental). Quart. Green. (3) (#1452) $850

211 Indian, bird, tree and dog. 5 dots. Reverse: eagle on monument. Quart. Aqua. (5) (#195) $200

213 Marked (Isabella Glass Works) around anchor. Reverse: picture of glassworks. ½ pint. Green. (3) (#164) $400

214 (Isabella Glass Works) around anchor. Reverse: glassworks and tree. Quart. Aqua. (4) (#2186) $80

215 (Isabella Glass Works) around anchor. Reverse: sheaf, rake and fork. Pint. Aqua. (4) (#2019) $90

216 (General Jackson) over bust. Reverse: 10 stars over eagle on beaded oval marked (B&M). Beaded edges. Pint. Clear. (GI-67). (1) (#1881) $5,400

217 (General Jackson) over bust. Reverse: 13 stars over eagle over beaded oval marked (J.T. & Co). Beaded edges. Pint. Green aqua. (GI-65). (1) (#1244) $1,000

218 (General Jackson) over bust. Reverse: 10 stars over eagle on beaded oval. Beaded edges. Pint. Aqua. (GI-64). (1) (#1996) $950

219 (General Jackson) over bust. Reverse: floral motif showing acorns. Beaded edges. Pint. Light green. (GI-68) (1) (#2596) $2,550

220 (Andrew Jackson) over Masonic arch and bust. Reverse: eagle and 6 cannon balls under (Knox & McKee Wheeling). Pint. Green aqua. (GI-69). (1) (#2321) $25,000

221 (General Jackson) over bust. Reverse: 10 stars over eagle over beaded oval. Marked (J. R) and (Laird Sc Pitt) below. Beaded edges. Pint. Faint violet tinge. (GI-66). (1) (#580) $4,700

**Andrew Jackson's portrait appears on this flask with Masonic symbols. (220).**

222 Key on flat panel. Reverse: plain. Pint. Aqua. (4) (#243) $40

223 Latticed on depressed panels. 19 beads either side. Reverse: 13 stars on panel surrounded by grapevines. Pint. Green. (5)

223V Similar, but 17 stars only. ½ pint. Light green. (5)

224 Calabash. (Kossuth) above bust. Reverse: tree. Quart. Blue green. (GI-113). (3) (#1724) $400

224B Same, amber. (3) (#244) $575

225 (Louis Kossuth) over bust with flags. Reverse (U. S. Steam Frigate Mississippi) and S. Huffsey). Quart. Clear olive green. (GI-112). (2) (#2881) $900

225A Same. Quart. Blue green. (2) (#547) $500

225B Same. Dark brown amber. (1) (#1641) $1,200

225V Same, except (S. Huffsey) omitted under (Mississippi). Quart. Aqua. Heavy glass. (1) (#2705) $1,550

**Flask with portrait of Louis Kossuth. (225V).**

226 (Lafayette) above bust. Reverse (DeWitt Clinton) over bust above (C-T). Corrugated edges. ½ pint. Olive green. (GI-82). (1) (#2481) $2,800

226X Plain flask marked on base (LGCo). Quart. Amber. (6) (#1498) $5

227 (Lafayette) above bust with (T. S.) below. Reverse (DeWitt Clinton) with reversed (D) over bust. (Coventry C-T) below. Corrugated edges. Pint. Amber. (GI-80). (1) (#1689) $800

Lafayette flask made in Coventry, Connecticut. (227).

228 (LaFayette) over bust, (S&C) below. Reverse (DeWitt Clinton) over bust, (C-T) below. Corrugated edges. ½ pint. Amber. (GI-81). (1) (#1353) $850

229 (Lafayette) over bust over (T.S). Reverse: Masonic arch, two 6-pointed stars above, 12-pointed stars below. Corrugated edges. ½ pint. Amber. (GI-84). (1) (#2673) $3,000

230 (Lafayette) over bust over (S). Reverse: star and moon above Masonic arch. Pint. Olive green. (GI-83) (1) (#1913 $2,500

231 (Lafayette) over bust. Reverse: Masonic arch. Pint. Olive green. (GI-88). (1) (#2369) $2,000

232 Similar to above. ½ pint. Olive green. (GI-89). (1) (#1849) $2,200

233 (Lafayette) above bust, (Coventry C-T) below. Reverse: 11 stars above liberty cap, (S&S) below. Pint. Amber. (GI-85). (1) (#1161) $550

235 (Lafayette) over bust, (Coventry C-T) below. 2 rings around base. Reverse: 9 stars over liberty cap, (S & S) below. ½ pint. Amber. (GI-86). (1) (#1900) $650

235V Same. Aqua. (1) (#1417) $2,800

236 Similar to above except 3 rings and no stars over liberty cap. ½ pint. Amber. (GI-87). (1) (#785) $3,800

237 (Genl Lafayette) over bust in arch. Reverse: 7 stars over eagle perched on 6 cannon balls. Pint. Light green. (GI-92). (1) (#465) $2,100

238 Same, except marked (Knox & McKee Wheeling). Pint. Clear. (GI-93). (1) (#2417) $4,400

239 (General Lafayette) over bust. On edge, (Republican Gratitude). Reverse: eagle over beaded oval marked (T. W. D.). On edge, (Kensington Glass Works, Philadelphia) and (E. Pluribus Unum) over eagle. Pint. Aqua. (GI-90). (1) (#1419) $450

239V Same, but no (E. Pluribus Unum) or inscriptions on edge. Pint. Aqua. (GI-91). (3) (#2443) $275

240 (Jenny Lind) over bust in wreath. Reverse: smoke from chimney going straight up instead of down as on all other Jenny Lind flasks. Quart. Aqua. Heavy glass. (GI-105). (2) (#1674) $190

240B (Jenny Lind) over bust in wreath. Ribbed sides. Reverse: tree with fruit and more fruit on ground at base of tree. Quart. Aqua. (GI-100). (1) (#321) $5,000

241 (Jenny Lind) over bust. Reverse (Kossuth) over bust. Quart. Aqua. (GI-100). (3) (#2620) $85

242A (Jenny Lind) over bust and wreath. Reverse (Fislersville Glass Works) and factory. Quart. Green. (GI-107). (2) (#1403) $350

242B Same. Amber. (2) (#2515) $410

243 (Jenny Lind) over bust and wreath. Reverse (Millfora G. Works) and factory. Quart. Aqua. (GI-101). (3) (#2834) $70

244 (Jenny Lind) over bust and wreath. Reverse (Glass Works S Huffsey) and factory. Quart. Emerald green. (GI-99). (2) (#705) $1,050

Jenny Lind flask is calabash shape. Emerald green glass. (244).

244A Same. Light amber. (3) (#1145) $600

244V Same as above but no inscription on either side. Aqua. (2) (#1162) $1,000

245 (Jenny Lind) over bust and wreath. Reverse (Glass ★ Factory) with star between words. Ribbed sides. Quart. Green. (GI-102). (2) (#515) $775

246 (Jenny Lind) over bust and wreath. Reverse: glassworks and no inscription. Quart. Bluish aqua. (GI-103). (3) (#978) $60

247 Bust of Jenny Lind over lyre. Reverse: same. Shape of violin flask. Pint. Sea green. (GI-109). (2) (#993) $60

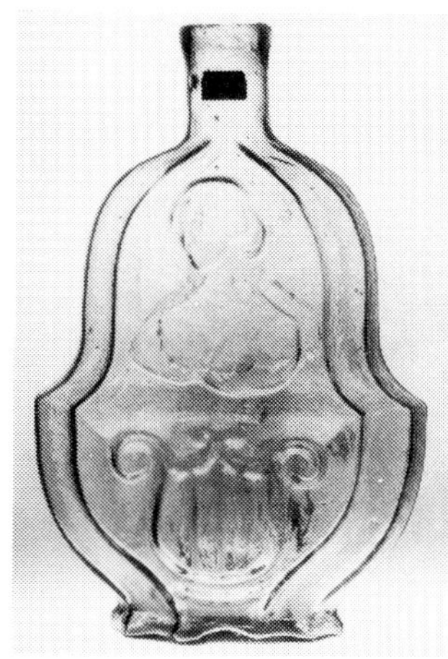

**Jenny Lind flask in violin shape is identical on both sides. (247).**

247A Same. Quart. Sea green. (GI-109). (2) (#2353) $1,700

247B Same, but with vines around edges. Quart. Deep aqua. (GI-110). (2) (#1337) $1,250

248 (Jenny Lind), similar to #246, but bust and head are narrower. Ribbed sides. Quart. Blue. Heavy glass. (GI-104). (1) (#2241) $950

248A Same. Yellow green. Heavy glass. (1) (2899) $1,250

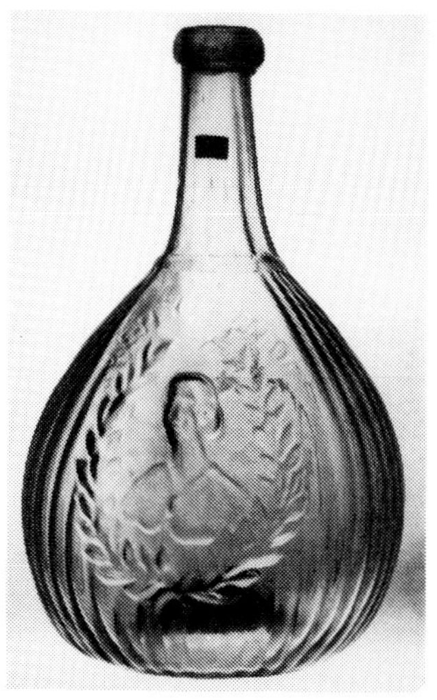

**Jenny Lind flask in heavy glass. Portrait is somewhat narrower than that on #244. (248).**

249 (Louisville, Ky) in semicircle over (Glass Works). Reverse: plain. Quart. Aqua. (5) (#1498) $5

250 (Louisville, Ky Glass Works) in circle near base. Flat rib. Pint. Aqua. (5) (#994) $40

251 Locomotive. (Success To The Railroad). Reverse: same. Pint. Blue. (GV-1). (2) (#2177) $2,500

**"Success to the Railroad" flask is same on both sides. (251).**

251A Same. Pint. Green. (GV-2). (2) (#529) $1,300

251B Same. Pint. Clear olive green. (GV-2). (2) (#1793) $1,000

251C Same. Pint. Medium amber. (GV-1). (2)

253 Log cabin. (Tippicanoe) over door. Cider barrels under window. Reverse (Harrison) over door. Height: 3½". Aqua. (2) (#429) $1,000

254 (Mechanics Glass Works Philada). Reverse: sheaf, rake and fork. Quart. Green. (3) (#2257) $575

255 (McCarty & Torreson Manufacturers Wellsburg, Va). Reverse: large sunburst. Pint. Aqua. (GIX-48). (2) (#2721) $1,050

256 Same. Quart. Aqua. (GIX-49). (2) (#1561) $1,000

257 (Murdock & Cassell) above ribbing. Reverse (Zanesville Ohio). Pint. Light green. (GX-14). (2) (#500) $1,250

259 Flat canteen shape. Marked (Picnic). ½ pint. Amber. (6) (#770) $85

259V Same. Pint. Aqua. (6) (#770) $85

259A Similar 4 oz. amber. Marked (Pap's Picnic). (6) (#2370) $60

259B Similar 6 oz. amber. Marked (Try It). (6) $75

Same, yellow amber. (#2370) $75

260 (New London Glass Works) around anchor. Reverse: 7 stars over flying eagle. Pint. Yellow amber. (GII-68). (3)

260A Same. Red amber. (3) (#1748) $475

260B Same, striated green. (2) (#353) $900

260C Same, olive green. (3)

261 (New London Glass Works) around anchor. Reverse: 9 stars over eagle on wreath. ½ pint. Aqua. (GII-67). (3) (#1932) $125

261A Same, sea green. (3) (#972) $210

261B Same, yellow. (3) (#1500) $1,150

261C Same, dark amber. (3)

261D Same, black olive green. (3) (#916) $600

261E Same, olive green. (3) (#2467) $400

262 New London Glass Co. hat. Green. 6″ by 2¾″. (4)

263 (New London Glass Works) around anchor. Reverse: 7 stars over eagle on wreath. Quart. Aqua. (GII-68). (3) (#1292) $325

263A Same, red amber. (3)

263B Same, light amber. (3) (#132) $375

263C Same, green. (3) (#1644) $650
Similar, yellow. (GII-66). (#2180) $500
Similar, light green.

264 Pig bottle. Marked (Beiser and Fischer N. Y.). ¾ quart. Deep amber. (2) (#2080) $270

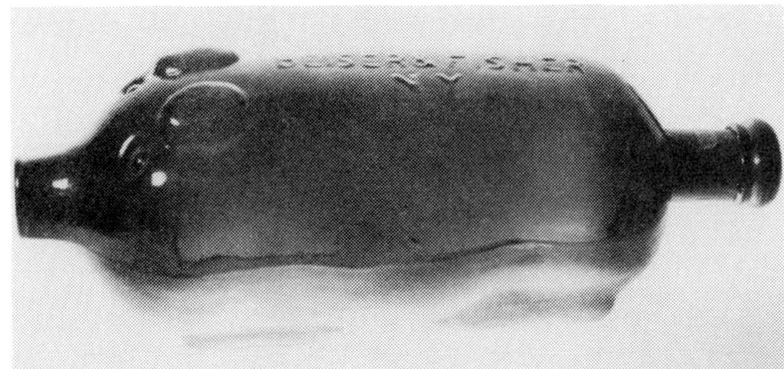

**Pig bottle embossed "Beiser & Fischer N. Y." Deep amber. (264).**

265A Woman on old-fashioned bicycle with small wheel. Marked (Not For Joe) coming from mouth. Reverse: plain. Pint. Blue. (2) (#2964) $1,600

266 Pig bottle. Marked (Good Old Bourbon in a Hogs ---). ½ pint. Amber. (4) (#2080) $270

266B Same, clear. No inscription. (5) (#910) $35

266C Same. Marked (Cresent Saloon 214 Jefferson Street, Louisville, Ky) and (Duffy). ½ pint. Clear. (4) (#1110) $525

267 Pineapple-shaped. Diamond quilting with space for label. ¾ quart. Golden amber. (3) (#1165) $200

267Z Similar, but neck, mouth and label panel vary. ¾ quart. Amber. (3) (#2069) $150

268 Similar, but marked (W&Co N.Y.) on panel. Flattened into chestnut shape with applied handle. ¾ quart. Amber. (2) (#949) $2,100

**Two bottles in pineapple pattern differ in that one has depressed and marked label while other has applied handle. (268).**

268A Similar to above, but not flattened or any handle. ¾ quart. Amber. (3) (#2645) $250

268E Same. Clear, deep olive green. (3) (#213) $1,000

268C Similar, but marked (J. C. CO). ¾ quart. Dark amber. (3) (#1997) $700

269 Pottery pig covered with map and marked (From Hon Gaubat No 115 Christy Ave. St. Louis, Mo). Made around 1872-1874. ½ pint. Brown Anna Jug Pottery. (4) (#2272) $950

269A Similar, but smaller with different map and inscription. Brown pottery. Marked (Jim Owens Chester Idol). (4) (#758) $1,050

269B Ordinary stoneware marked (To my friend with a little good old rye in a hogs ---) (ICRR) (Cairo) (Chicago) (Mounds) etc. (4) (#1685) $2,000

269C Small pig. (Something good in a hog's ---), (He won't squeal) (Pat W), clear. (5) (#1603) $40

269D Pottery pig marked (Brachman & Massard 81 West Third Street Cincinnati With a Little Fine Old Bourbon In). (3) (#2814) $900

270 (Success To The Railroad) around horse and cart. Reverse: eagle lengthwise and 17 stars. Pint. Olive green. (GV-8). (3) (#1307) $170

**Olive green "Success to the Railroad" has eagle on reverse side. (270).**

271 Similar, but no stars or lettering. Pint. Amber. (GV-9). (3) (#1595) $120

271A Same, olive green. (3) (#1739) $190

272 (Success To The Railroad) with railroad above cart. Reverse: same. Pint. Aqua. (GV-4). (2) (#323) $325

272V Same as above, olive amber. (2) (#163) $350

**"Success to the Railroad" flask, identical on both sides, shows horse pulling cart on tracks. (227V).**

272A Similar lettering with slight variation in arrangement. Pint. Olive amber. (GV-3). (3) (#1147) $150

272B Same, clear olive green. (3) (#1203) $190

272C Same, aqua. (3) (#2659) $225

273V Similar, but different arrangement of letters. Pint. Green. (GV-5). (3) (#707) $400
Reproduction, pint, aqua. (#797) $20
Reproduction, pint, olive green. (#1351) $40

274 (Success To The Railroad) small letters. Reverse: same (Success) above cart. Pint. Amber. (GV-6). (3) (172) $230
Same, olive green. (#2195) $175
Same, yellow. (#2193) $900

275 Similar horse and cart, but no inscription on either side. Pint. Green. (GV-7). (3) (#1964) $550

276 (Railroad) and (Lowell) around cart. Reverse: eagle lengthwise and 13 stars. ½ pint. Amber. (GV-10). (3) (#2051) $200

**Similar flask with eagle and stars on reverse. (276).**

277 (Success To The Railroad), (Success) below. Reverse: slightly different. Pint. Olive green. Sloping collared mouth unusual. (GV-5). (3)

278 (Ravenna Glass Works) in large letters. Reverse: 5-pointed star. Pint. Aqua. (4) (#1867) $25

279 (Robt Ramsey Wine & Liquor Mercht 281 8th Avenue N. Y.). Reverse: bust of Taylor. Pint. Dark amber. (2) (#1193) $900

281 Same. Quart. Golden amber. (4) (#1004) $275

281V (Ravenna Glass Company) and anchor. Reverse: 13 stars over eagle. Pint. Deep olive green. (4) (#2723) $325

282 (Ravenna Glass Company) and anchor. Reverse: 13-stars over eagle. Pint. Deep olive green. (4) (#419) $350

282A Same, light blue. (4) (#2771) $275

282B Same, dark amber. (4) (#1939) $350

283 (Geo. W. Robinson Main St. W. Va No 75). Reverse: plain, flat rib. Quart. Aqua. (5) (#178) $70

283A Same. Pint. Aqua. (4) (#1402) $45

284 (Major Ringgold) over bust. Reverse (Rough and Ready) over bust of Taylor. Pint. Amethystine. (GI-71). (3) (#577) $3,000

284A Same, moonstone. (3)

**Obverse of Taylor flask in moonstone color. Reverse (not shown) is bust of Zachary Taylor. (284A).**

284B Same, but no central rib. Pint. Aqua. (GI-72). (#1836) $1,450

285 Inverted cone shape with medallion on loop around neck marked (S. M & Co New York). Gallon. Golden amber. (3) (#1893) $975

285A Similar shape with applied handle. Marked (S. M. & Co N. Y.) on medallion. Quart. Amber. (3) (#1421) $150

285V Same. Pint. Amber. (3) (#1634) $175

287 Sailboat, no waves. Reverse: 8-pointed star. ½ pint. Light green. (GX-9). (4) (#297) $275

288 Sailboat. Reverse (Bridgeton, New Jersey). ½ pint. Aqua. (4) (#1499) $170

289 Sailboat. Reverse (Bridgeton, New Jersey). ½ pint. Aqua. (GX-7). (4) (#2123) $200

290 Sailboat. Reverse (Bridgeton, New Jersey) over bust of Kossuth. Pint. Green. (GI-111). (3) (196) $700

291 Sailboat. (Fells) above, (Point) below. Reverse monument over (Balto). ½ pint. Amethyst. (GVI-2). (3) (#2529) $1,250

291A Same, yellow green. (3) #740 $650

**Sailboat with reverse of bust of Kossuth and "Bridgeton, New Jersey." (290).**

292 Sailor dancing on platform above bar. Reverse: musician on bench above bar. ½ pint. Amber. (4) (#548) $350

292A Same, olive green. (4) (#1940) $775

292X Similar, but bar marked (Chapman). Reverse (Baltimore Md) on bar. ½ pint. Light green. (4) (#2441) $150

292Y Same, light olive green. (4) (#692) $550

293 Sheaf of rye, rake and fork. Reverse: 5-pointed star high on side. ½ pint. Amber. (4) (#820) $225

293A Same, light green. (5) (#1395) $120

293B Similar. Quart. Emerald green. (4) (#2449) $400

294 Similar. Pint. Amber. (5) (#2283) $125

295 Sheaf of rye with 10 stalks. Reverse: same except 12 stalks. Pint. Aqua. (5) (#2963) $140

296 (Liberty above sheaf on panel. Reverse: dot in center of 5-pointed star. Pint. Aqua. (GX-10). (3) (#2657) $500
½ pint. Aqua. (GX-11) (#788) $375

297 Latticed. Sheaf in panel on 1 side. Reverse: latticed, (DSGCo) on base. Pint. Amber. (6) (#866) $55

298 Plain sheaf of rye. Reverse: plain. On base (Tibby Bros Pitts Pa). ½ pint. Aqua. Broad collar. (6) (#962) $50

298V Same. Pint. Aqua. (5) (#962) $50

299 Calabash. Sheaf of rye, rake and fork under spray of leaves. Reverse: 8-pointed star under (Sheets & Duffy). Quart. Aqua. (4) (#1306) $250 (#1610) $100

300 Same, but (Sheets & Duffy) omitted. Quart. Aqua. (5) (#1018) $200

301 Same, but spray omitted and has applied handle. (3) (#17) $275

302 Same, but no handle. Quart. Blue green. (5)

302A Same, Quart. Amber. (4) (#2489) $220

304 (Franklin) under full-rigged ship. Reverse: Masonic arch around edges: (Free Trade and Sailors Rights), (Kensington Glass Works Phiadelphia). Pint. Pale green. (GIV-34). (3) (#2643) $500

**Ship, Franklin, under full sail. (304)**

305 Broad sheaf with 11 stalks over plain oval. Reverse: plain. Pint. Aqua. (5) (#1775) $110

306 (Franklin) under full-rigged ship. Reverse: rayed eagle over beaded oval marked (T. W. D.). Pint. Aqua. (GII-42). (3) (#787) $200

**Franklin flask with reverse marked "T.W.D." (306).**

308 Soldier over (Balt. Md). Reverse: ballet dancer over (Chapman). Pint. Green. (3) (#1988) $450

308A Same, olive green. (3) (#1852) $525

**Soldier and ballet dancer adorn this flask made in Baltimore. (308).**

309 Calabash. Soldier. Reverse: 11-pointed star. Quart. Green. (3) (#819) $210

310 (Will You Take a Drink - Will a [picture of a duck] Swim). Reverse: plain. Pint. Aqua. (5) (#1275) $125

310A ½ pint. Similar with variations. (4) (#1682) $150

310B Quart. Green. (4) (#2804) $750

310V Pint. Aqua. Similar with variations. Sloping collar blown in mold. (5) (#907) $175

311 (South Carolina Dispensary) around palmetto tree. Reverse: plain. ½ pint. Aqua. (6)

312 (S C) with palmetto tree. Reverse (E. P. Jr & Co) near base. Pint. Aqua. (6)

312G Same, ½ pint. Aqua. (6)

313 (South Carolina Dispensary) around palmetto tree with 8 branches. Reverse: plain. Pint. (6)

313V (SC) on either side of tree. Crossed logs, at base: (Dispensary). ½ pint. Aqua. (5) (#2210) $855

314 (S C) on either side of tree, (Dispensary) below. Reverse: plain. Original label. Quart. Olive green. (GX-24). (6)
Note: 311 to 314 were sold well before the auction. This excepts 313V

315 (Jared Spencer) on round medallion. Reverse (Manchester Con). Diamond quilting. Pint. Olive green. (GX-25). (1) (#1545) $26,000

315A Similar to above. No inscription. Concentric rings around cross. Quilting below. Pint. Olive green. (GX-25). (1) (#545) $16,000

**Group of three Jared Spencer flasks in shades of olive green. All made in Connecticut.**

315B Similar to above. No inscription. Circular medallion with 8 large pearls around larger one. Diapering. Pint. Olive green. (GX026). (1) (#2993) $18,500

318 (Springgarden Glass Works) around anchor. Reverse: cabin with tree to right. Bars below anchor and cabin. ½ pint. Aqua. (4) (#555) $95

318A Same. Amber. (4) (#1180) $475

318B Same. Olive green. (4) (#764) $550

319 Pint, similar, but no bars. Amber. (#2836) $400

319A Same. Blue (3) (#1513) $3,800

321 Rayed eagle to right on beaded oval. Reverse (Coffin & Hay, Hammondton) on oval panel. Pint. Aqua. (GII-51). (4) (#404) $1,200

322 (Coffin & Hay Hammonton) around stag. Reverse: rayed eagle head to right over plain oval. ½ pint. Aqua. (GII-50). (4) (#1436) $425

323 (Good Game) at right of stag. Reverse: willow tree. Ribbed edges. ½ pint. Aqua. (4) (#2444) $325

323C (Good Game) at right of stag. Reverse: willow tree. Ribbed edges. ½ pint. Aqua. (4) (#867) $725

324 Same as #322 only black. (GII-49). (3) (#897) $3,500

326 Stag, tree to left. Reverse: boar's head in hunting horn with sword and gun crossed in background. Canteen shape. ½ pint. Deep sapphire blue. (4) (#852) $47-50

327A (Genl Taylor) over bust facing left. Reverse (Fells Point) over monument and (Balto) below. Pint. Amethyst. (GI-73). (1) (#1241) $2,450

328 (Rough and Ready) above bust of Taylor turned to left. Reverse: 10 stars over eagle to right over oval with 19 beads. Diagonal ribbing at base. Corrugated edges. Pint. Deep aqua. (GI-76). (1) (#2244) $2,800

329 (Rough & Ready) over bust over star. Reverse (Masterson) over 13 stars over eagle. Corrugated edges. Quart. Aqua. (GI-77) (3) (#305) $2,200

330 (Zachary Taylor) above bust, (Rough and Ready) below. (Corn For The World) over cornstalk. Smooth edges. Pint. Brilliant olive green. (GI-75). (1) (#1945) $2,000
Similar, (GI-74), pint, aqua. (#1321) $850

**Taylor and "Corn for the World." Flask is brilliant olive green. (330).**

331 Bust of Taylor facing left. Reverse: sheaf, rake and fork. Deep green. (GI-57). (3) (#964) $1,400

332 Same. Pint. Aqua. (GI-58). (4) (#1266) $95

333 Same. ½ pint. Aqua. (GI-59). (4) (#754) $50

334 (Travelers) and (Companion). Reverse: plain. ½ pint. Aqua. (4) (#1804) $150

335 (Travelers Companion). Reverse (Railroad Guide). ½ pint. Light green. (4) (#2329) $400

336 (Travelers Companion). Reverse (Railroad Guide). ½ pint. Light green. (4) (#2329) $400

336 (Travelers Companion) around 8-pointed star. Reverse: sheaf, rake and fork. Quart. Deep amber. (4) (#340) $250

336D Same, olive green. (4) (#2610) $120

**Obverse of this flask reads "Travelers Companion." (335).**

338 (Travelers Companion) around crude duck. Reverse (Lockport Glass Works) around 8-pointed star. Pint. Green. Heavy glass. (3) (#452) $1,100

**"Traveler's Companion" flask is decorated with crude duck. (338).**

339 (Traveler's Companion) around 8-pointed star. Reverse (Lancaster Erie Co N. Y.) around star. Pint. Green. (3) (#2772) $575

340A (Summer) above tree in leaf with bird. Reverse (Winter) above tree with no leaves or bird. Pint. Light olive green. (4) (#1276) $1,600

340 Same, dense wine red. (3) (#2356) $900

341 Tree in leaf. Reverse: tree without leaves, bird on bough. ½ pint. Aqua. (GX-16). (4) (#498) $100

342 Similar. Quart. Golden amber. (GX-19). (4) (#84) $610

**Tree in leaf. Reverse, (not shown) has bare tree with bird on bough. (342).**

342A Same. Vaseline. (4) (#1564) $675

343V Tree with buds of fruit. Reverse: bird on tree with no buds or leaves. Varies from above. Quart. Emerald green. (GX-18). (4) (#2491) $875

345 Tree in leaf on panel. Reverse: same. Pint. Light green. (GX-17). (3) (#1884) $95

346 Tree in circular medallion. (The) (Oak) on either side of trunk. Flat rib. ½ pint. Amber. (4) (#1514) $60

347 Calabash. Tree in leaf. Reverse: heavy sheaf, rake and fork. Ribbed sides. Quart. Deep wine. (3) (#945) $1,300

348 Calabash. Tree in leaf with bird. Reverse: slender sheaf rye, rake and fork. Ribbed sides. Quart. Green. (4) (#1483) $250

349 Tree in leaf covering entire panel. Reverse: 3 stars over eagle. Quart. Aqua. (GII-47). (3) (#1516) $475

350 Tree in leaf on panel. Reverse: rayed eagle over beaded oval. Pint. Aqua. (GII-41). (4) (#723) $120

351 (Union), 13 stars, shield with clasped hands and oval. Reverse: same. Quart. Light amber. (4) (#979) $400

351A Same, blue. (3) (#2531) $550

353 (Union Glass Works, New London Ct). Reverse: plain. Pint. Aqua. (4) (#1068) $325

353A Same, olive amber. (3) (#2948) $750

353B Same, light green. (4) (#2564) $200

354 Similar, with wide expanded mouth for snuff. Pint. Olive green. (3) (#1977) $5,200

**Bottle made in New London, Connecticut, has expanded mouth and was probably used for snuff. (354).**

355 (Waterford). 13 stars and clasped hands. Reverse: eagle over oval. Quart. Aqua. (4) (#274) $55

356 Bell-shaped. Ribbed, marked (Chestnut Grove C. Wharton) on medallion hanging on ribbon around neck. Quart. Amber. (3) (#2301) $375

357 (Westford Glass Co Westford Conn). Reverse (Liberty) over eagle on wreath. ½ pint. Amber. (3) (#1066) $90
(#1466) $10

358 (Westford Glass Co Westford Conn). Reverse: sheaf, rake and fork. Star below. Pint. Dark amber. (4) (#1530) $60

358C Pint. Same, olive green. (4) (#387) $75

**Flask made in Westford, Connecticut. (358C).**

359 Similar markings, but no star. ½ pint. Dark amber. (4) (#1242) $85

359C Same, olive green. (4) (#1587) $70

360 Same, olive green. Pint. (4) (#2434) $85

360C Same, amber. Pint. (4) (#2098) $100
Same, red amber. (#2754) $95

360D Same, dark green. (4)

361 (Wharton's Whiskey 1850 Chestnut Grove) on round panel. Reverse: plain. Oval flask. ¼ pint. Blue. (4) (#2388) $200

361V Same as above, but original stopper marked (Chestnut Grove). ¼ pint. Amber. (3) (#899) $175

362 (Wheat Price & Co) around bust to right. Reverse (Fairview Works) around building. Bust with heavy hair. Pint. Green. (GI-116). (1) (#1017) $6,250

362V Same as above, but bust differs slightly and hair is shorter. Pint. Green. (GI-115). (1) (#1833) $2,000

363 (Willington Glass Works West Willinton Conn), 5 lines. Reverse (Liberty) over eagle on wreath. ½ pint. Olive green. (GII-63). (3) (#1915) $375

363A Same, olive green. (3) (#1834) $110

363B Same, olive amber. (3) (#450) $100

364 Similar, only with 4 lines. Pint. Olive green. (GII-62). (3) (#98) $120

364A Same. Pint. Clear green. (3) (#611) $275

365 Similar, olive green. Quart. (GII-61). (3) (#818) $160

365A Same. Quart. Brilliant red amber. (3) (#2914) $200
(#1626) $125

365B Same. Quart. Olive amber. (3) (#1322) $140

365V Same. Quart. Deep olive green. (3) (#2018) $200

366 Similar. Smaller eagle. Pint. Green. (GII-64). (3) (#2907) $150

366A Same, olive green. (3) (#906) $150

366B Same, dark amber. (3) (#258) $110

367 Plain flask marked on base (Whitney Glass Works). Pint. Amber. (5) (#1962) $35

367V Similar except inside threaded neck with stopper. Pint. Amber. (5)

368 Wreath on flat panel. Reverse: plain. Pint. Honey amber. (6) (#418) $17.50

369 (Zanesville City Glass Works) in oval. Reverse: plain. Pint. Amber. (5) (#546) $190

370 (Weeks & Gilson Co Stoddard N. H.) on base. Cylindrical bottle. Quart. Amber. (4) (#874) $150

371 Canteen-shaped with hole near base for spigot. Marked (S. Wolf & Sons Fine Whiskey). Reverse: wolf head on shield. 2 quarts. Clear. (3)

372 Pear-shaped. 3 rings around neck and base. On oval panel (Old Wheat Whiskey S. M. & Co). 2 quarts. Amber. (4) (#823) $425

373 Pig. Marked (Paperweight from Theodore Netter Philadelphia Compliments of Theodore Netter Distilling co). ½ pint. Clear. (5) (#2536) $80

374 Oval flask. One side in large oval, (Wheeling) (Va). Reverse (Old Rye). High central rib. Pint. Light green. Heavy glass. (4) (#2468) $425

## Chapter Eight

# Masonic Flasks

375 Masonic arch and emblems. Reverse: eagle over oval marked (KCCNC). Pint. Amber. (GIV-19). (3) (#1067) $200
Same, olive amber. (#1659) $150

376 Similar with variations. Oval, marked (KEENE). Pint. Olive green. (GIV-17). (3) (#1747) $130

376X Similar. Imprint heavier. Pint. Golden amber. (GIV-17). (3) (#2083) $160

377 Similar, but marked (KCCNC) with beehive below. Pint. Amber. (GIV-18). (3)

378 Similar, but designs more delicate. Arch more slender. No inscription in oval. Pint. Olive amber. (GIV-21). (3) (#115) $200

Same, amber. (#2323) $150

378V Same, clear olive green. (3)

380 Similar, marked (KCCNC). 2 dots to right of eagle. Design above eagle. Pint. Amber. (GIV-20). (3) (#595) $250

380V Similar, but no design above eagle. Pint. Amber. (GIV-20). (3) (#2403) $200

386 Masonic arch and emblems. Reverse: eagle over oval with 8-pointed star. Wide mouth. Pint. Sea green. (GIV-5). (3) (#1625) $550

385 Masonic arch and emblems. Reverse: eagle over beaded oval with 8-pointed star. Star smaller. Pint. Blue green. (GIV-8). (3) (#1820) $525

384 Masonic arch. Reverse: eagle over beaded oval with 8-pointed star. Wide mouth. Pint. Emerald green. (GIV-7). (3) (#2817) $850

383 Masonic arch and emblems. Reverse: eagle over oval with 8-pointed star. ½ pint. Light green. (GIV-13). (3) (#113) $750

382A Same, but aqua. (3) (#753) $550

382 Similar eagle with ball feet over oval. ½ pint. Olive green. (GIV-24). (3) (#2307) $190

381 Similar to #382 with different arrangement of emblems and oval. Marked (NEG). ½ pint. Olive green. (GIV-20). (3) (#2273) $900

387 Masonic arch and emblems. Arch much narrower than on GIV-3. Reverse: eagle over beaded oval. Variant of GIV-3. Pint. Clear

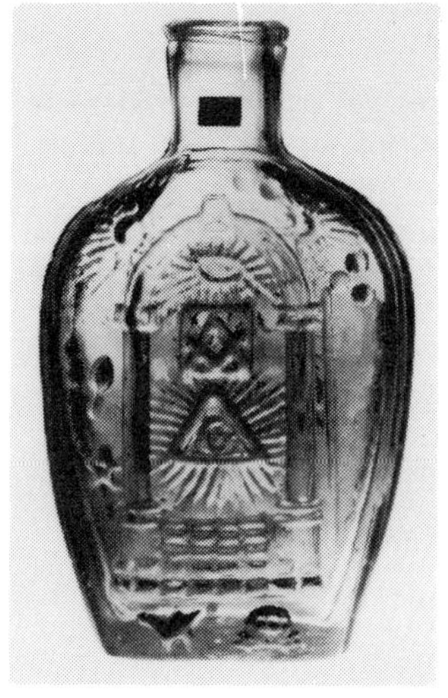

**Masonic flask in emerald green. This scarce bottle is a product of the Marlboro St. Glass Works of Keene, New Hampshire. (384).**

Tooled lip. (3) (#337) $850

388 Masonic arch and emblems. Reverse: eagle over beaded oval marked (J.K.B.). Pint. yellow green. (3) (#2788) $1,500

**This another scarce Keene Masonic that was made with a tooled lip. (388).**

388A Pint. Same, shaded olive green and amber. Tooled lip. (GIV-3). (3) (#625) $3,000

388B Same. Pint. Yellow green, tooled lip. (3) (#789) $1,600

389 Similar, but letters in oval smaller. Pint. Aqua. (GIV-4). (3) (#1721) $1,750

390 Similar. (E. Pluribus Unum) on banner over eagle. Marked (IP), beaded. Pint. Light green. (GIV-1). (3) (#2547) $275

391 Similar, but E. Pluribus Unum omitted and no beads on oval. Pint. Blue green. (GIV-1). (3) (#2260) $675

391A Same, dark olive green. Heavy glass. (3) (#2145) $800

392 Similar. Reverse: eagle over beaded oval marked (H.S.). Pint, blue green. (GIV-2). (3) (#2867) $675

392E Same, brilliant olive green. Heavy glass. (3) (#209) $700

393 Masonic arch, no designs outside arch except beehive. Corrugated edges. Reverse: eagle over plain oval. Pint. Olive green. (GIV-16). (3) (#2081) $2,500

393A Same, green. (3) (#433) $3,900

394 Masonic arch and emblems. Reverse: eagle over oval marked (N. E. G. Co). Pint. Deep blue aqua. (GIV-27). (3) (#1113) $2,000

395 Same, aqua. Pint. (3) (#2164) $200

**Masonic flask made and marked (on reverse) by the New England Glass Company. (395).**

395A Same. Pint. Olive green. (3) (#2625) $1,150

396 Similar. Eagle over leaflike design in beaded oval. Pint. Green. (GIV-11). (3) (#2873) $450

397 Similar. Eagle over beaded oval. Star similar to GIV-7, but tipped lower on left side. Tail on oval like GIV-10. Pint. Green. (3) (#665) $700

398A Farmers, arms over floral design. Reverse (Zanesville) over rayed eagle on oval and marked (Ohio), (J. Shepard & Co), (S) reversed. Pint. Red amber. (GIV-32). (3) (#1044) $450

398V Same, light blue green. Flanged neck. (3) (#1980) $475

**Light blue glass, farmers' arms on one side, reverse has eagle and is marked: Zanesville, Ohio. (398V).**

400 Masonic arch with elaborate decorations outside arch. Reverse: same. ½ pint. Green. (GIV-28). (2) (#929) $2,000

**Scarce Masonic flask, maker unknown. The decoration is the same on both sides. (400).**

400A Same. Emerald green. (3) (#1257) $1,050

401 Masonic arch and emblems. No "G" in triangle. Reverse: eagle over plain oval marked (1829). Pint. Clear. (GIV-22). (1) (#2225) $9,000

402A Calabash. 13 stars over shield with clasped hands, square and compasses and (Union).

Reverse: eagle with banner above and below shield over (A. R. S.) Quart. Citron. (GIV-42). (4)

403 Similar, but (A. R. S.) omitted. Quart. Aqua. (GIV-42a). (4) (#2146) $55

405 Masonic arch or farmers, arms. Reverse: rayed eagle over beaded oval marked (T. W. D.). Pint. Aqua. (GIV-37). (4) (#1467) $180

406 Similar to above. Reverse: square-rigged ship above, (Franklin). Corrugated edges. Pint. Light green. (4) (#2291) $160

409 Pitkin, 36 vertical ribs only. Height: 5 7/8″. Clear olive green. (#1683) $160

**Masonic arch and farmers' arms and ship *Franklin* decorate this flask made at the Kensington Glass Works, Philadelphia. (406).**

Chapter Nine

# Pitkin Flasks

410 Ribs swirled to right. 3 7/8″ high. Olive green. (2) (#1385) $900

411 Swirled to right, widely spaced ribs. Squat. Height: 5 5/8″. Light green. (3)

412 Swirled to right. Heavy ribbing producing pronounced pattern. Height: 5¼″. Dark olive green. (3) (#721) $300

413 Vertically ribbed. Height: 4 3/16″. Olive green. (3) (#2980) $400

414 36 ribs swirled to right. Height: 2½″. Olive amber. Smallest known Pitkin and therefore **extremely rare.** (1) (#2945) $2,100

**Group of Pitkin flasks. Flask on left is smallest known of its type. All are typical of the pocket flasks made in Connecticut and elsewhere. (414, 410, 433, 443).**

415 Swirled to right with vertical ribs which produce pronounced corncobbing. Crude neck sheared unevenly. Height: 5″. Light olive green. (3) (#1851) $160

416 Ribs swirled to right with vertical ribbing. Height: 4 1/8″. Olive green. (3) (#1211) $350

417 Swirled to left, ribbed. Height: 5 1/8″. Olive green. (3) (#2739) $175

418 Swirled to left and ribbed. Height: 5 1/8″. Olive green. (3) (#2243) $160

419 Swirled to left. Height: 5½″. Clear olive green. (3)

420 Swirled to left and ribbed. Height: 5½″. Light olive green. (3) (#1195) $250

421 Broad ribbing slightly to the right only. Height: 4 7/8″. Olive green. (3)

422 Swirled to right and ribbed. Height: 5½″. Light olive green. (3) (#1611) $150

423 Swirled to right only. Height: 5½″. Clear olive green. (3) (#83) $250

424 Swirled to right with pronounced ribbing. Flat, crude Midwestern glass. Height: 5½″. Clear, dark green. (3)

425 Swirled right. Dipped twice and crude around neck. Height: 5¾″. Light olive green. (3) (#2675) $425

426 Swirled right with pronounced ribbing. Midwestern. Height: 6″. Deep rich green. (3) (#259) $200

427 Swirled right. Ribbing partway up bottle. Height: 6 6/16″. Dark olive green. (3) (#1993) $190

428 Swirled right with ribbing partway up. Height: 6½″. Light olive amber. (3) (#1787) $275
Similar. (#1859) $150

429 Swirled left and ribbed partway up. Height: 7″. Dark olive green. (3) (#1163) $250

430 Swirled right with pronounced ribbing. Height: 7″. Clear sea green. (3) (#675) $400

431 Similar in shape and color to New England Pitkin, but wider ribs swirled left. Height: 6 5/8″. Olive green. Infolding collar. (3) (#403) $300

432 Wide ribs swirled slightly to left only. Height: 6½″. Olive green. (3) (#2915) $200
Similar. (#2497) $190

433 Swirled right. Pronounced ribbing. Height: 6″. Olive amber. (3) (#1131) $250
Similar. (#2163) $190

434 Swirled left with pronounced ribbing. Height: 6 7/8″. Green. (3) (#2067) $80

435 Swirled left with pronounced ribbing. Midwestern glass. Height: 5¾″. Clear dark amber. (3) (#1769) $475

436 Swirled right with faint ribbing. Exceptionally broad and flat. Height: 5″. Olive green. (3) (#1531) $180

437 Swirled to right with broad vertical ribs.

Height: 6 5/8″. Clear. Midwestern glass. (#559) $250

438 Swirled to right with broad vertical ribs. Height: 6½″. Green. Midwestern glass. (3) (#2419) $300

439 Squat bottle with 14 widely spaced ribs. Double dipped. Height: 5″. Sea green. Midwestern glass. (3) (#2285) $300

440 Swirled to left and ribbed partway up. Crude and out of shape. Mouth uneven. Probably Midwestern glass. Height: 7¼″. Clear green. (3)

441 Fine swirl to right. Vertically ribbed. Pronounced corncobbing. Height: 5¼″. Clear olive amber. Midwestern glass. (3) (#307) $350

442 Pitkin hat. Swirl to left. Height: 2 ¾″. edge ground. Olive green. (2)

443 Swirled to right, only, with very flat sides. Height: 6 ¾″. Clear olive green. (3) (#1371) $375

444 Swirled to right, only. Only known specimen of New England Pitkin in this color. Undoubtedly blown at Keene, New Hampshire. Height: 5¾″. Amethyst. (1) (#241) $4,500

445 Swirled to right with ribs partway up sides. 36 ribs. Height: 7 3/8″. Olive green. (3)

446 Swirled to left. Widely spaced and very pronounced ribbing. No vertical ribs. Height: 6½″. Clear olive green. (3) (#1387) $300

447 Swirled to right with vertical ribbing. Height: 6″. Deep greenish aqua. Midwestern glass. (3) (#594) $45

448 16 vertical ribs. Height: 5 3/8″. Green. Midwestern glass. (3)

449 Swirled to left with vertical ribbing. Height: 7¼″. Green. Midwestern glass. (3) (#1547) $230

Similar. (#1691) $170

Chapter Ten

# Pikes Peak Flasks

450 (For Pikes Peak) with prospector to left, cap, pack and cane. Reverse: eagle. Pint. Aqua. (5) (#1098) $40

451 No inscription. Prospector to left. Reverse: eagle. Pint. Emerald green. (4) (#2099) $1,025
Similar, ½ pint. Aqua. (#2340) $40

452 (For Pikes Peak) with prospector to left, pack and cane above oval with (Old Rye). Reverse: eagle over (Pittsburgh Pa) in oval. Pint. Greenish amber. (4) (#2820) $700

**Pikes Peak flask in greenish amber is marked "Pittsburgh" on the reverse. (452).**

453 Same. Quart. Aqua. (4) (#2898) $60

454 (For Pikes Peak) with prospector to left with pack and cane over plain oval. Reverse: plain. ½ pint. Aqua. (5) (#1578) $30

455 No inscription. Prospector to left on rectangle. Reverse: eagle over oval. Pint. Amber. (4) (#92) $330

456 (For Pikes Peak) with prospector to left, derby and long-tailed coat. Reverse: eagle over oval. Pint. Aqua. (5) (#1938) $35

457 (For Pikes Peak) with prospector to right, derby, pack and cane. Reverse: hunter shooting deer. Pint. Amber. (4) (#1745) $525

458 (For Pikes Peak) with prospector to left with derby on oval. Reverse: plain. Quart. Aqua. (5) (#2178) $25

459 (For Pikes Peak) with prospector right, derby, pack and cane. Reverse: hunter shooting deer. Pint. Olive green. (4)

459A Same. Light yellow green. (4) (#179) $525
Similar. (#755) $450

459B Same. Medium amber. (4) (#2419) $575

460 (For Pikes Peak) with prospector on left on low-crowned hat on rectangle. Reverse: eagle over rectangle. Pint. Aqua. (5) (#466) $40

**Aqua pint Pikes Peak bottle shows prospector on obverse wearing low-crowned hat. (460).**

461 (For Pikes Peak) with prospector on right. Reverse: hunter shooting deer to right. Quart. Yellow amber. (4) (#2308) $700

462 (For Pikes Peak) with prospector on right. Reverse: hunter to right shooting deer. ½ pint. Aqua. (5) (#1425) $120

463 (For Pikes Peak) with prospector left. Reverse: eagle left, banner overhead over oval. Pint. Amber. (4) (#2595) $475

464 (For Pikes Peak) with prospector left. Reverse: eagle left, banner overhead over oval. ½ pint. Aqua. (5) (#946) $40
Same. Pint yellow amber. (#2211) $525

465 (For Pikes Peak) with prospector left. Reverse: plain. Pint. Aqua. (5) (#2130) $45

466 (For Pikes Peak) with prospector left, short tails on coat, small head. Reverse: eagle to left over plain oval. ½ pint. Aqua. (5)

467 (For Pikes Peak) with prospector left, large head, right arm not visible over oval. Reverse: eagle left over plain oval. Pint. Amber. (4)

468 (For Pikes Peak) with prospector right. Reverse: eagle right above long oval. Quart. Deep amber. (4) (#2627) $440

469 (For Pikes Peak) with prospector left. Reverse: eagle to left over oval marked (W. Mc & Co Glass Works Pitts Pa). Pint. Aqua. (4) (#1858) $360

470 (For Pikes Peak) with prospector left. Reverse: eagle left over oval marked (C. Ihmsen & Co Pittsburgh Pa). Pint. Aqua. (4) (#2290) $400

472 (Pikes Peak) with prospector left in derby, pack on left, cane in right hand. Reverse: eagle over oval. Quart. Aqua. (5) (#114) $65

473 (For Pikes Peak) with prospector left, cap and cane. Reverse: eagle over oval. Quart. Aqua. (5) (#2617) $65

474 (Pikes Peak) with prospector left, cap and cane. Reverse: eagle over oval. ½ pint. Aqua. (5) (#1658) $80

475 (For Pikes Peak) with prospector left, derby and cane on oval marked (Old Rye). Reverse: eagle over oval (Pittsburgh Pa). ½ pint. Aqua. (5) (#242) $75

476 Unmarked. Prospector left on oval. Reverse: eagle over oval marked (Arsenal Glass Works Pitts Pa). Pint. Yellow green. (4) (#1497) $700
Similar. (#355) $450

476B Same. Dark amber. (4) (#1474) $380

476C Same. Brilliant green. (4)

476D Same. Olive green. (4) (#2905) $525

476A Similar. Quart. Amber. (4) (#2738) $550

476V Similar, but not marked. Pint. Aqua. (5) (#674) $40

477 (For Pikes Peak) with prospector left, cap and cane on oval. Reverse: eagle left, over oval marked (Ceredo). Pint. Aqua. (5) (#2402) $75

477A Same. Quart. Deep yellow green. (4) (#1963) $1,200

477B Same. Quart. Green amber. (4) (#291) $575

477D Same. ½ pint. Light green. (5) (#1978) $170

**Unusual Pikes Peak flask, #478, is not listed in Gardner catalog. Reverse has eagle with "My Country" embossed below. Otherwise it is similar to #477.**

477E Same. ½ pint. Dark amber. (4) (#1835) $850

479 (For Pikes Peak) with prospector left over plain oval. Reverse: eagle right over rectangle marked (&Co). ½ pint. Aqua. (5) (#1818) $45

480 Prospector to right holding bottle to mouth. Reverse: eagle on oval. Quart. Green. (3)

481 Similar to above. Very bubbly. Pint. Deep blue aqua. (3) (#499) $575

482 (For Pikes Peak) with prospector to left. Reverse: hunter shooting at deer. Pint. Deep aqua. (2) (#1002) $2,200

485 Unmarked. Prospector left on rectangle. Reverse: eagle over oval. ½ pint. Aqua. (5)

**Pikes Peak flask in clear glass is marked "Kauffeld" on reverse under hunter shooting deer. (488). This is an extremely rare bottle.**

486 (For Pikes Peak) with prospector right, cap and cane on rectangle. Reverse: eagle over rectangle. Pint. Aqua. (5) (#1675) $80

487 (For Pikes Peak), same as above with square around head from altered mold. Pint. Aqua. (5) (#1946) $35

488 (For Pikes Peak) with prospector right. Reverse: hunter shooting right at deer. Marked (L. Kauffeld). Quart. Clear. (2) (#161) $1,650

489 No inscription. Prospector to right on irregular oval. Reverse: eagle over large oval. Quart. Amber. (4) (#1323) $675

## Chapter Eleven

# Sunburst Flasks

490A Sunburst on panel. Design in center. Reverse: same. Pint. Dark amber. (GVIII-20). (3) (#481) $850

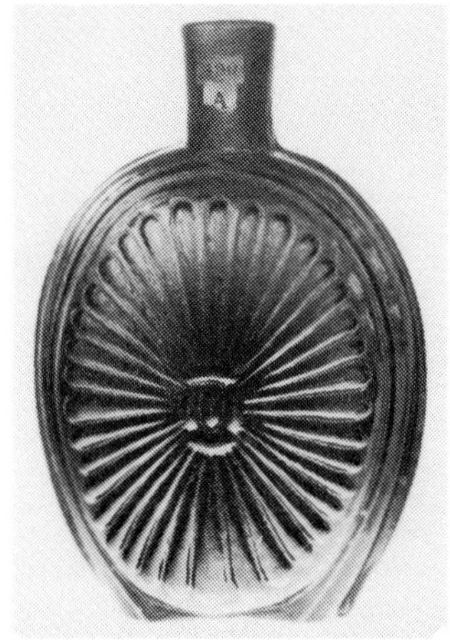

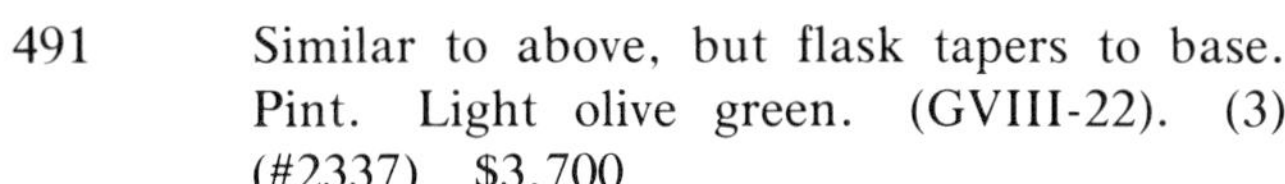

**Sunburst with 36 rays on dark amber glass has been attributed to Baltimore and is comparatively scarce. (490A).**

491 Similar to above, but flask tapers to base. Pint. Light olive green. (GVIII-22). (3) (#2337) $3,700

491A Same. Puce. (1) (#817) $3,000

492 Similar to 490A. ½ pint. Deep amber. (3) (#1753) $1,000

492A Sunburst on panel. Floral motif in center. ½ pint. Deep wine. (GVIII-25). (3) (#2465) $2,000

493 Elongated sunburst in ovoid panel. Reverse: same. Heavy vertical ribbing on both sides. ½ pint. Green. (GVIII-29) (3) (#532) $300

493C Same. Clear olive green. (3) (#1593) $1,100

493D Same, except no beading around oval. ½ pint. Pale green. (3) (#1204) $900

494 Large sunburst covering side. Reverse: same. Corrugated edges. Narrow base. ½ pint. Aqua. (GVIII-27). (3) (#1548) $300

494A Same. Deep olive green. (3) (#2001) $1,950

495 Similar. Pint. Green. (3) (#177) $600

495A Same. Deep olive green. (3) (#1449) $3,200

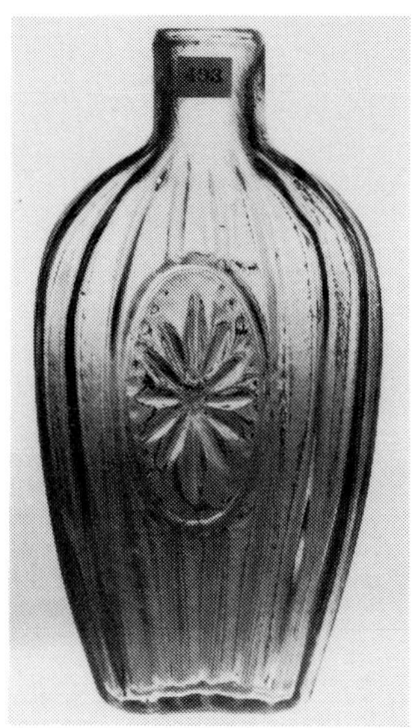

**Elongated sunburst on oval panel. Maker is not known and bottle is scarce. (493).**

**Scarce sunburst flask in green glass with corrugated edges. (495).**

495B Same. Clear. Folded lip. (3) (#2409) $350

496 Similar to 494, but 3 ribs instead of corrugations. ½ pint. Aqua. (3) (#2212) $225

499 Small sunburst, oval in center marked (Keen). Reverse: oval marked (P&W). Corrugated edges. 2 bars around base. Pint. Olive green. (GVIII-8). (3) (#2484) $500

500 Similar. 1 bar at base. ½ pint. Amber. (3) (#796) $425

500A Same. Aqua. (3) (#257) $650

**Sunburst flask in amber glass was made at Keene, New Hampshire glassworks. (500).**

500D Same. Olive green. (3) (#1148) $325

500E Same, but ovals unmarked. ½ pint. Green. (3) (#1001) $2,600

**Variant of Keene sunburst. (500E).**

501 Similar to #500, but broader shoulders. ½ pint. Olive amber. (GVIII-10). (3) (#52) $425

502 Sunburst with heavy shoulders sloping. Corrugations extend up neck. 2 bars at base. ½ pint. Golden amber. (GVIII-18). (3) (#2876) $120

503 Sunburst, heavy shoulders, square. 1 bar at base. ½ pint. Olive amber. (GVIII-16). (3)

503A Same. Deep green. (3) (#2121) $450

504 Sunburst. Corrugations extend up shoulders. 2 rings at base. Pint. Olive green. (3) (#2577) $550

505 Similar. 3 rings at base. 5 dots above sunburst, 2 below. Pint. Amber. (GVIII-6). (1) (#2385) $2,200

506 Sunburst. Heavy corrugations extend up neck. Dot and 2 concentric rings in center. 2 rings at base. Pint. Shaded olive green. (GVIII-1).. (3) (#33) $4,400

506A Same. Emerald green. (3) (#2884) $1,050

507 Sunburst. Lighter glass with sloping shoulders. Similar in shape to #505 with concentric rings in center. Pint. Amber. (GVIII-5a). (2) (#2641) $1,100

508 Sunburst similar to #499, but no inscriptions in ovals. Pint. Sea green. (GVIII-12). (4) (#849) $950

508A Same. Deep olive green. (1) (#1865) $4,500

**Sunburst flask with "Keene" in center of motif. (508A).**

509 Sunburst. Heavy glass. No center motif. Corrugations extend up neck. 2 bars. Pint. Green. (GVIII-2). (3) (#2692) $400

509A Same. Aqua. (3)

509B Same. Light green. (3) (#996) $600
Same, clear. (#1883) $975
Reproduction, pint. Amethyst. (GVIII-2). (#217) $20
Reproduction, pint. Cobalt blue. (#589) $150

511 Sunburst, large. No central motif. Corrugations extend up neck. 2 bars. Like #509 only lighter and smaller. Pint. Amber. (GVIII-3). (3) (#1388) $450

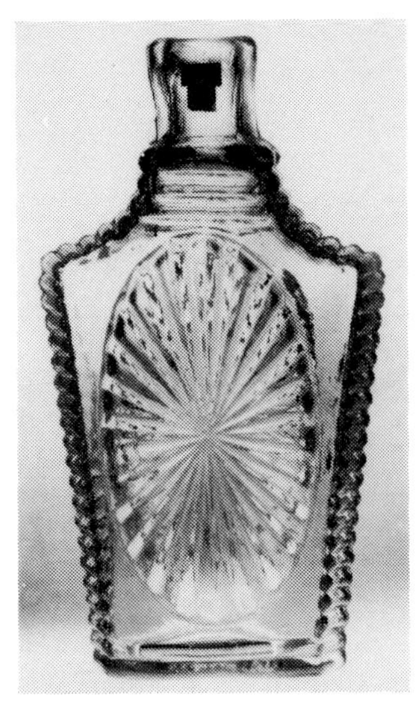

Rare sunburst, made at Keene, is of heavy light green glass. (509B).

511X Same. Olive green. (3) (#2818) $525

512 Sunburst, dot in circle. Corrugated edges. 2 rings at base. ½ pint. Green. (GVIII-14). (3) (#641) $1,000

512A Same. Olive green. (3) (#356) $1,000
Same. Clear, ½ pint. (#1929) $650

512V Same, except only one ring around base. ½ pint. Blue green. (GVIII-14a). (3) (#2068) $1150

513 Heavy, slightly smaller than #511. Maltese cross in center of sunburst. Pint. Clear. (GVIII-4). (1) (#1273) $9,900

514 Shaped like #504. Depressed circle in center of sunburst. 2 large depressed dots at top on either side. Corrugated edges. Reverse: same, but dots omitted. Pint. Olive green. (GVIII-7). (2) (#2961) $1,250

## Chapter Twelve

# Vertically Ribbed Bottles and Flasks

515 Heavy vertical ribs. Raised label panel near base. Reverse: same. ½ pint. Aqua. (6) (#1034) $45

516 Ribbed, long neck. Slightly oval decanter shape. Quart. Probably South Jersey glass. (5)

517 Closely ribbed. Flat central rib. Reverse: same. Pint. Light green. (6)

518 Similar. ½ pint. Amber. (6)

519 Ovoid. Broad ribbing. Height: 8½″. Sea green. (5)

520 Ovoid. Finer ribbing. Height: 6½″. Sea green. (5)

521 Ovoid. Broad ribbing. 18 ribs. Height: 6 5/8″. Citron. (4)

522 Ovoid. Fine ribbing. Height: 7″. Deep aqua. (5) (#1202) $75

523 Fine ribbing on oval panel. Reverse: same. ½ pint. Aqua. (6) (#2242) $75

524 Heavy, broad shoulders, sides flat, wide ribbing. ½ pint. Green aqua. (5)

525 Same. Pint. Green. (5) (#765) $425

526 Similar, but slightly taller and thicker. Ribs more widely separated. Very heavy glass. Pint. Deep olive green. (Made in Keene, N. H.) (#2220) $325

526V Similar, but slightly smaller and lighter. Pint. Olive green. (4)

527 Round. Broad ribbing. Oval panel on 1 side. On base: (M&GM). Quart. Aqua. (4)

528 Round decanter shape. Heavy ribbing. Long neck. Quart. Aqua. (Possibly English.) (4)

529 Oval with wide vertical ribs from base to neck. Light yellow tint. Pint. Folded lip. (5)

531 Inverted bell shape. Expanded ribbing. ¾ quart. Deep amber. (4) (#697) $15

530 Similar to above with seal on shoulder marked (Gin Cocktail S M & Co N. Y.). Quart. Clear amber. (4) (#1597) $600

532 Round. Vertically ribbed except label panel. Paper label "Superior Cologne/Samuel Kidder & Co/Druggist and Chemist/Charlestown, Mass." ¾ quart. Aqua. (5) (#96) $25

## Chapter Thirteen

# Violin Flasks

535 6-pointed star over fleur-de-lis. Reverse: same, only star has 5 points. ½ pint. Brilliant yellow green. (GIX-32). (4) (#612) $550

535A Two 6-pointed stars, inverted heart-shaped scroll. Reverse: same. (GIX-31). (5) (#2578) $95

535B Same. Amber. (4) (#2420) $500

536 8-pointed star, 2 dots below. (BP&B) in scroll. Reverse: 1 dot and fleur-de-lis. ½ pint. Aqua. (GIX-38). (4) (#2003) $270

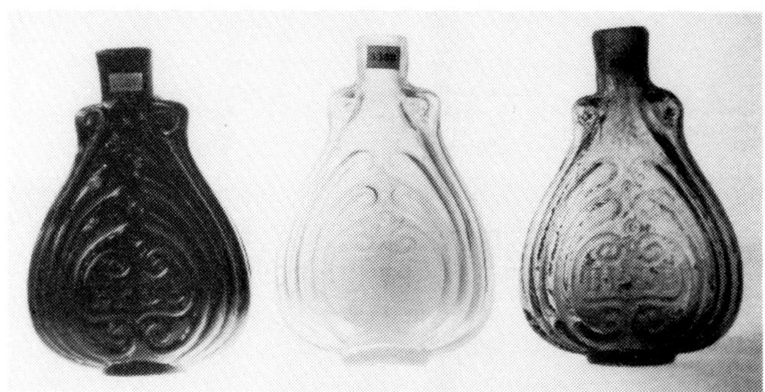

**Three variants of scroll flask marked (B.P.&B) for Bakewell, Page & Bakewell, glassmakers. (536V, 536B, 536A)**

536B Same as above but in moonstone. (4) (#1692) $575

536V Same, but with circular rather than oval base. ½ pint. Deep blue. (GIX-39). (2) (#1961) $7,000

536A Same as above. Green. (GIX-39). (3) (#2996) $1,050

537 8-pointed star and dot over fleur-de-lis. Reverse: same. ½ pint. Amber. (GIX-34). (4) (#1684) $425

537V Similar. Greenish amber. (GIX-35). (4) (#1225) $500

537A Same. Olive green. (3) (#1948) $425

538 Similar. Variations. ½ pint. Aqua. (GIX-36). (5) (#482) $75

539 6-pointed star over fleur-de-lis. No dot. Reverse: same. ½ pint. Aqua. (GIX-37a). (5) (#66) $80

540 Two 6-pointed stars. 2 extra stars in heart. Reverse: same. Pint. Aqua. (GIX-23). (3) (#1401) $325

541 Two 6-pointed stars. Reverse: same. Quart. Light amber. (GIX-2). (4) (#2857) $700

542 Same. Quart. Deep blue. (2) (#2785) $2,400

543 Same. Quart. Light blue. (3) (#2882) $230

544 Same. Quart. Light amber. (3) (#2868) $600

545 Same. Quart. Deep brown. (GIX-4). (3) (#1356) $725

546 Same. Quart. Blue. (GIX-1). (3) (#2932) $850

546D Same. Quart. Light green. (4) (#2787) $400

547 Same. Olive green. (GIX-1). (3) (#260) $275

547A Same. Reddish amber. (3) (#2020) $475

548 Two 8-pointed stars. Reverse: same. Pint. Vaseline. (GIX-10). (4) (#2042) $25

549 No star above. Small star below. Pint. Sapphire blue. (GIX-18). (3) (#1177) $1,450

550 Two 6-pointed stars. Pint. Green. (4) (#2281) $600
Similar. (#148) $375

551 Two 8-pointed stars. Pint. Dark amber. (GIX-10). (4) (#2548) $350
Reproduction, pint, cobalt blue. (GIX-II). (#2221) $30

552 Same. Amber. (4) (#1979) $375

553 Same. Sapphire blue. (3) (#881) $1,700

554 Two 5-pointed stars. Reverse: same. Pint. Blue. (GIX-15). (3) (#1268) $950

554A Extra 5-pointed star below. Pint. Aqua. (GIX-22). (4) (#2338) $450

555 6-pointed star over 8-pointed star. Pint. Clear green. (GIX-12). (4) (#1707) $410

555A Same. Deep olive green. (4) (#1532) $750

556 2 large dots over lettering (C) in scroll. Reverse: letter omitted. Pint. Light green. (4) (GIX-25). (#578) $310

557 Similar, but letter (A) in scroll. Reverse: letter omitted. Pint. Aqua. (GIX-24). (4) (#1475) $400

558 Broad shoulders, 4 dots and anchor. Reverse: fleur-de-lis over 2 dots. ½ pint. Deep aqua. (GIX-41). (3) (#428) $225

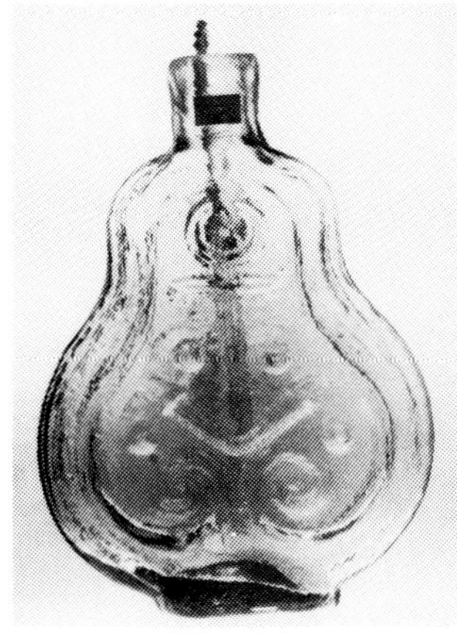

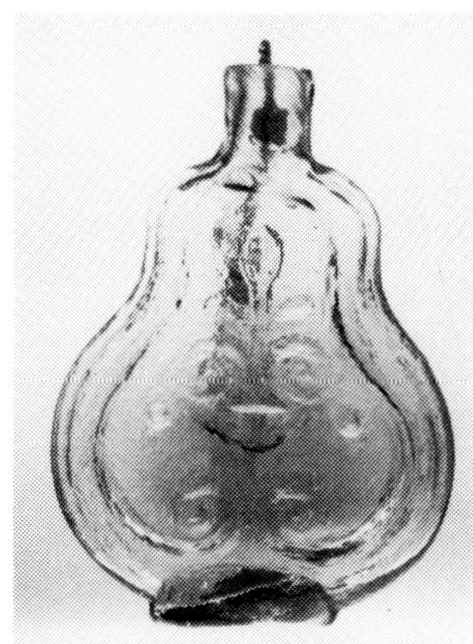

**Most scroll flasks are the same on both sides, but this rare flask has anchor on one side and fleur-de-lis on the other. (558).**

559 6-pointed star over 7-pointed star. Pint. Amber. (GIX-14). (4) (#793) $350

559A Same. Yellow green. (4) (#1484) $750

560 Two 8-pointed stars over (Louisville Ky). Reverse: same, except (Glass Works). Pint. Aqua. (GIX-8). (4) (#1051) $240

560I Two 6-pointed stars over (Louisville Ky). Reverse: same, except (Glass Works). Quart. Aqua. (GIX-6). (4) (#100) $140

560H 2 dots on base. Variant of above. Quart. Aqua. (GIX-7). (4) (#435) $225

560V Two 8-pointed stars over (Louisville Ky). Reverse: same, except (Glass Works) letters curved. Pint. Pale green. (GIX-9). (4) (#2875) $330

561 Narrow-waisted, urn-shaped frame enclosing (JR&Son). Reverse: fleur-de-lis. Pint. Aqua. (GIX-43). (3) (#865) $600

561V Same, but inscription omitted. Pint. Aqua. (GIX-44). (3) (#1660) $550

562 Corseted, scroll design covering entire sides. Reverse: same. Pint. Green. (GIX-45). (3) (#737) $1,850

563 Like #558 except on one side (JR&S). ½ pint. Aqua. (GIX-42). (2) (#708) $675

564 Two 8-pointed stars. Reverse: same. 7 ribs on edges. ½ gallon. Aqua. (GIX-29). (3) (#1628) $375

565 Shape of violin with strings. Pint. Amber. (5)

566 Corseted. Similar to #562. Quart. Green. (GIX-46). (3) (#2833) $900

567 Corseted with scrolls. Marked on 1 side. (Soyers Sauce). ½ pint. Amber. (5) (#1649) $625

568 Two 8-pointed stars. On 1 side only (S. M'Kee). Pint. Aqua. GIX-26). (2) (#915) $575

569 Violin-shaped. (R. Knowles & Co Union Factory South Wheeling Ca) in circle. Reverse: star above fleur-de-lis. Pint. Deep aqua. (GIX-47). (2) (#2513) $2,000

570 Very small complete violin holding 1 drink. Lettered (Pat. Appld. For). Height: 6½". Amber. (5) (#2063) $110

571 Top center scroll is a raised heart. Below 8-pointed star and in center below is a 6-pointed star or rosette. Pint. Aqua. (GIX-20). (4) (#1339) $110

572 8-pointed star over dot over fleur-de-lis. Reverse: same. ½ pint. Green. (GIX-16). (4) (#1116) $650

573 Two 5-pointed stars. Reverse: 6-pointed star above 5-pointed star. Pint. Deep olive green. (GIX-16). (4) (#1260) $600

574 8-pointed star over small dot above fleur-de-lis. Reverse: same. ½ pint. Deep olive green. (GIX-37). (4) (#2276) $550

574A Same. Emerald green. (3) (#193) $550

575 5-pointed star over oval spot. Reverse: two 5-pointed stars. Pint. Aqua. (GIX-21). (4) (#1898) $350

576 Two 8-pointed stars. Reverse: same. Pint. Deep olive green. Heavy glass. (GIX-II). (4) (#913) $600

578 Two 7-pointed stars. Reverse: same. Pint. Golden amber. (GIX-13). (4) (#2132) $475

579 Two 6-pointed stars. Reverse: same. Pint. Tobacco brown. (4) (#756) $400

Chapter Fourteen

# Washington Flasks

580A (General Washington) over bust. Reverse (E Pluribus Unum) over rayed eagle and beaded oval marked (TWS). Around edges (Adams & Jefferson July 4 AD 1776), (Kensington Glass Works, Philadelphia). Pint. Green. (GI-14). (3) (#2452) $1,700

581 (General Washington). "N" in "General" inverted above bust. Corrugated edges. Reverse: eagle to right on beaded oval with olive branches on either side. Pint. Deep aqua. (GI-3). (2) (#900) $1,550

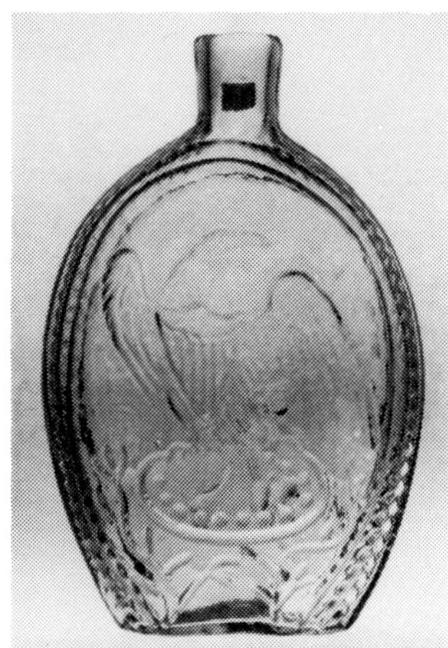

**Extremely rare Washington portrait flask has "n" reversed in "General." (581).**

582 (General Washington) over bust. Reverse: eagle over beaded oval marked: (TWD). Pint. Aqua. (GI-16). (2) (#1315) $120

583 (General Washington) over bust. Reverse: eagle over beaded oval. Corrugated edges. Pint. Light green. (GI-2). (3) (#36) $550

584 (General Washington) over bust. Reverse: 9 stars over eagle right over heavily beaded oval. Corrugated edges. Pint. Green. (GI-1). (2) (#2852) $1,150

585A (G. Washington) over bust. Reverse: stars over eagle on small beaded oval. Corrugated edges. Pint. Brilliant amber. (GI-10). (2) (#2737) $5,100

586 (G. G. Washington) over bust. Reverse: 9 stars over eagle on beaded oval. Corrugated edges. Pint. Green. (GI-9). (2) (#1468) $2,800

587 (G. Geo. Washington) over bust. Reverse: 12 stars over eagle on beaded oval marked (FL). Corrugated edges. Branches below. Pint. Aqua. (GI-7). (2) (#324) $950

589 (General Washington) above bust. Reverse: 9 stars above eagle on beaded oval, marked (J.R). (Laird S. C. Pitt) below. Heavy beading around high central rib. Pint. Pale yellow green. (GI-6). (1) (#1052) $1,650

590 Bust of Washington with vines either side. Reverse: 13 stars over rayed eagle. Corrugated edges. Pint. Aqua. (GI-11). (2) (#2116) $820

592A Bust of Washington (The Father of His Country). Reverse: bust of Taylor (General Taylor Never Surrenders). Outside panel (Dyottville Glass Works Phila). Quart. Honey amber. (GI-37). (3) (#1049) $700

**Washington-Taylor flasks showing obverse of one and reverse of other. Both were made by the Dyottsville Glass Works in Philadelphia. (597A, 592A).**

592B Same. Light yellow green. (3) (#564) $375

592C Same. Sapphire blue. (3) (#68) $800

592E Same. Deep claret. (2) (#2161) $900
Reproduction. Quart, amethyst. (#1640) $50

593 Similar. Pint. Light yellow green. (3) (#857) $575

593A Same. Claret. (3) (2217) $750

593B Same. Green. (3)

593C Same. Deep olive amber. (3) (#772) $550

593D Same. Deep puce. (3) (#1316) $700

593E Same. Cornflower blue. (3) (#2228) $850

594 (The Father of His Country) over bust. Reverse (General Taylor Never Surrenders) over bust. Dyottville Glass omitted. Quart. Olive green. (GI-39). (3) (#2937) $600

594B Same. Dense brown. (3) (#836) $600

596 Similar, with variations. Pint. Aqua. (GI-40a). (4) (#914) $60

596A Similar, different bust and smaller letters. Pint. Brilliant blue. (2) (#385) $1,750

597A Similar. ½ pint. Light green. (GI-41). (4) (#1930) $120

597B Same. Deep olive green. (4) (#884) $1,250

597C Same. Aqua. (5) (#2762) $85

598 Bust of Washington. Reverse: bust of Taylor. No inscriptions. Quart. Olive green. (GI-55). (3) (#1612) $475
Similar, yellow amber. (GI-54). (#1868) $475

598B Same. Light green. (4) (#947) $150

598C Same. Deep emerald green. (3) (#1164) $600

599 Similar. Pint. Light amber. (GI-56). (3)

600 Similar. ½ pint. Green. (GI-53). (4) (#1340) $1,350

600A Same. Amber. No queue on Washington. (GI-56). (4) (#628) $600
Similar. Citron, ½ pint. (#1860) $1,100

600F Similar. Ribbon on queue. Washington. Pint. Dense olive green. (GI-52). (3) (#1740) $575

600V Same. Emerald green. (3) (#2036) $475

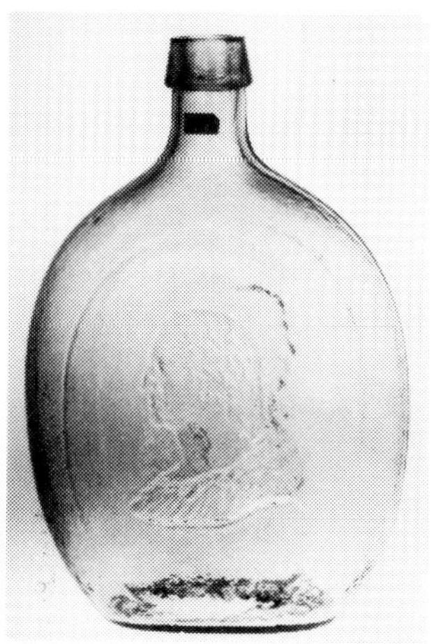

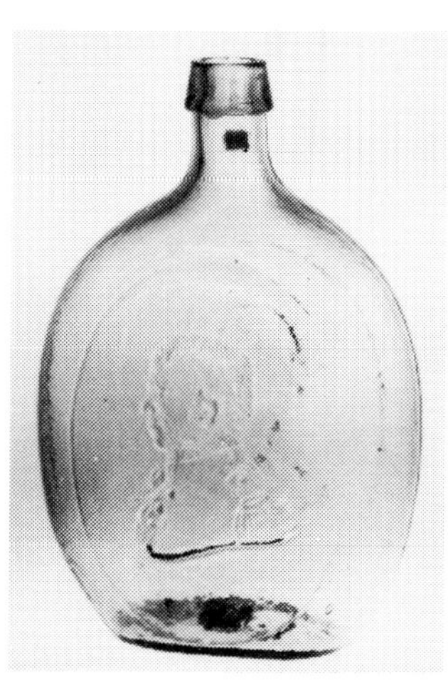

**Washington-Taylor flask showing Washington with long queue. (601).**

601 Bust of Washington with long queue. Reverse: bust of Taylor. Quart. Cornflower blue. (GI-51). (3) (#2260) $1,000

601V Same. Yellow green. (3) (#1212) $475

602 Bust of Washington (The Father of His Country). Reverse (Gen. Z. Taylor) over bust. Quart. Aqua. (GI-46). (4) (#2690) $80

603 Bust of Washington. (Washington) above. Reverse (Gen. Z. Taylor) over bust. Pint. Aqua. (GI-49). (4) (#554) $75

604 Bust of Washington with (Washington) above. Reverse: bust of Taylor with (G. Z. Taylor) above. Pint. Deep green. (GI-50). (3) (#484) $500

605 Bust of Washington under (The Father of His Country). Reverse: bust of Taylor under (I Have Endeavored to Do My Duty). Quart. Puce. (GI-43). (2) (#2769) $1,900

606 Similar. Different queue. Pint. Brilliant amber. (GI-44). (3) (#1796) $800

606A Same. Sapphire blue. (2) (#2609) $1,550

606B Same. Emerald green. (3) (#2324) $650

607 Bust of Washington under (The Father of His Country). Reverse: bust of Taylor under (A Little More Grape Captain Bragg). Quart. Aqua. (GI-42). (4) (#322) $95

607V Same. Aqua. But neck 2½". (GI-42V). (4) (#1338) $100

608 Bust of Washington (The Father of His Country). Reverse: bust of Taylor. No inscription. Quart. Aqua. (GI-45). (2) (#1802) $150

609A Bust of Washington. (The Father of His Country). Reverse: plain. Pint. Sea green. (GI-48). (3) (#1035) $250
Same. Citron. (#2612) $750

609B Same. Very deep green. (3) (#2404) $550

609C Same. Light amber. (3) (#2916) $1,450

610 Similar. Quart. Green. (3) (#1003) $225

610C Similar. Quart. Blue. (GI-47). (3) (#2916) $1,450

611 (Lockport Glass Works) over bust of Washington. Reverse: bust of Washington only. Quart. Yellow green. (GI-60). (2) (#1657) $1,700

612 Bust of Washington on both sides. No inscription. Quart. Blue. (GI-61). (2) (#2033) $3,900

612A Same. Emerald green. (2) (#1) $850

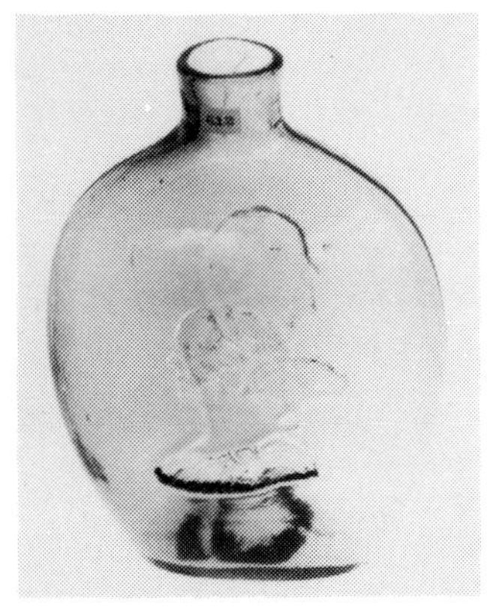

**Rare Washington flask made at the Lockport (N.Y.) Glass Works. Flask is the same on both sides. (612).**

615A Bust of Washington. Reverse: 7 stars above eagle, 5 stars below. Quart. Green. (GI-27). (3) (#212) $750

615 Same, except heavy central rib. Quart. Aqua. (GI-26). (3) (#596) $170

616 Bust of Washington (Fells) above and (Point) below. Reverse: monument and (Balto). Quart. Light yellow green. (GI-21). (3) (#1324) $1,100

617 (Bridgetown New Jersey) around bust of Washington. Reverse (Bridgetown New Jersey) around bust. Quart. Light green. (GI-25). (3) (#2516) $250

618 (Washington) above bust. Reverse (Bridgetown ★ New Jersey) over bust of Taylor. Pint. Light green. (GI-24). (3) (#1396) $400

618A Same. Dense amber. (3) (#1596) $825

619 (Washington) above bust with Roman nose. Reverse (Baltimore Glass Works) over monument. Pint. Green. (GI-18). (3) (#2339) $850

619A Same as above. Blue. (2) (#977) $5,000

620 (Washington) above bust. Reverse (Baltimore Glas(s) Work(s)). Small "s" above bust of Taylor. Pint. Pale puce. (GI-17). (3) (#2860) $2,050

620A Same. Brown amber. (3) (#1036) $2,200

621 (Fells) above bust, (Point) below. Reverse: monument above (Balto). Pint. Green. (GI-20). (3) (#2052) $850

621A Same. Puce. (4) (#2897) $550

622 Bust of Washington. Reverse (Baltimore X Glass Woks). No "r" in "Works." Quart. Olive green. (GI-23). (2) (#2900) $2,600

623 (Baltimore Glass Works). All 3 "s's" are reversed above bust of Washington. Reverse: bust of Taylor. Quart. Aqua. (GI-22). (2) (#948) $400

625 (Albany Glass Works) above bust of Washington. (Albany N. Y.) below. Reverse: full rigged ship. Pint. Green. (GI-28). (3) (#868) $675

625A Same. Golden amber. (3) (#1788) $750

625B Same. Deep yellow green. (3) (#2644) $1,650

626A Bust of Washington. Reverse (Albany Glass Works N. Y.). ½ pint. Light amber. (GI-30). (3) (#1428) $950

626B Same. Light green. (3) (#51) $370

627 (Washington) over bust, bars on lapels. Pint. Dark amber. (GI-31). (3) (#2371 $150

628 Same. Green. (3) (#489) $380

628A Same. Brilliant amber. (3) (#483) $170

629B Same. Aqua. (GI-32). (3) (#1043) $270

629 Similar, no bars on lapels. Pint. Clear olive green. (GI-32). (3) (#2763) $250

629A Same. Amber. (3) (#67) $150

630 Similar, smaller letters. Pint. Amber. (GI-33). (3) (#803) $200

631 Similar. ½ pint. Amber. (GI-34). (3) (#1427) $275

633 Calabash. Bust of Washington. Reverse: tree in leaf. Quart. Aqua. (GI-35). (4) (#2530) $80

634 Calabash. Small bust of Washington. Reverse: tree in leaf. Quart. Aqua. (GI-36). (4) (#99) $55

## Chapter Fifteen

# Bininger Bottles

Collectors who specialize in early whiskey bottles will be especially interested in the number of Bininger bottles in the Gardner collection. This group was produced specifically for whiskey sold by the grocery stores in New York owned by the Bininger family between 1840 and 1870 and the embossments include the addresses of these stores. There are earlier examples of Bininger bottles dating from around 1820 that prove that this family of merchants existed through most of the nineteenth century. The bottles made for their great variety of wines and spirits were produced in many interesting shapes.

The Gardner collection of Bininger bottles included most of the examples of shapes used. There were almost 40 Biningers in barrel, clock-face, cannon shape, pear shape and chestnut shape. They are in a variety of shades of amber or green and the embossments show that some of the molds were altered as the address of the firm changed.

990 Square face gin. (Bininger & DeWitt New York). ¾ quart. Olive green. (4) (#1009) $750

991 Square, beveled corners. (Bininger's Golden Apple Cordial A. M. Bininger & Co 338 Broadway N.Y.) ¾ quart. Light olive green. (4) (#2666) $280

992 Flattened chestnut type with applied handle. Paper label only, "Old Kentucky Bourbon 1849 Reserve A. M. Bininger & Co 338 Broadway N.Y." Quart. Amber. (4) (#522) $110

993 Square. Beveled corners. (A. M. Bininger & Co No 375 Broadway N.Y.) ¾ quart. Golden amber. (4) (#208) $210

994 Same as #992 but label reads: "Bininger's Pioneer Bourbon A. M. Bininger & Co Established 1778 338 Broadway N.Y." ¾ quart. Amber. (4)

995 Square, beveled corners. (Bininger's Old Kentucky Bourbon 1849 Reserve Distilled in 1848 A. M. Bininger & Co No 19 Broad St N.Y.) Mold altered from 338 Broadway. ¾ quart. Dark green. (4) (#1462) $100

996 Oval flask, flattened at shoulders, bevel around base. (Bininger's Night Cap No 19 Broad St N.Y.). Reverse: plain. Pint. Dark amber. (4) (#2064) $270

**Amber jug with applied handle is one of many Bininger bottles in Gardner collection. (994).**

997 Square, beveled corners. (A. M. Bininger & Co No 17 Broad St) (Old London Dock) (Gin). Crown on shoulder. ¾ quart. Emerald green. (4) (#1877) $150

998 Square, beveled corners. (Bininger's Bana Juice) (A. M. Bininger & Co) (No 338 Broadway, N.Y.) Paper label. ¾ quart. Dark green. (2) (#2366) $790

1000 Barrel, marked (Distilled in 1848 Old Kentucky Bourbon 1849 Reserve A. M. Bininger & Co 19 Broad St N.Y.). ¾ quart. Dark amber. (3) (#11) $130

1000V Same, but marked # (338 Broadway). ¾ quart. Amber. (3) (#439) $150

1001 Pear-shaped jug. (Bininger's Day Dream A. M. Bininger & Co, No 19 Broad St N.Y.). ¾ quart. Amber. (3) (#2765) $3,200

1003 Same as #1000. Quart. Golden amber. (3) (#1170) $150

1003V Same as #1000V. Quart. Amber. (3) (#1984) $290

1004 Pear-shaped with applied handle. (Bininger's Knickerbocker A. M. Bininger & Co 19 Broad St New York). Pint. Amber. (3) (#703) $900

1005 Cylindrical with applied handle. (A. M. Bininger & Co 19 Broad St New York). Paper label, "Strawberry Brandy." ¾ quart. Amber. (3) (#184) $210

1005V Same. Paper label, "Peach Brandy." (3)

1005C Same. Clear olive green. (3) (#1016) $1,300

Same. Amber. (#2730) $340

1006 Vase. (A. M. Bininger & Co 19 Broad St New York). 9¾″ high. Amber. (3) (#25) $950

1007 Vase with applied handle. Marked (A. M. Bininger & Co 19 Broad St. New York). Wide mouth. ¾ quart. Amber. Height: 9″. (3) (#1509) $1,250

1008 Square, beveled corners. (Heidelberg Branntwein) (A. M. Bininger & Co No 338 Broadway N.Y.) ¾ quart. Deep olive green. (3) (#1320) $100

1009 Similar. (Bininger's Old Dominion Wheat Tonic A. M. Bininger & Co No 18 Broad St N.Y.) ¾ quart. Amber. (3) (#46) $65

1009V Same, but (338 Broadway). ¾ quart. Olive green. (3) (#826) $70

1010 Half-round, beveled. (Bininger's Peep O'Day No 19 Broad St N.Y.). Pint. Golden amber. (3) (#880) $325

1011 Cannon. Marked (A. M. Bininger & Co 19 Broad St N.Y.). Reverse: ribbon over star. Original label. (2) (#140) $500

1012 Flat oval flask. (Bininger's Traveler's Guide A. M. Bininger & Co No 19 Broad St N.Y.) ¼ pint. Amber (4)

1013 Clock, hands set at 11. (Bininger's Regulator 19 Broad St New York). Reverse: plain. Marked (Gin). Pint. Golden amber. (3) (#1895) $325

1013A Pint. Same. Marked (Bourbon). (2) (#95) $300

1013V Same. Aqua. (3) (#669) $900

1014 Square. (A. M. Bininger & Co No 19 Broad St N.Y.) (Distilled in 1848 Bininger's Old Time Family Rye). ¾ quart. Olive green. (3) (#159) $350

1015 Square. (A. M. Bininger & Co No 19 Broad St N.Y. Old London Dock Gin). ¾ quart. Amber. (3) (#894) $40

1015V Same, but (338 Broadway). ¾ quart. Olive green. (3) (#2171) $35

1015A Same, but (17 Broad St.). ¾ quart. Olive green. (3) (#1538) $60

1016 Square. (A. M. Bininger & Co No 19 Broad St. N.Y. Old London Dock Gin.) Pint. Amber. (4) (#2622) $45

1016V Same. Amber. (5) (#607) $30

1017 Square. (A. M. Bininger & Co No 19 Broad St N.Y.) (Old London Dock Gin). Pint. Amber. (4) (#2010) $50

1018 Square face gin. (A. M. Bininger & Co New York). Original label. ¾ quart. Bright green. (3) (#2437) $1,400

## Chapter Sixteen

# Case Bottles

The rectangular bottles with flat sides were a common bottle type in the late eighteenth and early nineteenth century. They were made in a variety of sizes and were mostly used for transporting and holding gin. They ranged from a half-pint to several gallons in capacity and most were made in the inexpensive utilitarian green commercial glass.

The reason for the development of the case bottle shape was that many could be packed in a box for safe shipping.

Included in this listing of case bottles in the Gardner collection are several decorated tea caddies called generally, Stiegel-type. Most of these are not commercial bottles, but were made as decorative glass. They are rarely found today and most known examples are in museums.

Auction prices for this category of bottles have not been included due to the difficulty of identifying the bottles from the auction catalog descriptions. Measurements and colors differed and rather than place monetary values where they were not accurate these few listings were left unpriced.

1150 Rectangular. Cutting on all 4 sides. 5″ x 2½″ x 1¾″. Clear. Double dipped. (6)

1151 Similar, but 8½″ x 3½″ square. Clear. (5)

1152 Square holding about a gallon. Ground stopper. Heavy ring around mouth. Not double dipped. Clear. (4)

1154 Rectangular with edges coming to a point rather than being flat. 10″ x 5¾″ x 3¼″. Flower on each side. Cut on all corners. Clear. Ground pontil. Double dipped. (4)

1155 Rectangular. 7 3/8" x 3¼″ x 2½″. Not dipped. Clear olive green. (6)

1156 Rectangular tea caddy. No cutting. Threaded mouth with glass screw cap. ½ pint. Clear. (4)

**East wall of Gardner bottle room holds display of early demi johns, case bottles and drug jars.**

1157 Rectangular, Stiegel-type tea caddy. Wide threaded mouth with glass screw cap. Engraved on all 4 sides. Widely beveled corners. ½ pint. Clear. (4)

1158 Rectangular. 6½″ x 3″ x 2½″. Engraved on all 4 sides. Double dipped. Clear. (5)

1158A Rectangular 8″ x 4¼″ x 3″. Gilt decorations around shoulders. Double dipped. Clear. Ground pontil. (5)

1158B Same as above, but gilt decorations differ. 7¼″ x 4″ x 2¾″. Double dipped. Clear. Ground pontil. (5)

1158C Cylindrical. 8½″ x 4½″. Very extensive and elaborate cutting with gilt decorations added. Not double dipped. Clear. Ground pontil. (4)

# Chapter Seventeen
# Chestnut Bottles

The term "chestnut shape" is a convenient name for the many bottles that were free-blown in a bubble shape with an elongated neck. These were commercial bottles made in the seventeenth, eighteenth and nineteenth centuries for a variety of purposes in all of the inexpensive glass colors. As one can see by glancing at the listing of pontilled chestnut flasks in the Gardner collection, bottles made in the chestnut shape varied in size from less than three inches to almost 17 inches.

Some chestnut flasks were made as table bottles while many others were flattened to serve as pocket or saddle flasks. Because they were the most basic bottle shape to make, they were, at one time, very common. Today's collectors like chestnut flasks because they were blown quickly from cheap glass material and many are rough and bubbled.

Where the bottles could not be identified correctly through comparison of the auction listings with the Gardner descriptions no prices have been given. Obviously, what was "olive amber" to Charley may have appeared to be "golden amber" to the auction cataloger.

1159 2 5/8". Amber. (4) (#2303) $25

1160 3 3/8". Bubbly green glass. (3) (#75) $220

1161 3 9/16". Bubbly amber. (3) (#2320) $210

1162 3¼". Olive green. Round. (3) (#2247) $45

1163 3 9/16". Amber. (3) (#1638) $95

1164 3¼". Olive amber. (3) (#1524) $170

1165 3½". Deep aqua. Spanish. (6) (#617) $70

1166 3¼". Olive amber. Round. (3) (#1122) $40

1167 4". Deep aqua. Spanish. (6) (#1205) $40
Similar (#1888) $55

1168 3¾". Green. Round. (3) (#219) $210

1169 7". Green. Short neck. (3)

1170 4 7/8". Green. (3) (#1334) $30

1171 1 7/8". Globular with 4 flattened sides. Green. (3) (#138) $50

1172 5 1/8". Green. (3) (#781) $65
Similar (#2383) $65

1173 5¼". Olive green. (3) (#847) $65
Similar (#1062) $90

1174 2". Amber. Round. (3)

1175 2½". Olive amber. Round. (3) (#13) $200

1176 3 5/8". Olive amber. Round. (3) (#382) $60
Similar. (#864) $250
Similar. (#2544) $160

1177 5 3/8". Light amber. (3) (#1688) $100

1178 4 1/8". Olive green. Applied rigaree on sides. Short neck. (3) (#1012) $110

1180 5¼". Pale olive green decanter shape. (3)

**Group of free-blown bottles, mostly chestnut flasks, from Gardner collection.**

1181 5½". Oxblood amber. Short neck. (3) (#2911) $50

1182 3". Olive amber. Round. (3) (#1181) $80

1183 5 5/8". Olive amber. Round. (3)

1185 5 7/8". Light olive green. (3) (751) $65
Similar. (#1590) $70

1186 3". Pale green. Round. Applied base. (4)

1192 6½". Clear amber. Short neck. (3) (#651) $65

1194 6". Dark olive green. (3) (#2872) $80

1196 6½". Olive green. Seal marked (S:B). Made at Willington, (Conn.). (2) (#2985) $425

1197 6½". Green. (3) (#203) $75

1198 6 5/8". Pale aqua. (4)

1199 6 5/8". Golden amber. (3) (#1540) $60

1200 7¼". Deep olive green. Decanter. (3) (#606) $75

1201 6 7/8". Light amber. (3) (#2188) $45

1202 5¾". Olive green. Decanter. (3) (#1094) $85

1203 6 7/8". Light olive green. (3) (#1030) $65
Similar. 6¾". (#2288) $30

1204 8″. Light green. (3) (#1832) $65

1206 8 7/16″. Light olive green. Decanter. (3)

1208 10 5/8″. Light amber. Decanter. (3) (#506) $35

1209 7½″. Dark amber. (3) (#2154) $60
Similar. 7¼″. (#2607) $85

1210 10 3/8″. Green. Decanter. (3)

1211 7 ¾″. Light olive green. (3) (#534) $70
Similar. (#2511) $55

1212 10″. Green. Decanter. (3) (#2027) $80

1213 8½″. Light amber. (3) (#1991) $55

1214 10¼″. Olive green. Decanter. (3) (#1848) $90

1215 8¾″. Deep green. (3) (#2473) $75

1216 7 5/8″. Olive green. Very heavy. Early. (2) (#2240) $40

1217 8 ¾″. Clear. (4) (#1570) $35

1218 8½″. Olive amber. Round. (3) (#38) $100

1220 9½″. Olive green. Wide tapering neck. (3) (#2198) $55

1221 9¼″. Clear olive green. (3) (#448) $110

1222 9½″. Olive green. Round. (3) (#2975) $55

1223 9 5/8″. Olive green. (3) (#1809) $60

1224 9 5/8″. Olive green. (3) (#1380) $60

1225 9¼″. Olive green. (3) (#1175) $70

1226 8½″. Olive green. Cone shape. (3)

1227 10½″. Amber. (3) (#1443) $50

1228 10 3/8″. Olive green. (3) (#2684) $55

1229 10¾″. Aqua. (4) (#2251) $30

1230 10½″. Olive green. (3) (#634) $25

1231 11″. Dark green. Heavy glass. (3)

1233 11 1/8″. Amber. (3) (#1112) $100

1234 16½″. Light olive green. 2-mold. (4)

1235 12 5/8″. Amber. (3) (#437) $120
Similar. 12¼″. Olive amber. (#246) $150

1236 14½″. Light sea green. (4)

1237 12½. Light olive green. (3) (#539) $60
Same. (#2488) $140

1238 13″. Light amber. Swirled. (3)

1239 16″. Sea green. (4) (#2270) $40

## Chapter Eighteen

# Decanter Types

The most outstanding bottles in this category in the Gardner collection are the decanters blown in the mold at Keene, New Hampshire. These dark green bottles with sunburst and other early glass decoration were made in the early nineteenth century and are extremely rare today. They were patterned generally after European cut glass and are some of our earliest examples of decorative tableware made in molded designs.

Also included in this category are some early blue, Sandwich, Massachusetts, toilet water bottles. The sapphire blue examples which have their original stoppers would be considered very good rare examples of the early production of the famous glass house.

The reader will find no price for the Bristol decanter, the one bottle Nina Gardner decided to keep.

1241 Pillar-type cut glass decanter. 11″. Topaz. Flared lip. (4)

1243 Sandwich toilet water bottle. Ribbed with 2 rings on neck. Sapphire blue. Stopper. (4) (#123) $270

1244 Similar to above. Diagonal ribbing, 2 rings. 5 3/8″. Deep blue. Stopper. (4) (#1941) $175

1245 Similar to above. Vertical ribbing. 2 rings. 6″. Purple. Stopper. (4)

1245V Similar. 1 ring. No stopper. Deep violet. (4) (#2973) $280

**Keene, N.H., decanter with alternate square of sunbursts and diamond diapering. Olive green. (1248).**

**Pair of similar Keene decanters. (1251, 1249).**

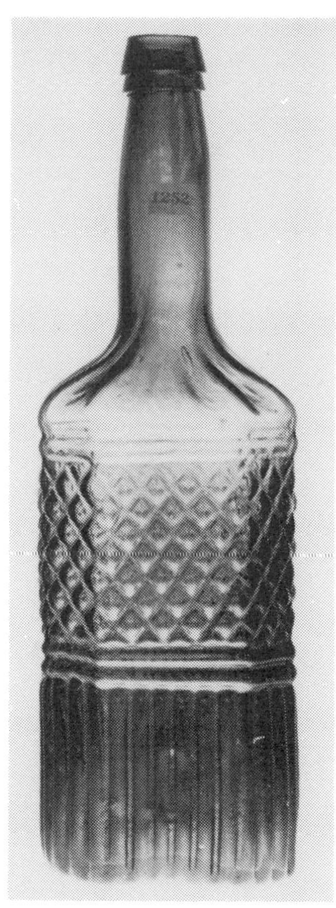

**Extremely rare, dark green decanter made in three-part mold by Louisville, Kentucky, Glass Works has design of ribbing and diamond diapering. (1252).**

1246 Similar. Diagonal ribbing. Stopper. Deep sapphire blue. (4) (#2464) $130

1246A Same. Pale green. Stopper. Rare (3)

1247 Similar in shape. Blown in a vertical ribbed mold and expanded. Stopper. Inside folded lip. Sapphire blue. (3)

1248 Keene (N.H.) decanter. Alternate squares of diamond diapering and sunbursts. Pint. Olive green. (2) (#2537) $400

1250 Same as above. (2) (#525) $625

1249 Similar with varying design. Quart. Olive green. (1) (#41) $650

1251 Same. (1) (#1537) $650

1252 Square. 3 mold. Diamond diapering and ribbing. 10½″. Dark green. (1) (#2021) $2,000

1253 Round. 4 panels of diamonds above band of small diamonds with another above. Quart. Deep olive green. (1) (#1029) $1,500

1255 Round Bristol decanter with 3 rings around neck. Flat oval cut stopper. Quart. Emerald green. Ground pontil. (4)

## Chapter Nineteen

# Demijohns

This grouping includes all of the free-blown bubbles of glass in shapes typical of bottles used commercially from ancient days. The kidney, cylindrical and globular shapes were derived without molds and the glass used was of the cheapest commercial type. Colors range from pale aqua to a dark olive green that appears to be almost black.

The sizes of the demijohns in the Gardner collection vary enormously from a few inches to 25 inches. Demijohns were used for storing and transporting a variety of liquids throughout history and many of those found in this country today were, at one time, encased in wicker to protect them and their contents during transportation and storage.

1258 Kidney-shaped. 4 1/8". Green. (3)

1259 Kidney-shaped. 7 7/8". Amber. Early. (2)

1260 Kidney-shaped. 7". Amber. Early. (2)

1261 Kidney-shaped. 4 9/16". Olive green. (3)

1262 Kidney-shaped. 7¼". Dark olive green. Early. (2)

1263 Kidney-shaped. 3 5/8". Olive amber. (3)

1268 Kidney-shaped. 10½". 2-mold. Amber. (3) (#367) $100

1269 Kidney-shaped. 11". Dark olive amber. (3) (#53) $170
Same. Light green, 10½", olive amber (#2638) $120

1270 Kidney-shaped. 8½". Light green. (4) (#2815) $70

1271 Kidney-shaped 18". Brilliant yellow green. (2) (#620) $50

1272 Kidney-shaped. 10½". Clear green. (3) (#1080) $60

1273 Kidney-shaped. 10¼". Olive green. (3) (#232) $210
Similar, cracked (#1960) $55

1274 Kidney-shaped. 5 1/8". Green. (4)

1275 Kidney-shaped. 11½". Olive amber. Crude. (3) (#1629) $75

1276 Kidney-shaped. 10 3/8". Green. (3) (#2353) $230

1279 Kidney-shaped. 12". Light green. Crimped. (4) (#1325) $60

1280 Kidney-shaped. 12". Olive amber. (3) (#2602) $120

1281 Kidney-shaped. 12 5/8". Olive green. (3) (#878) $270

1283 Kidney-shaped. 7". Clear olive amber. Early. (2)

1285 Kidney-shaped. 15¼". Olive amber. Short neck. (3)

1286 Globular shape. 17". Medium amber. (3) (#584) $90

1291 Kidney-shaped. 16". Green. (This bottle was used for porch light in front of Gardner home in New London.) (3) (#461) $80

1293 Kidney-shaped. 16½". Dark green. Crude. (3) (#2798) $170

1296 Kidney-shaped. 17". Olive green. (3) (#1239) $210

1297 Kidney-shaped. 17¼". Dark olive green. (3) (#1921) $130

1299 Kidney-shaped. 17¼". Dark amber. (3) (#73) $60

1303 Kidney-shaped. 17¾". Clear light amber. (3)

1307 Kidney-shaped. 18". Aqua. (4) (#526) $60

1309 Kidney-shaped. 18". Amber. Marked ( V. K. 1859). (3) (#127) $140

1311 Kidney-shaped. 18". Olive amber. (3)

1313 Kidney-shaped. 18". Clear olive amber. (3) (#941) $80

1314 Kidney-shaped. 18". Clear. (Made into lamp.) (4)

1315 Kidney-shaped. 18". Olive green, shaded. (3) (#2204) $120

1316 Kidney-shaped. 18½". Deep olive green. (3) (#395) $130

1318 Kidney-shaped. 18½". Clear blue green. (3)

1319 Kidney-shaped. 18½". Warm red amber. (3) (#1490) $140

1325 Kidney-shaped. 20". Olive green. (3)

1330 Cylindrical. 13". Amber. Short neck. (4) (#1725) $85

1332 Cylindrical. 16½". Amber. Short neck. (4) (#2992) $40
Similar (#774) $190

1345 Globular. 17″. Dense amber. (3) (#186) $160

1351 Globular. 22″ high, 17½″ in diameter. Light amber. (3) (#326) $500

1352 Globular. 19″. Light olive green. (3) (#2014) $65

1354 Globular. 22½″. Olive green. (3) (#1014) $130

1356 Globular. 18″. Olive green. (3) (#2111) $75

1358 Globular. 18″. Light olive green. (Made into lamp.) (4)

1359 Globular. 18½″. Aqua. (3) (#2599) $45

1360 Globular. 18″. Golden amber. (3) (#2700) $150

1361 Globular. 23″. Aqua. (4)

1362 Globular. 17″. Dark olive amber. Pear-shaped. (4) (#1141) $200

1363 Globular. 17″. Light olive amber. (Made into lamp.) (4) (#699) $35

1364 Globular. 15″. Olive amber. (Lamp) (3)

1365 Globular. 12″. Light green. Pear-shaped. (5) (#821) $40

1366 Globular. 18″. Olive green. (3)

1367 Globular. 17½″. Clear olive amber. (3) (#842) $60

1368 Cylindrical. 25½″. Red amber. Marked (Old Valley Whiskey This Bottle Is The Property of The Cook & Bernheimer Co New York USA Gold Lion Cocktails) around lion. (3) (#780) $225

## Chapter Twenty

# Drug Bottles and Jars

This group includes the great variety of bottles and jars used by the local apothecary or chemist to hold the many concoctions that either killed or cured in the late eighteenth and early nineteenth century. Every glass house in America supplied these jars and bottles to druggists and doctors. This group is of special interest to the many collectors of the later medicine and bitters bottles.

Most of the drug bottles in this group are of a large size and they were used to store medicines at the druggist's. It was from these large covered jars that smaller amounts were doled out into bottles and jars for the patient. Few of the druggists' jars and bottles have any embossments or identification as to where they were made or who made them. Later in the nineteenth century almost every bottle of medicine would be embossed with a name or identification of the client and manufacturer of the cure and the bottle.

1376 Cylindrical. 13 vertical panels. 7¾″ high. Olive green. (5) (#2743) $120

1377 Cylindrical with wide mouth, decorated with painted flowers and a shield. 10″ high. 5¾″ diameter. Clear blue. (4) (#544) $310

1378 Cylindrical. 7½″ high, 4¾″ diameter. Mouth, 4 3/8″. Brilliant olive green. Flanged. (4) (#16) $120

1379 Jar, wide mouth. Short neck. Dark olive green. 16¼″ high. 7¾″ in diameter. (4) **(#1286) $160.**

1380 Tall, tubular, pointed stopper. 18″. Aqua. (5)

1382 Cylindrical. Quart. Amber. (Gardner's Aphrodisiac). Fake, epoxy embossment. (#2175) $15

1383 Urn-shaped. Heavy cut glass in 2 sections. Hollow, pointed stopper. 30½″ high. Clear. (2) (#1526) $250

1384 Apothecary jar with wide mouth and stopper. Height: 10″. Deep blue. (3) (#2773) $70

1385 Same as above. (3) Sold with above for 1 price.

1386 Cylindrical medicine. (C. W. Merchant Chemist Lockport, N.Y.). Pint. Emerald green. (5) (#182) $220

1387 Rectangular. (C. Brinkerhoff's). Reverse (Price $1.00) (Health Restorative) (New York). Height: 7¼″. Olive green. (1) (#137) $140

1388 Cylindrical. Funnel mouth. Height: 12 5/8″ Olive green. (6)

1389 Jar. Blown lid. Height: 12″. Light green. (3) (#2139) $75

1390 Jar. Hollow blown stopper. Height: 9½″ Aqua. (4)

1391 Jar. Broad mouth. Height: 8½″. Red amber. (6) (#2202) $80

1392 Jar. Broad mouth. Height: 9 ¾″. Deep aqua. (5)

1393 Jar, wide mouth. Height: 9 11/16″. Light olive green. (5) (#2025) $170
Similar. 10″. (#2177) $200

1394 Square. 6 3/8″. Height: 15″. Short neck. Dense olive green. Crude. Willington (Conn.) bottle. (2) (#1157) $525

1395 Jar, wide mouth. Height: 9″. Olive green. (5) (#1535) $210

1396 Jar, wide mouth. Height: 13 5/8″. Clear olive green. Folded lip. (4) (#103) $65

1397 Jar, wide mouth. Height: 9½″. Clear green. (4) (#1651) $75

1398 Jar, wide mouth. Height: 11″. Blown cover. Blue green. (3)

1399 Jar, wide mouth. Height: 9 13/16″. Blue green. (2)

1400 Jar, wide mouth. Height: 9 1/8″. Square. Light olive green. (5)

1401 Jar, wide mouth. Height: 9 1/8″. Square. Light green. Label, "Herrick Lane Salaratus." (4) (#2309) $150

1402 Jar, wide mouth. Height: 10″. Green. (5) (#1350) $45

1403 Jar, wide mouth. Mineral water marked (G. W. Weston & Co Saratoga, N.Y.) Quart. Olive green. (4) (#157) $400

1404 Jar, wide mouth. Attributed to Stoddard. Crude, long neck. Ring applied around expanded mouth. Height: 16 7/8″. Deep olive. (1) (#909) $525

1404A Similar. Height: 21″. Olive green. (1) (#976) $550

1405 Jar, wide mouth. 10 panels on shoulders. Height: 10″. Deep olive green. Heavy, applied collar for inside cap. (3)

Three sunburst flasks. 508, 513, 506A.

Slender cornucopia, tail left. Reverse has 13 stars over crude eagle. McKearin number GII-58.

Keene decanters in olive green, alternate squares of diamond pattern and sunburst designs. 1251, 1249.

Rare bottle marked "Union Glass Works, New London, Ct." has expanded mouth, iron pontil. 354.

Sunburst flasks. 514, 508A, 506.

Two flasks with flag decoration. Made in Stoddard, New Hampshire. 166, 167.

Rare Jared Spencer flask is variant of bottle that brought $26,000 at Gardner auction. This bottle sold for $16,000. 315A.

Group of Pitkin bottles. One on left is 2½″ high and is smallest known of its type. 414, 410, 433, 445.

Rare Connecticut bottle, similar to 315 but with no inscription, brought $18,500. 315B.

Left: Masonic flask. Obverse, five-pointed star over crossed keys. Reverse: square and compasses around reversed G. 160. Right: Masonic pillars either side with stars, moon and hourglass. 202.

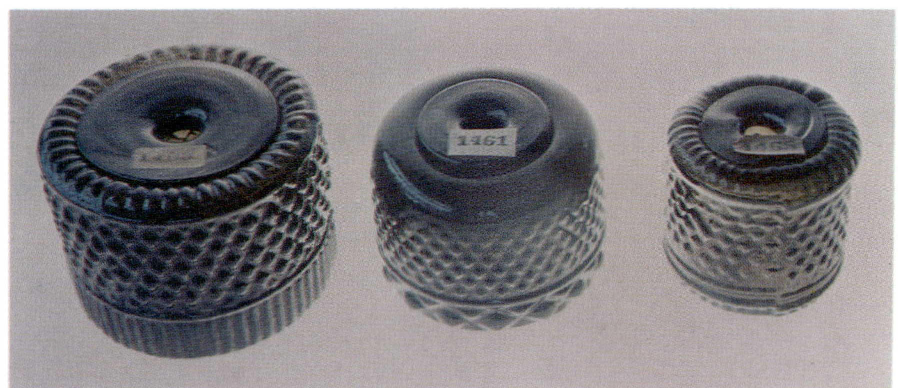

Group of three-mold inks. 1436, 1461, 1465.

Group of horizontal ring ink bottles. 1445, 1456, 1445A.

Group of three expanded pattern bottles. 1604, 1600, 1599.

Group of early bottles, some with push-up bases in aqua and amber. 2027, 1182, 2028, 2030.

Three vertically ribbed bottles. 1571, 1574A, 1564.

Three expanded pattern flasks. 1559, 1574A, 1564.

Washington flasks, Dyottville Glass Works, Philadelphia. 592E, 592C.

Group of violin or scroll flasks. 572, 537, 537A.

Two elongated neck bottles. 1583, 1535.

Group of violin flasks. Deep blue color on left makes bottle a great rarity. 536V, 536B, 536A.

Pikes Peak flask with embossment "For Pikes Peake." Reverse has hunter shooting at deer. 482.

Rare blue Columbia flask established record price for any American bottle at auction in first session. 164.

Pikes Peak flask. Prospector on obverse. Reverse, hunter shooting at deer. Marked: L. Kauffeld. 488.

Pineapple pattern bottles. Left, deep olive with mark "W & Co. N.Y." Right, bottle flattened into chestnut shape with handle. 268E, 268.

Left, General Taylor flask. Reverse has Fells Point over monument. Center, Major Ringgold and General Taylor flask in opalescent blue (moonstone) color. Right, Ringgold and Taylor flask in pale amethyst color. 327A, 284A, 284.

Group of bitters bottles with labels intact. 3342, 5200 (this number doesn't show up on Gardner catalog), 3277.

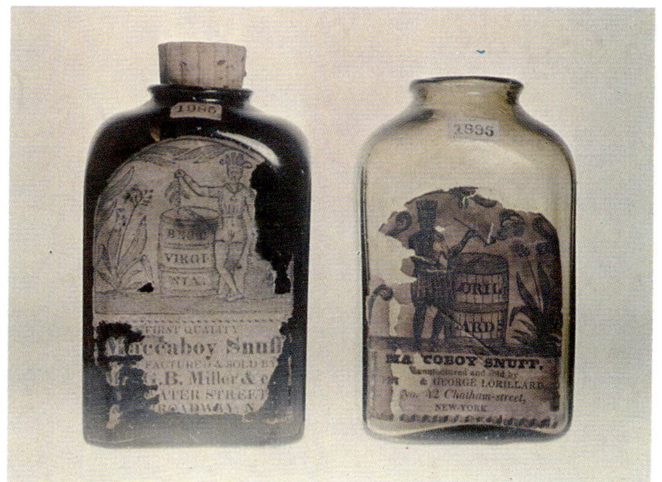


Snuff and blacking bottles with fragments of labels. 1985, 1995.

Log cabin bottles for "Smokine" in quart and pint sizes. 1852, 1852V.

Log cabin bottles made for Kelly's Old Cabin Bitters. 1078, 1078V.

William Allen's Congress Bitters bottles in puce and deep emerald green. 2865A, 2865.

Indian figurals. Left, Indian Herb Bitters. Rare variant in aqua. 1075 Variant A. Right, Indian queen is not a bitters bottle but is listed among them. It was made for Mohawk Whiskey Pure Rye. 1075, 2951.

Poland Water "Moses" bottles. 1777, 1777E.

Bottle in shape of cannon was made for Buchanan Distillery Handmade Sour Mash Whiskey. 154.

Bitters bottles, bust of Washington. Simons Centennial Bitters. 1113B, 1113.

Left, bottle in shape of log with canoe on one side (Tippecanoe Medicine). Center, bottle in shape of ear of corn. Right, hexagonal bottle for Wheeler's Berlin Bitters. 4046C, 4069, 3002.

Fish bitters bottles in three colors. 1055B, 1055A, 1055.

Sazarac Aromatic Bitters bottles. 2841V, 2841B, 2841A.

Group of Harrison's Columbia Ink bottles. Bottle on left is rare gallon size. 1472, 1476, 1472A.

Pig bitters bottles. 1116, 1025.

Group of peppersauce bottles. 1896, 1895, 1899V, 1899.

Saratoga Seltzer Water bottles. 4505, 4506.

1406 Jar, wide mouth. Height: 7 3/8". Olive green. (4) (#16) $120

1407 Jar, wide mouth. Long sloping shoulders. Height: 8¼". Olive green. Welted rim. Pitkin. (1) (#891) $280

1407A Same as above, but heavier glass and deeper color. Height: 8½". (1)

1408 Square jar. Wide flanged mouth. 5¾" x 3 ¾". Pale sea green. (5)

1409 Jar, wide mouth. Uneven sheared mouth. Height: 10 1/8". Olive green. (3) (#736) $35

1410 Octagonal bottle. Height: 6". Olive green. (4)

1411 Octagonal bottle. On 4 panels (Lewi's) (Cough) (Syrup) (Rochester N.Y.). Original label. ½ pint. Deep emerald green. (5)

1412 Like Van Rensselaer's plate 105 #3 except has wide neck with 2½" mouth. Heavy applied ring around neck. Early wine jar. (1)

1412V Similar to above but neck and mouth more fully expanded. Wide mouth with similar flattened applied ring. Height: 9 7/8". Deep olive green. (1) (#2585) $700

1413 Jar, wide mouth. Height: 5½". Clear olive green. (4) (#1136) $100

1414 Jar, wide mouth. Height: 7¼". Green. Folded collar. (4) (#1981) $70

1415 Jar, wide mouth. Height: 13 1/8". Olive green. (3) (#1074) $100

1416 Rectangular like snuff bottle. (Widely beveled corners. Height: 8". Olive green. Bubbled glass. (3) (#1107) $85
Similar. (#1478) $40

1417 Jar, wide mouth. Height: 8". Olive amber. (3) (#266) $230

1418 Jar, wide mouth. Height: 9½". Olive green. (3) (#301) $220
Similar. 9¼". (#2234) $200

1419 Rectangular bottle. Beveled corners. 3 sunken panels. (C. W. Stone's) (Liquid Cathartic & Family Physic) (Lowell Mass). Pint. Heavy glass. Brown amber. (4) (#1909) $825

1420 Square, like gin bottle with very wide mouth. Height: 10½". Olive green. (3) (#687) $450

1421 Rectangular, beveled corners. Paper label, "Jedediah R Gay MD New London Ct Electro Chemico Compound." Height: 8". Olive green. (4)

1422 Similar to 1404. Heavy ring around mouth. Height: 15¼". Olive green. (1) (#1231) $325

1423 Similar. Height: 12¾". Olive amber. (1) (#1460) $525

1424 Similar. Height: 13½". Olive amber. (1) (#1905) $450

1427 Jar, wide mouth. Height: 13½". Square. Short neck. Olive green. (1) (#2704) $750

1430 Square. (London Mustard). Height: 5½". Clear. Folded lip. (#848) $30

1433 Similar to above, but marked only (London). Height: 5½". Striated green. Folded lip. (5) (#2734) $220

1435 Jar. Height: 5¾". Short neck. Olive amber. (1)
Similar, yellow green, 5 1/16". (#2800) $40

1436 Square. Label, "Tilden & Co West Bebanon N.Y. Ferrated Wine of Wild Cherry." Height: 6½". Light blue. (6)

1437 Cylindrical. (Johnson's American Anodyne). Height: 5½". Aqua. Folded lip. (6) (#1282) $15

1438 Jar tapering from mouth. Marked (B&D). Height: 5¼". Aqua. Inside fold in lip. (5) (#1600) $45

1439 Jar, wide mouth. Marked (Queru's Cod Liver Oil Jelly). Height: 5 3/8". Aqua. Rolled lip. (5) (#1251) $120

## Chapter Twenty-One

# Square Face Gin Bottles

Although most beginning collectors might think that all bottles in this category look pretty much the same, a study of the limited examples in the Gardner collection would show that there is a great variety in color and size of bottles of this type.

Not all square face gin bottles of the last century were made in this country. Many were made abroad and the gin was then imported in the bottles which, because of their shape, could conveniently be packed in great boxes for shipping. The huge bottles of several gallons capacity were used to hold an ample supply of gin and smaller bottles were taken to local taprooms for filling.

1425 Height: 9″. Olive amber. (4) (#1424) $20

1426 Height: 9½″. Green. (Glastonbury). (3) (#2950) $75

1428 Height: 10¼″. Olive amber. (4) (#1766) $30

1429 Same. (4)

1431 Height: 10″. Olive amber. Beveled corners. (6)

1432 Height: 11½″. Olive amber. (4) (#2361) $140

1434 Height: 11 7/16″. Early screw type. No neck. Pewter collar and screw cap. Olive green. (4) (#2190) $270

1440 Height: 14″. Olive green. (2) (3011) $140

1441 Height: 19¾″. Holds 3 gallons, 1 quart and 1 pint. Olive green. (1) (#31) $350

1442 Same as above. Cracked. (1) (#2445) $525

1443 Height: 13″. Olive green. (5)

# Chapter Twenty-Two
# Inks

Most dedicated ink bottle specialist-collectors would agree that inks were not Charles Gardner's first love and the collection is small, but extremely choice. It includes very few examples of later nineteenth century bottles and concentrates instead on the eighteenth and early nineteenth century mouth-blown inks. The rather large group of Pitkin-type inks in shades of amber or green is extremely choice.

There were only a few master ink bottles in the Gardner collection. Most of those available were made too late to be of any interest to a collector who specialized mainly in blown glass bottles. The most important of the few master inks owned by Charley was undoubtedly the gallon-size, 12-sided Harrison's Columbia Ink in deep blue.

Generally, however, the Gardner ink collection consisted mainly of the early blown individual bottles that were the delight to all collectors of American ink bottles who were able to purchase them at auctions.

1444 Shape of small log cabin. Height: 3¼″. Clear. Ground mouth. Heavy glass. (3) (#2633) $350

1445 Round. 7 rows of horizontal rings. 2 mold. Amber. (4) (#57) $600

1445A Similar, but slightly taller. Olive green. (4) (#1105) $500

Group of two-mold concentric-ring inkwells. (1445, 1456, 1445A).

1446 Round, like an apple. Short depressed neck. Height: 1 7/8″. Olive green. (4) (#2037) $300

1447 Pitkin. Swirled left and ribbed. Olive green. Height: 1½″. (1) (#2079) $275
Same. 1 7/16″. (#519) $275

**Two swirled Pitkin inkwells with hat made in similar mold and shaped by hand into hat shape.**

1448 Same. Swirled left. Height: 2″. Amber. (1)

1449 Same. Swirled right. Height: 1¾″. Olive green. (1) (#608) $325

1450 Same. Swirled left. Height: 1¾″. Square. Olive green. (1) (#896) $550

1451 Same. Swirled right. Height: 1½″. Olive green. (1) (#1982) $100

1452 Same. Swirled left and ribbed. Height: 1¾″. Olive green. (1) (#2573) $375

1453 Same. Swirled left. Square. Height: 1½″. Olive green. (1) (#1718) $300

1454 Same. Swirled left. Height: 1 3/8″. Olive amber. (1) (#1176) $375

1455 Same. Swirled left. Height: 2″. Olive green. (1) (#255) $300

1456 Like #1445 except 5 rows only. Height: 1 5/16″. Olive amber. (4) (#2679) $375

1457 Pitkin. Swirled right. Height: 2 1/8″. Olive green. (1) (#2953) $350

1458 Round. Dome shape. (D. F. Halsey Patent). Unusual ring around collar. Olive amber. (3) (#2581) $425

1460 3-mold. Ribbed around base, dots and squares above. Amber. (4)

1461 3-mold. Square and triangles around base. Diamonds above. Olive green. (4) (#442) $120

1462 Similar. Ribbing around base, diamonds above. Olive green. (4) (#2944) $125

1463 Same with diamonds on base. (4) [Note: there were several of these so similar that they cannot be identified from catalog. Prices ranged from $100 to $130.]

**Group of three-mold inkwells with similar designs.**

1463V Same with concentric rings on base. (4)

1464 Same with smaller diamonds. Olive green. (4) (#1779) $90

1465 3-mold vertical ribbing over diamond diapering. 2 rings and narrow band of vertical ribbing at base. Olive green. (4) (#1557) $130

1466 Pitkin. Swirled to left with vertical ribbing. Height: 1 7/8″. Olive green. (1) (#2312) $550

1467 Pitkin swirled left. Height: 1½″. Olive amber. (1) (#48) $325

1468 Tiny green ink. Diameter: 1 3/8″. Imbedded in 3 layers of cork. (5) (#942) $30

1470 Octagonal 3½″. (Farley's Ink). Golden amber. (1) (#1441) $475

1470A Similar. 1¾″. Olive amber. (2) (#2009) $210

1471 Small log cabin, 2½″ x 2½″ x 1¾″. Tiny hole in corner. Clear. (6) (#2457) $170

**Group of representative commerical ink bottles. #1472, on left, is gallon size and very rare. (1472, 1476, 1471A).**

1471A Cylindrical. 5½″ x 2¾″. (Harrison's Columbia Ink). Deep blue. (5)

1472 12-sided. (Harrison's Columbia Ink). Gallon. Deep blue. (1) (#2534) $2,200

1473 9-sided. Height: 2½″. (Harrison's Columbia Ink). Aqua. (6) (#175) $60

1473A Same. Shoulders paneled. Height: 1¾″. Aqua. (6) (#2246) $40

1474 Same. Height: 4″. Aqua. (5) (#1304) $85

1475 12-sided. (Jones Empire Ink N.Y.). Quart. Deep green. (2) (#1045) $800

**Group of commercial ink bottles. (1475A, 1478, 1477, and uncataloged bottle.)**

1475A Similar, but pint size. Green. (2)

1476 Round. (Harrison's Columbia Ink). Height: 4″. Blue. (6)

1477 Barrel. (W. E. Bonney). Original label. Height: 5″. Aqua. Spouted lip. (5) (#2416) $150

1478 Cylindrical. 16 flutes on shoulder. (E. Waters Troy, N.Y.) Pint. Aqua. (4)

1469 Cylindrical. Marked on base (Newburgh Glass Co Pat Feb 27 66). Pour spout. Height: 9¼″. Black. (2) (#2208) $300

6000 Cylindrical. Marked (Hohenthal Brothers & Co Indelible Ink). Quart. Dark olive green. Pour spout. (5) (#205) $225

6001 Cone. Height: 2 3/8″. Olive green. (5)

6003 Umbrella. Height: 2½″. Light green. (6) (#587) $40

6004 Umbrella. Height: 2 3/8″. Original label "Johnson's Empire Black Ink." Aqua. (6)

6005 Umbrella. Height: 2 3/8″. Dark olive green. (4) (#2512) $80

6006 Pottery drum shape. "Warden's Brilliant Scarlet Ink London" on label. (6) (#813) $10

## Chapter Twenty-Three

# Handled Jugs

This group included a wide variety of bottles made to hold many types of alcoholic beverages in the latter half of the nineteenth century. Some of these jugs with applied handles have embossments to identify their original contents and others still have the old labels applied. The jugs were made in a variety of shapes and colors and what all of them have in common are the applied glass handles that made them easy to hold and pour from. A few of them were made with spout mouths to make pouring easier. While all of these jugs might easily fit into some other category in the collection they are cataloged together, here, to identify that one feature that separates them from all of the other liquor bottles in the Gardner collection.

1479 Flattened chestnut with applied handle. Seal (Chestnut Grove whiskey C. W.) Reverse: circular sunken panel. Quart. Amber. (2)

1480A Similar. ¾ quart. Amber. Original label. (2) (#1156) $70

1481 Similar. Crown differs from 1479. Quart. Amber. Spout mouth. (2) (#2026) $150

1482 Similar. (Ambrosial BM & EAW & Co). Original label. ¾ quart. Amber. (2) (#2844) $125

1483 Similar. Unmarked. Pint. Clear amber. (4) (#1715) $60

1483X Similar. Paper label "Old Kentucky Bourbon." ¾ quart. Amber. (3) (#361) $55

1484 Similar. Unmarked. Light amber. (4) (#30) $100

1484A Similar. Unmarked. Blue. (2) (#409) $700

1485 Similar. Squat and heavy. Red amber. (4)

1487 Similar with long octagonal neck. On base (F. P. Admas & Co Boston Mass USA). Pint. Aqua. (5) (#1236) $20

1488 Similar. (Whiskey) engraved on side in wreath. Combination stopper with bird on top. Quart. Clear. Ground pontil. (2)

1489 Similar. Height: 5 5/8". Red amber. (4)

1490 Similar. Height: 6½". Red amber. (4) (#230) $110

1491 Pear-shaped. Similar to Bininger Knickerbocker. Pint. Dark amber. 2 mold. (4)

1492 Similar. Quart. Dark amber. (4)

1493 Globular. On seal (Cognac W & Co). Pint. Clear amber. (2) (#511) $200

1494 Pear-shaped. Height: 8¾". Wine color. (2) (#1507) $120

1495 Inverted bell shape. Marked on seal (Pure Cognac). ¾ quart. Amber. (2) (#1280) $600

1496 Similar. Expanded ribbing swirled to left. On seal at base of handle (BF & Co N.Y.). Height: 10". Amber. Spout. (1) (#749) $475

1497 Pear-shaped. (Griffith Hyatt & Co Baltimore). Reverse: round panel. One label intact. ¾ quart. Amber. (2) (#493) $525

1498 Round tapering. (R. B. Cutter Pure Bourbon). ¾ quart. Amber. (3) (#2795) $250

1499 Pear-shaped. Off-hand. Pint. Amber. (2)

1500 Flattened chestnut. Expanded ribbing swirled to right. Quart. Amber. (2) (#375) $275

1502 Pear-shaped. Off-hand. Pint. Dark amber. (2)

1503 Wicker design with irregular panel. Flat. Pale green. (5)

1504 Similar, but round. (5)

1505 Pear-shaped with vertical ribbing. On seal (J. F. T. & Co. Philad). ¾ quart. Amber. (2) (#2681) $100

1506 Ribbed like #1500 with original paper label. "Fine Old Wheat Whiskey," etc. Quart. Amber. (3) (#998) $110

1507 Flat Chestnut marked (S.S.W. & Co.) Quart. Amber. (3) (#1889) $200

1508 Round, similar to Cutter bottle. On base (Macy & Jenkins New York). ¾ quart. Amber. Heavy glass. (4) (#576) $40

1508B Similar, base marked (The Holz & Freystedt Co N.Y.). Heavy glass. (4) (#2286) $22.50

1508V Similar, paper label. "Old Club House Whiskey." (4) (#991) $17.50

1508A Similar. Base marked (Moore Trimble & Co). ¾ quart. Amber. Heavy glass. (4) (#124) $140

1509 Flask shape with long neck. On base (Whitney Glass Works Glassbororo, N.J.). Quart. Amber. Spout. (4) (#1727) $100

1509A Similar, but not marked. Light green. (4)

1509V Similar. Marked. Pint. Amber. Spout. (4)

1510 Inverted bell shape. On oval (Star Whiskey New York W. B. Crowell Jr). Vertical Ribs. ¾ quart. Amber. Spout. (2) (#272) $125

1510V Similar, but expanded ribbing. (2) (#505) $250

1511 Flattened chestnut. On seal (J. T. Bickford & Bartlett Boston). Quart. Amber. (2) (#2672) $75

1512 Inverted bell. Cord around neck. Marked on seal (The Old Mill Whitlock & Co). Quart. Dark amber. (1) (#2013) $475

1513 Oval. (Pure Malt Whiskey Bourbon Co Kentucky). ¾ quart. Smoked amber. (3) (#2222) $250

1514 Similar to Cutter jug. Pour spout. (4)

1515 Flask shape. On side (Wharton's Whiskey 1850 Chestnut Grove). On base (Whitney Glass Works Glassboro, N.J.). ¾ quart. Deep amber. Pour spout. (1) (#2526) $275

1515V Similar, but marked on seal under handle. (Chestnut Grove Whiskey C. W.). On base: same as above. Quart. Deep amber. Pour spout. (1) (#954) $220

1516 Inverted bell shape, corseted. Quart. Deep amber. (2) (#1032) $80

1517 Same as above, but larger. (2) (#2446) $100

1518 Typical chestnut with applied handle. Quart. Clear amber. (3) (#1800) $70

1519 Pear-shaped, off-hand blow. Height: 6″. Golden amber. (2)

1520 Bell-shaped. On seal (Dr. Girard's Ginger Brandy). Paper label. ¾ quart. Amber. (2) (#181) $325

1521 Cylindrical like old schnapps jug. Marked (Very Old Gin). ¾ quart. Olive green. (4) (#1087) $160

1522 Large jug tapering from shoulder to base. Marked (Oldner's Superior Old Rye) over 2 miners in oval. (Is The Miners Protector). 2 quarts. Dark copper amber. (1) (#2189) $2,300

1523 Flattened chestnut type with deep aqua applied handle. Marked (Bulkley Fiske & Co) over (Brandy). Quart. Light greenish amber. (1) (#2925) $5,600

1524 Flat oval, like Flora Temple with applied handle. Marked (Vidvard & Sheehan) on side. ¾ quart. Pale yellow green. (3) (#1089) $850

## Chapter Twenty-Four

# Miscellaneous Liquor Bottles

This was a rather large grouping of bottles that seemed not to fit into other categories of this section of the Gardner collection. It included some handsome and rare specimens of Midwestern blown and expanded glass flasks and bottles, a couple of tubular glass bottles used for testing wine in the barrels, some nursing bottles, saddle flasks, many swirled bottles in a variety of handsome colors and even some glass hand grenades used for putting out fires in the nineteenth century.

Most of the blown and expanded ribbed bottles are very rarely found today and new collectors would happily settle for just one of the many to be found in this section. Of special interest are several bottles found in old Indian graves in Connecticut. Indians were unacquainted with glass in the early days and the bottles made here or brought to this country by the early settlers were considered so valuable by American Indians that they took them with them to their graves.

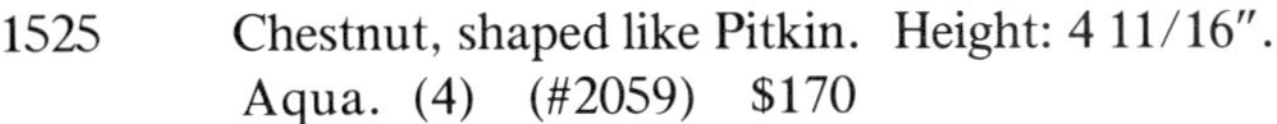

1525 Chestnut, shaped like Pitkin. Height: 4 11/16″. Aqua. (4) (#2059) $170

1526 Chestnut flattened with short neck. Height: 5″. Aqua. (5) (#2755) $250

1528 Chestnut, shaped like Pitkin. Faint ribbing. Height: 4 5/8″. Amber. (4)

1529 Chestnut, short neck. Height: 6 ¾″. Olive amber. (4)

1530 Chestnut, swirled broad ribs to left. Height: 6 3/8″. Clear yellow green. (1)

1531 Globular, 24 ribs swirled to left. Height: 7 3/8″. Deep aqua. Heavy applied ring. (3)

1533 Elongated like club soda bottle. Olive green. (4)

1534 Globular, 24 ribs swirled to right. Height: 9″. Olive amber. (1) (#97) $450

1535 Similar. Height: 7 ¾″. Citron. (1) (#2209) $500

1536 Globular, 16 ribs to right. Height: 5½″. Light amber. Mexican. (6)

1543 Ovoid. Plain. Height: 6½″. Deep purple blue. (3) (#2674) $50

1544 ½ pint flask. Height: 7 1/8″. Blue. (3)

1545 Ovoid. Height: 8″. Deep smoked amber. (4)

**Molded and expanded bottles. (1583, 1535).**

1546 Similar. Height: 8¾″. Dense amber. (4) (#154) $55

1548 Testing bottle. Length: 5¾″. Aqua. Crimped folded lip. (3)

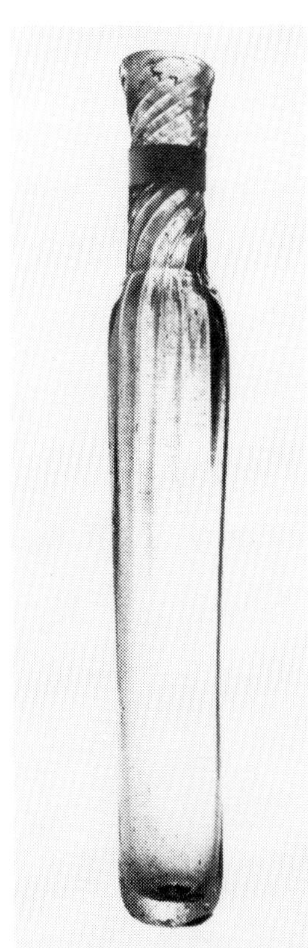

**Rare testing bottle with crimped neck and folded lip. Aqua glass. (1548).**

1549 Same. Length: 5¼″. Aqua. (3)

1551 Nursing bottle. Collared opening on top. Length: 8¾″. Aqua. (4) (#778) $210

1552 Similar. Heavy flange around nipple. Length: 8″. Aqua. (4) (#586) $160

1553 Similar. Length: 8″. Clear. (4) (#953) $190

1554 Saddle flask. Early type, long neck, flat. Height: 13½″. Olive amber. (4) (#2520) $95

1555 Similar. Thicker glass. Height: 10¼″. Crimped neck. Olive amber. (4) (#1188) $35

1556 Similar. Height: 11¾″. Olive amber. (4) (#1413) $45

1557 Similar. Thicker. Height: 8″. Olive amber. Ringed neck. (4) (#670) $50

1558 Nursing bottle. Canteen shape with threaded mouth on top and tin cup marked (The Favorite Patented Oct 21st 1890 McKinnon & Co New York). Aqua. (5) (#1533) $60

1559 Canteen shape. Broken swirl, 16 ribs to left. Height: 5½″. Blue. (2) (#1227) $55

**Group of molded and expanded flasks. One on left is broken swirl pattern in blue glass. Center flask is swirled and ribbed and flask on right is ribbed and swirled to left.**

1560 Chestnut type. Swirled to right with wide vertical ribs. Pint. Aqua. (3)

1561 Flattened canteen shape. Swirled to left. Height: 4 7/8″. Blue. (4) (#961) $225

1562 Ovoid. Finely ribbed and swirled. Height: 5½″. Green. (3)

1563 Chestnut, broken swirl to right. Height: 6¾″. Aqua. (3)

1564 Similar. Swirled to right. Height: 4″. Blue. (3) (#1394) $375

1565 Similar. Swirled to right. Height: 6½″. Aqua. (4) (#2594) $85

1566 Similar. Swirled to right. Flattened globe. Height: 9 1/8″. Sea green. (3)

1567 Similar. Swirled to left. Height: 5″. Brilliant amber. (2) (#2500) $240

1568 Similar. Broken swirl. Height: 8 7/16″. Ohio granddaddy flask. Deep amber. (1) (#1209) $1,400

1569 Similar. Swirled left, 18 ribs. Height: 6½″. Aqua. (3)

1570 Similar. Vertically ribbed. Height: 6¾″. Deep amber. (1) (#2443) $275

1571 Similar. Height: 5¼″. Deep amber. (2) (#1265) $275

**Three vertically ribbed flasks in molded and expanded shapes.**

1572 Similar. Height: 6″. Aqua. (4)

1573 Similar. Height: 7¼″. Light green. (2) (#2803) $550

1574 Similar. Height: 4½″. Deep aqua. (4) (#2122) $140

1574A Similar. Swirled to left and ribbed. Height: 4 5/8″. Amber. (1) (#908) $500

1574B Similar. Swirled to left and ribbed. 24 ribs. Height: 5″. Amber. (1) (#2100) $350

1574C Similar. Swirled to right and ribbed. 16 ribs. Height: 5¼″. Deep blue. (1) (#1947) $450

1575 Globular. Swirled to right. 24 ribs. Height: 7¾″. Dense amber. (1) (#2532) $350

1575A Similar. Swirled to left. 24 ribs. Height: 7¾″. Dense amber. (1) (#2593) $2,250

1576 Similar. Swirled to left. Height: 8 1/8″. Amber. (1) (#2492) $375

1577 Similar. Vertically ribbed. 16 ribs. Height: 8 5/8″. Aqua. (3) (#1777) $85

1578 Similar. Vertically ribbed. 24 ribs. Height: 8″. Red amber. (1) (#1737) $450

1579 Similar. Vertically ribbed. Chestnut. Height; 12″. Aqua. (3)

1579V Similar. Club shape. Swirled left. Height: 10½″. Aqua. (3) (#302) $50

1580 Similar. Swirled right with faint ribs. Height: 8 1/8". Aqua. (4) (#509) $130

1581 Similar. Swirled right with wide vertical ribs partway up sides. Height: 8¾". Aqua. (2) (#1281) $40

1582 Similar. Swirled to left. Globular. Height: 7¾". Green. (1) (#2084) $400

1583 Globular. Swirled to left and vertically ribbed. Height: 7¾". Brilliant amber. (1) (#561) $1,125

1584 Similar. Swirled to left and vertically ribbed. 6 7/8". Green. (1) (#1756) $325

1586 Similar. Swirled to left. Height: 8". Light amber. (1) (#609) $750

1587 Similar. Swirled to right. Height: 10¼". Amber. (1)

1588 Similar. Wide vertical ribs. Height: 7 1/8". Aqua. (3) (#16) $190

1589 Similar. Fine swirl to left, faint vertical ribbing partway up sides. Height: 7½". Amber. (1)

1590 Similar. Swirled lightly to right. Height: 8". Amber. (1) (#1033) $550

1591 Similar. Swirled right. Height: 7¼". Brilliant aqua. (2) (#1627) $130

1591T Similar. Fine swirl to right. Vertically ribbed. Applied thread of glass around neck. Quart. Aqua. Heavy glass. (2) (#1465) $350

1592 Chestnut. Vertically ribbed. Height: 4¾" Golden amber. (1)

1593 Similar. Vertically ribbed. Double dipped Height: 5". Aqua. (5)

1594 Similar. Wide ribbing. Height: 6¾". Sea green. (4)

1595 Similar. 24 ribs, mold marks on sides. Height: 7½". Light green. (4) (#1099) $210

**Globular chestnut flask shows reflection of Gardner bottle room on surface. (1596).**

1596 Globular. Plain glob. Height: 11½". Amber. (2)

1597 Chestnut type. Swirled to left. Height: 5". Amber. (3) (#1772) $140

1598 Chestnut. Expanded diamond type. Height: 4 7/8". Blue green. 10 diamonds. (1) (#2131) $400

1599 Similar, 10 diamonds. Height: 4 7/8". Yellow green. (1) (#2289) $550

1600 Similar, 10 diamonds. Height: 4 7/8". Golden amber. (1) (#1985) $425

**Group of expanded diamond blown and molded flasks.**

1601 Similar. Smaller diamonds, 16. Broader shoulders. Height: 4½". Aqua. (2) (#2218) $95

1602 Canteen shape. Small diamonds. Height: 6 5/8". Aqua. (4) (#786) $30

1603 Chestnut. Expanded oval or diamond pattern, 10. Height: 5¼". Deep reddish amber. Flanged lip. (1) (#2849) $950

1604 Chestnut type. Same, 10 diamonds. Height: 5 5/8". Deep red amber. (1) (#65) $925

1605 Same. Small diamonds. Double dipped. Height: 5¼". Clear. (4) (#2600) $70

1606 Same. Swirled to right and vertically ribbed. Height: 7". Light green. Broken swirl. (1) (#1795) $175

1607 Same. Stiegel daisy in square. Height: 5 1/8". Amethyst. (1) (#1801) $2,000

1608 Same. Swirled right, 16 ribs. Height: 5¼". Sapphire blue. (2) (#1931) $175

1609 Same. Swirled right, 16 ribs. Height: 3 5/8". Cobalt blue. (3) (#2004) $375

1610 Same. Vertically ribbed. Height: 5 1/8". Golden amber. (2) (#1267) $225

1611 Same. Swirled to right. Marked with blue and white flecks. Height: 5". Olive amber. (2) (#667) $240

1612 Same. Vertically ribbed. Height: 7 3/8". Amber. (2) (#2148) $300

1613 Chestnut. Swirled to left with vertical ribbing. Unusually long neck. Height: 7". Clear amber. (1) (#1476) $100

1614 Same, 24 vertical ribs. Height: 4 3/8". Olive amber. (1)

1618 Elongated chestnut, bands of small diamonds and elongated hexagons. Height: 7". Light green. (1) (#1258) $100

1619 Same. Height: 7½". Greenish yellow. (1)

1620 Same. Diamonds in lattice design. Height: 7". Aqua. (5) (#1482) $35

1621 Same. Smaller diamonds. Height: 6¼". Green. (5)

1622 Same. Tiny diamonds. Lightweight glass. Height: 6". Aqua. (4) (#1482) $35

1623 Same. Small diamonds. Height: 5¼". Deep aqua. (4)

1624 Same. Larger diamonds. Height: 6½". Light green. (3)

1625 Chestnut type. Hobnails. Double dipped. Height: 4 1/8". Aqua. (5)

1626 Same. Knobbed inside. Height: 4". Aqua. (4) (#162) $162

1627 Same. Knobbed. Height: 5 5/8". Clear green. (4) (#1803) $120

1628 Same. Height: 5½". Dark amber. (4) (#1643) $95

1629 Elongated chestnut. 16 diamonds. Height: 7¾". Green. (3) (#18) $80

1630 Globular. Plain. Quart. Aqua. (5)

1631 Similar. 24 ribs to right. Height: 7¼". Deep aqua. (3)

1632 Globular, with wide base. 18 vertical ribs. Pint. Light green. (4)

1633 Similar to 1631. Height: 5¾". Olive green. (3)

1634 Similar. Short tapering neck. Height: 5¼". Olive green. Miniature. (3) (#1738) $180

1635 Similar. Short tapering neck. Height: 6". Light olive green. (5)

1636 Similar with wide expanded mouth. Height: 6½". Ruby red. Ground pontil. (5)

1637 Similar. Sides straighter, neck longer. Height: 7 3/8". Smoked amber. (4)

1638 Similar. Short neck. Height: 4". Dense amber. (4)

1639 Similar. Height: 8". Aqua. Heavy glass. (4) (#2268) $100

1640 Similar, but about 3 quarts. Height: 9¼". Light olive green. (3)

1641 Similar. Heavy collar. Gallon. Height: 10½". Dark olive green. (3)

1642 Similar. Height: 10½". Light amber. (3)

1643 Similar. Height: 10½". Dark green. (3)

1644 Cylindrical. (Louis Weber Louisville Ky) on base. (W. McCulley & Co Pittsburgh). Quart. Dark amber. (5)

1645 Globular. Height: 11". Golden amber. (3)

1646 Same. Height: 11½". Red amber. (3)

1647 Squat bulbous etched (John Dewars Scotch Whiskey). Quart. Dark olive green. (6)

1648 Globular. Long tapering neck, swirled. Height: 12½". Aqua. Gallon. (5)

1648E Cylindrical early wine. Seal marked (JAs Oakesbury 1739). Medallion on chain marked (Whiskey). Quart. Deep olive green. (1)

1649 Globular. Rather straight sides. Swirl right. Quart. Aqua. (4) (#715) $45

1650 Rectangular with widely beveled corners. Wide mouth. Height: 7 7/8". Olive green. (5) (#2571) $70

1651 Globular. Lightweight with short neck. Height: 5 5/8". Amber. (4)

1652 Squat. Straight-sided. (Dr. Cutler) on seal. Height: 6 3/8". Olive green. (3) (#2522) $270

1653 Globular with 24 raised ribs. Vertical. Height; 7½". Opaque red. (3)

1654 Fire grenade. (Harden's Hand Fire Extinguisher Grenade Patented) on 4 panels. Remainder covered with diamonds. ½ pint. Blue. (3) (#2894) $375

1654A Similar, except 44 ribs only. Pint. Brilliant olive green. (3) (#1617) $140

1654B Egg-shaped. (Patented Septr 29th 1863). Length: 4¾". Aqua. (4) (#94) $110

1655 Fire grenade. (Diamond) (Fire Extr) (Pat June 29th 1869). Pint. Aqua. (4) (#2095) $310

1655A Similar, 8 diamonds and monogram (H.S.N). Pint. Light amber. (4) (#605) $80

1656 Similar. (Hardens Hand Grenade), covered with large diamonds. Pint. Blue. (4) (#1969) $20

1656V Similar to above, but marked (American Hand Grenade Fire Extinguisher Co.). Pint. Clear. (4) (#3005) $100

1657 Similar. (Hardens Hand Grenade). Ribbed. Pint. Blue. (4) (#191) $15

1657V Hardens grenade ribbed above and below center band. Pint. Blue. (4) (#1365) $45

1658 Similar. Horizontal ribbing. No name. Pint. Blue. Paper label. (4) (#2621) $300

1659 Similar. (Korbaline). Thumbprints. Quart. Golden amber. (4) (#1134) $100

1660 Similar. (Harkness Fire Extinguisher). Horizontal ribbing. Pint. Purple blue. (4) (#109) $350

1661 Similar. (Haywoods Hand Fire Grenade). Round panel on 4 sides. Pint. Blue. (4) (#650) $70

1662 Similar (Hardens Star). Vertical ribs and star. Quart. Green. (4)

1663 Same. Amber. Quart. (4) (#332) $190

1663A Same. Blue. Quart. (4)

1664 Similar. (Haywards Hand Fire Grenade). 4 panels with diamond-shaped depressions. Pint. Aqua. (4) (#2604) $40

1664A Same. Yellow amber. (4) (#2125) $45

1664E Same. Blue. (4) (#508) $240

1665 Similar. (Haywards Hand Grenade Fire Extinguisher). Vertical ribs with 2 diamond-shaped panels. Pint. Brilliant aqua. (4) (#928) $40

1665A Same. Blue. (4) (#2426) $65

1665G Large squat. Height: 7″. Bottle green. (1)

1666 Early squat bottle from Indian grave. Height: 8″. Olive green. Heavy applied collar. (1) (#2508) $425

1667 Similar. Height: 9″. (1) (#2942) $1,100

1668 Similar. Height: 4 5/8″. Olive green. (1) (#2750) $150

1669 Similar. Height: 5 3/8″. Olive green. (1) (#2540) $130

1670 Similar. Height: 6 5/8″. Olive green. (1) (#2810) $200

1670V Same. (1) (#2687) $675

1671 Same, except half-bottle. Height: 7¼″. Olive green. (1) (#2982) $70

1672 Same as #1666 except ball-shaped body. Height: 9¼″. Olive green. (1) (#2655) $775

1673 Similar to #1671. Height: 7¼″. Olive green. (1) (#2863) $220

1675 Miniature. Height: 4 1/8″. Olive green. (4)

1677 Similar. Squat. Height: 5½″. Dark olive green. (1) (#2780) $340

1678 Same, but marked on seal (T. Biddle Evershott 1720). Height: 6 1/8″. Dark olive green. (1) (#2749) $700

1679 Similar seal marked (PCM*). Height: 6″. Dark olive green. (1) (#2983) $375

1681 Similar. Height: 7¾″. Dark olive green. (1) (#2718) $240

1683 Similar with applied handle. (1) (#2653) $1,600

1684 Rectangular. Widely beveled corners. On seal (Jno Collings 1736) Qaurt. Green. (1) (#2957) $650

1685 Cylindrical. Height: 7″. Olive green. (3) (#2682) $100

1686 Squat. Height: 12 3/8″. Olive amber. (1)

1687 Similar. Height: 5¼″. Green. (1)

1688 Squat. Long neck. Height: 7″. Dark olive green. (2) (#2778) $65

1690 Same. Height: 8¾″. Olive amber. (2) (#2883) $850

1691 Same. Height: 7¾″. Olive amber. (2) (#2538) $170

1692 Cylindrical. On seal (J. Head 1825). On base (Patent Imperial H Ricketts' Co Glass Works Bristol). Height: 11″. Olive green. (1) (#2903) $200

1693 Similar. On seal (C). Quart. Olive green. (3) (#2830) $110

1694 Similar. On seal (R. Patterson). Quart. Olive green. (1) (#2654) $55

1695 Squat body tapering from shoulders. Long neck. Applied ring. Height: 9¼″. Olive green. (3) (#2632) $175

1695C Same, but earlier and heavier. Height: 10½″. Olive green. (3) (#2592) $190

1696 Octagonal. Early type. Height: 9¾″. Dark olive green. (3) (#2506) $250

1697 Cylindrical. On seal (John Winn Jr). On base (H Ricketts Glas Works Patent). Height: 8¾″. Olive green. (2) (#2811) $70

1698 Same. One seal (R. Lenox). Paper label. Quart. Dark olive green. (2) (#2919) $100

1700 Flask. Marked on side (Newburg Glass Co Patd Feb 17th 1866). Pint. Amber. (4) (#643) $175

1701 Cylindrical. On seal (Sherry). Height: 12½″. Clear olive green. (3) (#2999) $90

1708 Cylindrical. On shoulder (Patent). On base

(Bushwick Glass Works). Height: 11¾″. Golden amber. (5) (#1885) $40

1709 Cylindrical. On base (Willington Glass Works). ¾ quart. Dark amber. (5) (#1406) $40

1711 Similar. On seal (Wine P. C. Brooks 1820). 2 quarts. Deep olive green. (1) (#2751) $140

1712 Similar. On base (Whitney Glass Works). Inside screw cap. ¾ quart. Light amber. (5) (#280) $15

1712A Similar. On base (Whitney Glass Works). Sloping shoulders. Monogram (WKG). Quart. Blue green. (5) (#1349) $70

1712V Same, but shoulders don't slope. Olive green. (5)

1713 Globular, like water carafe. On circular panel (Forest Lawn JVH). ¾ quart. Olive green. (3) (#2698) $180

1714 Long tapering neck. Barber's bottle. Height; 11½″. Semi-opaque blue. (3)

1714V Same. Height: 16″. (3)

1715 Same. Height: 11″. (3)

1716 12-sided, slim. Height: 7 5/8″. Blue. (4)

1717 Similar. Height: 11½″. Blue. (4)

1718 Cylindrical. On base in reverse lettering (Dyottville Glass Works Phila). Quart. Light olive green. (4) (#1528) $45

1719 Barrel. Marked on base (Lancaster Glass Works Lancaster N. Y.). ¾ quart. Amber. (3) (#2043) $160

1720 12-sided. Slim. Height: 7½″. Amethyst. (4)

1720V 10-sided. Slim. Height: 7½″. (Ricketts Bristol) on base. Olive green. (4) (#537) $140

1721 Cylindrical. On base (Dyottville Glass Works Phila). ¾ quart. Amber. (5) (#1496) $140

1721V Similar. Markings on base same. Panel marked (Glass of 1846 W). Quart. Olive green. (4) (#2904) $310

1722 Similar. On shoulder (Patent). On base (Dyottville Glass Works Philada 5). ¾ quart. Amber. (4) (#15) $30

1722V Cylindrical. (Patent) on shoulder. On base (Dyottville Glass Works Phila). Letters larger than on #1722. Quart. Dark olive green. (4) (#188) $15

1723 Similar. On base (Ellenville Glass Works). ¾ quart. Olive green. (5) (#2245) $30

1724 Similar. On base (Cunningham & Ihmsen Pitts Pa). Original label. ¾ quart. Deep amber. (5) (4749) $70

1725 Cylindrical. Early and large. On seal (Paul Richards 1741). Height: 9″. Olive green. (1) (#2893) $950

1726 Similar. On seal (I Alsop 1763). Height: 10 5/8″. Dark olive green. (1) (#2831) $1,000

1727 Cylindrical. On base (Willington Glass Works) n's in Willington and s's in Glass reversed. Dot in center. ¾ quart. Amber. (5) (#2509) $45

1728 Squat. On seal (I. W. 1695). Height: 6¼″. Dark olive green. (1) (#1921) $1,950

**Early seal bottle dated 1695. (1728).**

1729 12-sided. Medium amber. Like #1720. (4)

1730A Crude cylindrical. Seal (Sir Will Stickland Bart 1809). Height: 9¾″. Dark olive green. (3) (2683) $190

1730B Similar. On seal (IF 1822). On base (H. Ricketts & Co Glass Works Bristol). Height: 9″. Olive green. (3) (#2779) $85

1730C Similar. On seal (Sir Wm Strickland Br 1809). Entirely different seal from one on 1730A. (3) (#3003) $280

1730L Similar. Seal marked (S. R. Fay). 1½ gallons. Height: 16¾″. Olive green. (3) (#2539) $220

# Chapter Twenty-Five

# Mineral Water Bottles

Natural mineral spring water was thought to have great curative powers in the nineteenth century when it was bottled at the famous spas and sold all over the world. In Europe it had been fashionable since the eighteenth century to visit famous watering holes and to "take the cures" that were offered for a variety of illnesses. Wherever the natural springs burst forth with bubbly sulphuric water, great hotels and spas were built and one would go many miles to drink water that was advertised to cure anything from "chronic catarrh of the nose" to "gout, obesity or diabetes."

One of the most famous American spas was Saratoga Springs, New York, but mineral spring water was bottled in many places. While some brands were sold only locally, many others were distributed nationally and a few internationally. Fortunately, the bottle-makers identified the bottles used for mineral waters with the name and, frequently, the addresses of the bottlers. Collectors search for all known varieties of bottles and embossments. One of the most interesting of all bottles used for mineral waters is the figural "Moses" bottle used for Poland Spring water.

Mineral water bottles made up a fascinating segment of the Gardner collection. They were made in a variety of colors and sizes and the embossments identified a great variety of watering holes that have long since been forgotten.

1730 Cylindrical (B. L. Winn Union Glass Works Philada). ½ pint. Dark green. (4) (#185) $65
Same. (#528) $35

1731 Same. Unlettered. Flying eagle with arrows and olive branch. ½ pint. Green. (3) (#809) $60

1732 Same. (W. Eagle New York) (Union Glass Works Phila A Superior Mineral Water). ½ pint. Blue. (3)

1733 Same. (W. Eagle's Superior Soda or Mineral Water). ½ pint. Green. (3) (#2448) $30

1734 Same. (F. Sherwood Bridgeport & New Haven Union Glass Works Philad.a). ½ pint. Greenish blue. (3) (#473) $170

1735 Octagonal. (T. W. Gillette New Haven). Star on reverse: ½ pint. Blue. (3) (#985) $170

1736 Same. (3) (#2092) $165

1737 Similar. (J. W. Harris Soda Water New Haven Conn). ½ pint. Blue. (3) (#201) $120

1738 Similar. (Premium Mineral Waters). Pint. Green. (3) (#1493) $90

1739 Octagonal (Hugh) (Goodwin) (Aromatic) (Ginger) (Ale) (No 47) (Montgomery Str) (Brooklyn). ½ pint. Aqua. Heavy glass. (4) (#1639) $17.50

1740 Round. (E. S. & H Hart Superior Soda Water Union Glass Works). ½ pint. Blue. (3) (#2023) $95

1761 Similar. (Lancaster Glass Works N. Y.). ½ pint. Clear blue. (3) (#364) $90

1762 Octagonal. (WM W. Pappeus - Premium - Soda or Mineral Waters - Albany). ½ pint. Blue. (3) (#1458) $230

1763 Cylindrical. On side (Hathorn Spring Saratoga N. Y.). Quart. Dark amber. (5) (#1303) $5

1763A Round. (Hathorn Springs Saratoga N. Y.). Quart. Deep emerald green. (4) (#779) $30
Similar (#1891) $20

1763B Same. Pint. Black. (4) (#128) $20

1764 Same. (Lynch & Clarke New York). Pint. Olive green. (4) (#560) $45

1766 Same. (Clarke & Co New York). Pint. Olive green. (4) (#520) $45

1768 Same. (G.W. Weston & Co) (Saratoga N. Y.). on side. Quart. Olive green. (4) (#333) $25

1771 Same. (Excelsior Spring Saratoga N. Y.). Pint. Emerald green. (4) (#2191) $30

1771A Same. Quart. Yellow green. (3) (#1810) $40

1772 Same. (Quaker Springs I. W. Meader & Co Saratoga Co N. Y.). Reverse (Old Saratoga Spring Water). Pint. Emerald green. (4) (#2431) $120

1773 Same. (Clarke & White New York) around large open block (C). Quart. Olive green. (4) (#2525) $20

1775 Same. Cylindrical. Short neck. (Guyser Spring Saratoga Springs State of New York). Reverse (The Saratoga Spouting Spring). Pint. Aqua. (4) (#202) $15

1775V Same. Quart. Aqua. (4) (#925) $25

1775X Same. (Missisquoi Springs) around (A). Quart. Olive green. (4) (#1555) $30

1776 Same. (Kissengen Water) above (Hanbury Smith). Pint. Green. (4) (#1846) $30

1776A Same. Olive green. (4) (#476) $35

1777 Shape of old man. (Poland Water H. Ricker & Sons Proprietors). Quart. Aqua. (2) (#507) $75

1777B Same. Clear. (2) (#1959) $25

1777E Same. Amber. (2) (#2237) $325

1778 Same. (Address C. W. Merchant & Co Lockport N.Y. Oak Orchard Acid Springs). Quart. Deep green. (4) (#62) $40

1778V Same. (H. W. Bostwick Agt No 574 Broadway New York Oak Orchard Acid Springs). On base (Glass from F. Hitchins Factory Lockport N. Y.). Quart. Deep amber. (4) (#2955) $45

1779 Same. (Henry Rawls & Co Albany). Quart. Olive amber. (4) (#2250) $160

1741 Round, 10 panels at base. (M. T. Crawford Hartford Ct). Reverse (Union Glass Works Philada Superior Mineral Water). ½ pint. Blue. (3) (#460) $130

1742 Round. (Hamilton Glass Works N. Y.). Pint. Aqua. (3) (#717) $45

1743 Round, squat. On base (Dyottville Glass Works). ½ pint. Pale green. Heavy glass. (3) (#2358) $40

1743V Similar. On side (Dyottville Glass Works Phila). ½ pint. Pale green. Heavy glass. (3) (#495) $25

1744 Round, (C. V. Demott) over 5 stars. Reverse (DeM). Pint. Green. (3) (#59) $40

1745 Similar. Around base (Union Glass Works Philad). ½ pint. Green. (3) (#2888) $10

1746 Similar. (Union Glass Works New London Ct). ½ pint. Aqua. (3) (#105) $200

1746F Same as above. (3) (#2493) $210

1747 Similar. (Morgan Bros & Co New York Superior Mineral Water Union Glass Works Phila). ½ pint. Green. (3) (#2842) $45

1748 Similar. (J. Tweedle Jr's Celebrated Soda or Mineral Waters Barclay St 41 New York). ½ pint. Green. (3) (#1399) $90

1749 Similar. (Tweedles Celebrated Soda or Mineral Waters Courtland St 38 New York). ½ pint. Blue. (3) (#1127) $127

1750 Similar. Marked (Clapp) on 1 side only. ½ pint. Red amber. (4) (#271) $50

1751 Similar. (J. Deane 164 Broadway). ½ pint. Green. (4) (#592) $35

1752 Similar. (M. T. Crawford Hartford Ct) (Brown Glass Works) over (D) over (New York). ½ pint. Blue. Heavy glass. (4) (#1730) $40

1755 Similar. (Dyottville Glass Works Philadelphia A. W. Rapp New York). Reverse (Mineral Waters R This bottle is never sold). Pint. Blue. (3) (#943) $120

1756 10-paneled sides. (Broughton) (& Chase) (Rochester N. Y.) (Bottles) (Registered) (According) (To Law). ¾ quart. Deep blue. (3) (#1489) $950

1757 Round, like club soda. (Luke Beard). ½ pint. Green. (3) (#911) $100

1757V Cylindrical. (Luke Beard, Howard St. Boston). Reverse: star, (This bottle never sold). ½ pint. Dark green. (3) (#1527) $50

1758 Round, like club soda. (Haddock & Sons). ½ pint. Olive green. (3) (#110) $220

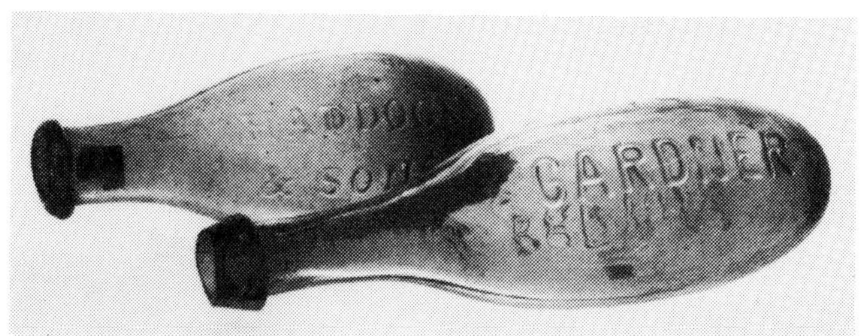

**Round-bottomed soda bottles. (1758, 4526).**

1759 Round, short neck. (Hansbury Smith's Mineral Waters). ½ pint. Dark olive green. (3) (#122) $40

1759V Same inscription but variant. Olive green. (3)

1760 Similar. (Simons G & Co Hartford Conn). ½ pint. Green. (3) (#1559) $70

1780 Same. (Guilford Mineral Spring Water Guilford Vt). Small circle enclosing (GSMW) around cross. Quart. Bright green. (4) (#701) $40

1781 Same. (Saratoga Red Spring). Quart. Emerald green. (4) (#267) $15

1781V Same. Pint. Deep green. (4) (#1605) $30

1782 Same. Short neck. (Buffalo Lithia Water Natures Meteria Medica Trade Mark) around seated woman. 2 quarts. Aqua. (6) (#218) $5

1783 Same, but woman's figure heavier and stippled. 2 quarts. Aqua. (6) (#1187) $15

1784 Same. (Saratoga) over 5-pointed star. (Springs) below. Quart. Emerald green. (4) (#889) $75

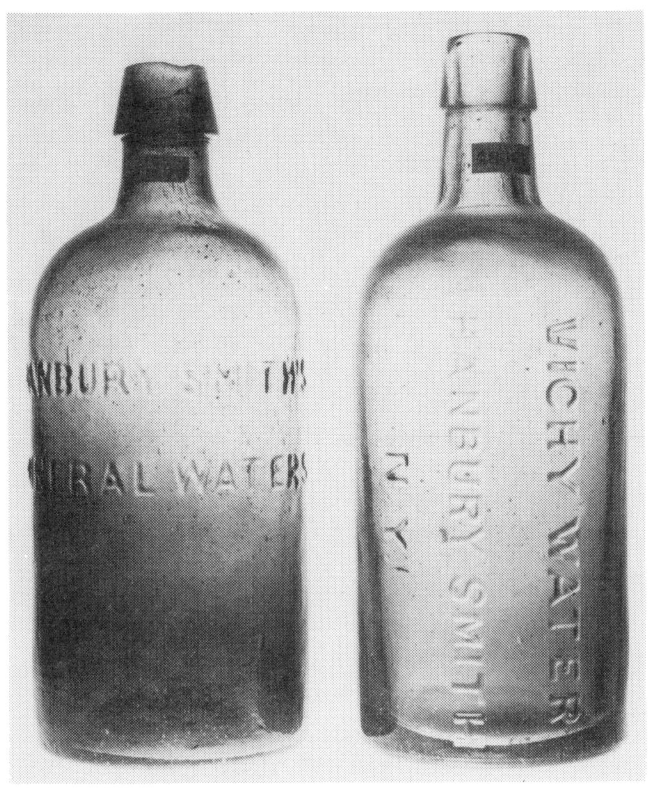


**Mineral water and Vichy water bottles. (1806V, 1759V).**

1784B Same. Quart. Dense amber. (3) (#2015) $25

1784V Same. Pint. Brown amber. (4) (#950) $50

1784A Same. Pint. Deep green. (4) (#1477) $60

1785 Same. (Middletown Healing Springs Grays & Clark Middletown Vt.). Quart. Rich golden amber. (4) (#733) $45

1785V Same. Deep green. (2) (#2079) $95

1786 Round. (Philadelphia XXX Porter & Ale). Reverse (Honesdale Glass Works. Pa) ½ pint. Green. (4) (#2112) $70

1786V Same. (Honesdale Glass Works Pa). Reverse (Mineral Water). ½ pint. Green. (4) (#2535) $40

1787 Same. (Lancaster) above (X) over (Glass Works) over (NY.). On reverse (XX). Pint. Blue. (3) (#775) $75

1788 Same. (H. W. Bostwick Agt No 574 Broadway New York). Reverse (Oak Orchard Acid Springs). On base (Glass from F. Hitchins Factory Lockport N. Y.). Quart. Deep emerald green. (4) (#2587) $45

1789 Same as above. Quart. Amber. Lighter glass. (4) (#2736) $40

1790 Same. (Avon Spring Water). Quart. Deep olive green. (4) (#2205) $200

1791 Same. (Gettysburg Katalysine Water). Quart. Olive green. (4) (#2463) $50

**Pair of mineral water bottles. (1780, 1785V).**

1791A Same. Bright green. Contents and label intact. (3) (#1445) $60

1792 Same. Octagonal. (J & A. Dearborn Mineral Waters New York) and star over (Union Glass Works). ½ pint. Deep blue. (4) (#2968) $35

1793 Same. (Congress & Empire Spring Co) above (Hotchkiss' Sons) above block (E) above (New York) (Saratoga N.Y.). ½ pint. Brilliant red amber. (4) (#1511) $45

1794 Same. (St Regis Water Massina Springs). Quart. Emerald green. (4) (#1927) $75

1795 Same. (Magnetic Springs Henniker N.H.). Quart. Golden amber. (4) (#85) $110

1796V Same. (Highrock Congress Spring) above (1767) above rock and (C&W Saratoga N.Y.). ½ pint. Amber. (4) (#2891) $85

1797 Same. (John Clarke New York). Quart. Olive green. (4) (#2987) $60

1798 Round. (Congress & Empire Spring Co) over (C) above (Saratoga N.Y.). Reverse (Congress Water). Quart. Emerald green. (4) (#1154) $20

1798V Same. Pint. Emerald green. (4) (#1025) $30

1799 Same. (Congress & Empire Spring Co) over different (C) from 1798 above (Saratoga N.Y.). Quart. Light greenish amber. (4) (#1703) $45

1800 Same. Pint. Deep olive green. (4) (#1827) $15

1801 Same. (Blount Springs Natural Sulphur Water). Reverse (Trade Mark) and monogram (BS). ½ pint. Blue. Heavy glass. (4) (#2555) $35

1802 Same. Like #1775X except neck has been cut off and expanded to form a jar. (Missisquoia Springs) around (A). Quart. Olive green. Tooled lip. (2) (#2249) $575

1803 Same. Squat. Marked on base (Hagertys Glass Works N.Y.). ½ pint. Clear green. Heavy glass. (4) (#1090) $55

1804 Same. Pointed base. (J. T. Brown Chemist Boston) (Double Soda Water). ½ pint. Blue green. (3) (#2989) $170

1805 Same. (Missisquoi Springs) around (A). Reverse: figure of Indian woman. Quart. Green. (3) (#1989) $350

1806 Same. 2 vertical lines (Vichy Water) (Hanbury Smith). ½ pint. Deep brown. (4) (#2318) $45

1806A Same. Grass green. (4) (#1048) $40

1807 Same. (Patent) on shoulder. On base (Phoenix Glass Works Phila). Pint. Green. (3) (#784) $100

1808 Same. (Artesian Spring Co) above (AS) over (Ballston N.Y.). Reverse (Ballston Spa) above (AS) over (Mineral Water). Pint. Dark green. (4) (#2813) $30

1808V Cylindrical. (Artesian Spring Co) above monogram (AS) above (Ballston N.Y.). Reverse (Ballston Spa Lithia Water). Pint. Deep green. (3) (#844) $40

1809 Same. (D. A. Knowlton Saratoga N.Y.). On base (4). Quart. Dark olive green. (4) (#824) $40

1810 Same. (Priets Natural Soda). Reverse (Natural) above head (Mineral Water) below. ½ pint. Aqua. (4) (#1575) $25

1811 Same. (Congress & Empire Spring Co) above (Hotchkiss Sons) over (C) above (New York Saratoga N.Y.). Pint. Olive green. (4) (#1652) $35

1811A Same. (Empire Spring Co) above (Saratoga, N.Y.). Reverse (Empire Springs). Quart. Blue green. (4) (#1542) $25

1812 Same. (Pentucket Spring Water). Reverse (C. S. Cushing) (Lowell) (Patent). ½ pint Green. (4) (#1789) $40

1813 Same. (Moxie Nerve Food Lowell Mass Patented) (#) on base. ¾ quart. Funnel mouth. (4) (#2060) $50

4500 Cylindrical. Marked (J & J. W. Harvey Norwich Conn). ½ pint. Green. (6) (#1697) $130

Similar. Aqua. ( I. W. Harvey & Co. Norwich, Conn.). (#1190) $30

4501 Similar. Rayed eagle on shield with flags. ½ pint. Green. (5) (#1189) $120

4502 Similar. (Congress & Empire Spring Co Hotchkiss Sons C New York Saratoga N.Y.). Reverse (Congress Water). Pint. Deep green. (5) (#1906) $30

4503 Similar. (Washington Mineral Water). In circle around (Lithia Well) (Ballston Spa N.Y.). Pint. Aqua. (5) (#443) $150

4504 Similar. (Washington Spring Saratoga N.Y.). Pint. Deep green. (5) (#398) $55

4505 Similar. (Saratoga Seltzer Water). Pint. Blue green. (5) (#986) $22.50

**Pair of seltzer water bottles. (4505, 4506).**

4506 Similar to above. ½ pint. Blue green. (5)

4507 Similar. (Saratoga Vichy Spouting Spring V Saratoga N.Y.) ½ pint. Dark amber. (5) (#2173) $20

4508 Similar. (Syracuse Springs) (Excelsior). Pint Dark amber. (5) (#1572) $70

4509 Similar. (Gardner & Landon Sharon Sulphur Water). Quart. Olive green. (5) (#2360) $140

4512 Similar. (Dr. Stowe's Ambrosial Nectar Patented May 22, 1866) around beaker. Pint. Rich amber. (5) (#2156) $30

4513 Similar. (Saratoga Lincoln Spring Co. This bottle not to be sold F.E.R.). Marked china stopper. Pint. Amber. Heavy glass. (5)

4514 Cylindrical, sloping shoulders. On base (Congress Spring Co S S N. Y. 4). Pint. Brilliant dark green. Heavy glass. (4) (#1206) $15

4515 Similar. (Vermont Spring Saxe & Co Sheldon Vt). 2 dots on base. Quart. Deep green. (5) (#2478) $20

4516 Similar. (Henry Gardner West Bromwich) (RBS). On base (Trade Mark MC). ½ pint. Yellow green. Heavy glass. (5) (#2048) $25

4517 Square. (J. W. Kelly's) (Portable) (Soda Water). Paper label. Height: 5¼″. Aqua. (4)

4518 Cylindrical. (Taylor Never Surrenders) (Union Glass Works Philada). ½ pint. Blue. (6) (#685) $40

4519 Cylindrical. (Adirondack Spring) over (Westport N.Y.). Quart. Deep green. (2) (#42) $35

4520 Cylindrical. (Haskins' Spring Co) over (H) over (Shutesbury, Mass). (H. S. Co). on reverse. Quart. Bright green. (2) (#2701) $95

4521 Cylindrical. Soda. (Bridgeton Glass Works) over (N.J.). ½ pint. Aqua. (3) (#1015) $10

4522 Cylindrical. (Pavilion & United States Spring Co) over (P) (Saratoga N.Y.). Reverse (Pavilion Water). Pint. Deep olive green. (3) (#630) $55

4523 Cylindrical soda. (Congress & Empire Spring Co Saratoga N.Y.) around large (E). Reverse (Empire Water). (X) on base. Pint. Blue green. (#535) $17.50

4524 Same. (Empire Spring Co Saratoga N.Y.) around large (E). Reverse (Empire Water). Pint. Blue green. (4) (#1283) $25

4524V Cylindrical. (Congress & Empire Spring Co) above big block (E) over (Saratoga N.Y.). Reverse (Empire Water). Quart. Deep green. (3) (#2285) $25

4525 Cylindrical. Soda. (Joseph Weber Philada). Reverse: 3-leaf clover marked (J. W.) above crossed cannons above 10 stacked cannon balls. ½ pint. Aqua. (4) (#672) $30

4526 Cylindrical. Soda. (John H. Gardner & Son) in semicircle above (Sharon Springs N.Y.). Reverse (Sharon Sulphur Water). Pint. Light green. (3) (#640) $60

4527 Cylindrical. Soda. (Chadsey & Bro. New York). ½ pint. Deep blue. (3) (#1879) $70

## Chapter Twenty-Six

# Nailsea, Bristol, Etc.

This interesting grouping in the Gardner catalog includes many examples of British glass bottles and other items of even greater interest to today's bottle collector. There are many entries for fascinating figural bottles and some examples of American and European art glass made just before the turn of the century.

In the figural category are bottles in the shapes of butterflies, clamshells, animals, a lantern and even a whisk broom. There are also a few examples of nineteenth century barbers' bottles, which is a category of specialization that has become popular in the past few years. The following listing is an interesting group of art glass, early European glass and novelty bottles in which shape, color or decoration is the outstanding feature of the glass.

1814 Squat, with long neck. White specks and dots. Quart. Olive green. (2)

1815 Similar, but wider base. Same coloring. Quart. Olive green. (2)

1816 Cruet-shaped with applied handle. Splotched with white. Height: 6″. Dark green. (2) (#2783) $310

1817 Ovoid. Swirled to right. Height: 6″. Ruby red. (2) (#2519) $190

1818 Gimmel. Turquoise and milk white striations. Length: 10″. Crystal. (3) (#2794) $55

1819 Shaped like Pitkin. Fine turquoise swirls to right. Height: 4 7/8″. Black. (2) (#2802) $160

1820 Ovoid. Swirled to right. Height: 7¼″. Emerald green. (2)

1821 Decanter shape. Olive green with white striations. Height: 8″. (4)

1822 Decanter type. White striations. Height: 10½″. Olive green. (2)

1823 Ovoid. White striations. Height: 6¼″. Olive green. (2) (#2611) $200

1824 Ovoid. Pointed vase. Pink and white lattice similar to Lutz scent bottles. Height: 6¾″. Clear. (2) (#762) $90

1825 Ovoid. Flecked with turquoise blue, white and brick red. Height: 7″. Medium green. (2) (#2823) $250

1826 Rectangular with widely beveled corners. Long neck. Covered with white specks. Height: 8¾″. Olive green. (2) (#2542) $290

1827 Small bellows with rigaree. Height: 7″. Clear. (4) (#286) $30

1828 Large bellows on base. Clear rigaree. Height: 14½″. Clear. (5) (#2204) $40

1829 Similar. Striated with opaque white. Clear rigaree. Height: 13½″. Clear. (3) (#2703) $120

1830 Barber's bottle. Decanter shape. Enameled decorations. Yellow green. (3) (#458) $90

1831 Butterfly. Corseted. Clear and frosted. Ribbed at base. Pint. Clear. (6)

1831A Same as above, but no frosting. (5)

1832 Clamshell, aqua, painted white. Screw cap. (6) (#875) $15

**Group of three clamshell bottles with screw caps. (1832, 1833, 1834).**

1833 Same. Blue. (6) #440) $120

1834 Same, but smaller and clear. (6) (#1013) $15
Same, Clear. (#1798) $15

1835 Blown bull, amber. (5) (#917) $250

1836 Shoe. Painted toe coming through. Length: 5¾″. Purple. (4) (#2603) $75

1837 Square base to monument. White metal statue. Quart. Milk glass. Ground pontil. (4) (#2126) $375

1838 Hourglass. 2 blown bottles in wooden frame. Aqua. (4) (#1208) $160

1839 Half-section of hourglass. Height: 2½″. Light green. (5) (#1211) Sold in lot with item below for $25.

1840 Same. Larger. Made at Pairpoints. (5)

1841 Complete hourglass blown in 1 piece. Wooden frame covered in plaid paper. Height: 6½″. Clear. (5) (#1828) $40

1843 Bear. Paws on knees. Snout molded and applied. Bib on chest. Heavy glass. ¾ quart. Dense amber. (3) (#2460) $130

1844 Bear. Similar but with variations. Applied face. Height: 10½″. Olive green. (3) (#1073) $675

1844A Bear. Similar with variations. Applied face. Very shaggy. Height: 11½″. Black. (3) (#800) $85

1845 Rolling pin. Crude, small knobs at ends. Length: 14½″. Green. (4) (#80) $75

1846 Similar. Length: 14¾″. Olive green. (4) (#919) $75

1846A Similar. Length: 15″. Opalescent milk glass. (3) (#1298) $70

1847 Similar. Length: 16″. Blue. Hollow handles. (4) (#1669) $110

1848 Similar to above. Clear. (5) (#384) $20

1848A Similar. Length: 17″. Amber. (4) (#2094) $70

1848B Similar. Length: 14½″. Amethyst. (4) (#571) $210

1849 Similar. Length: 18½″. Olive green Nailsea, splotched. (3) (#2998) $130

1850 Pig. (Drink While it Lasts From a Hogs). Length: 6¾″. Clear. (4) (#235) $80

1851 Duck. Bill holding mouth, label panel on breast. On base (Patd April 11th 1871). ¾ quart. Milk glass. Attaberry. (2) (#240) $250

1852 Log cabin. (Smokine Imported and Bottled by Alfred Andreson & Co). Quart. Amber. (2) (#2748) $225

Pair of Smokine log cabin bottles. (1825V, 1852).

1852V Same. Pint. Amber. (2) (#777) $160

1853 Bear. Varying from others. Crown on head. Height: 10½″. Greenish blue. (3) (#729) $1,250

1854 Shape of lantern. Tole frame containing olive green bottle. (4) (#3013) $200

1855 Whisk broom. Sunbursts and bull's-eyes. Pint. Clear. (6) (#2235) $20

1855V Same. ½ pint. Clear. (6)

1856 Patented non-refillable bottle marked (L. C. Edwards Non Refillable Bottle Patented April 28th 1903). Have necking tool for this item. Quart. Amber. (4) (#2105) $65

1857 Tall figure of Indian with feathered headdress forming cap. Leaning on long bow, tomahawk in belt, quiver on back. Height: 13½″. Frosted. (2) (#2174) $160

1858 Tall figure of colored butler in dress coat. Black head forms cap. Height: 15½″. Frosted. (2) (#438) $150

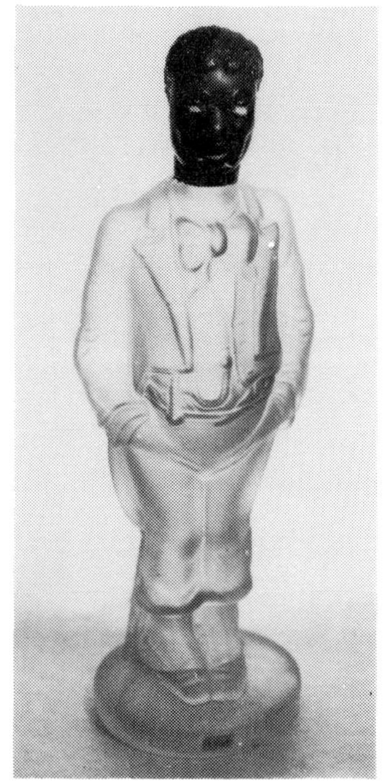

Unusual figural flask in frosted glass. (1858).

1859 Small canteen-shaped flask with Indian head on one side in beaded circle. Holds 4 oz. Clear. Threaded mouth. (5)

1842 Half-section, 3″, light green. (5) (#1092) Sold in lot with item below for $32-50.

1842V Same, 3½″. Pale green. (4)

1860 Lens shape with threaded handle in mouth. (Babbit's Chromo Lens. Patent App For). Dense amber. (4) (#618) $100

## Chapter Twenty-Seven

# Pottery Bottles

Any bottle collection of the size and scope of the Gardner collection would have to include some pottery examples along with the glass bottles. This grouping shows that Charley concentrated mainly on American pottery and he collected all of the classic flask shapes that were made in Bennington, Vermont, in the middle of the last century.

A glance at the listing illustrates that there was less interest in pottery than there was in glass, and the figural pottery bottles were listed with little regard for details. The majority of this group are book flasks with mottled brown glaze. While many of these were made in Vermont, others were probably produced in England. Most are unmarked except for a pseudo "title" on the spine. Any historian of American decorative arts is aware that while this country has always been able to produce glass of very high quality in great quantity, its production of pottery has not been as outstanding. However, the Gardner collection represented all vessels used to hold liquids in the past centuries and would not have been complete without this representative section.

It will be noted that there are few prices given for bottles in this category. The reason for this is that many of the Bennington flasks were considered decorative objects in the Gardner house and were not included in the auction.

1861 Book bottle. (Companion For Life) on spine. Height: 5½". (2)

1862 Book bottle. (Departed Spirits) on spine and (G). Height: 5½". (2)

1862A Book bottle. Same. Height: 5½". (2)

1863 Book bottle. (Coming Thro The Rye) on spine. Blue glaze. Height: 5". (2)

1863V Same. Height: 4". (2)

1864 Book bottle. (History of Holland) on spine. Height: 6". (2)

1865 Book bottle. Height: 8". (2)

1866 Book bottle. (History of Holland) on spine. Height: 5½". (2)

1867 Book bottle. Height: 5½". (2)

1868 Book bottle. (Departed Spirits) on spine. Height: 5½". (2)

1869 Book bottle. (History of Bourbon Co) on spine. Blue mottled glaze. Height: 7". (2)

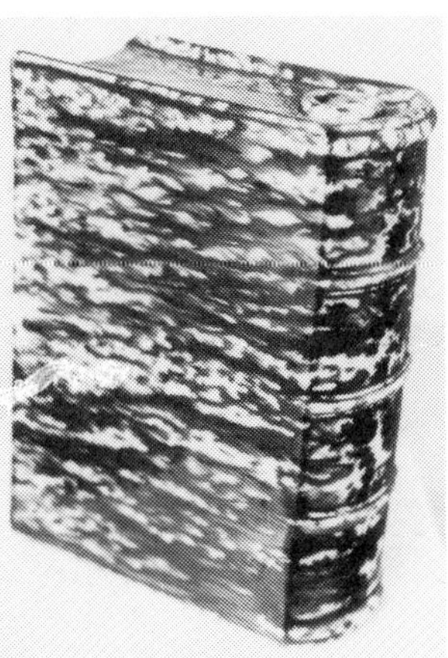

**Bennington pottery book bottle is one of many in Gardner collection. Brown mottled glaze.**

1870 Book bottle. Unglazed. (Civil Rights) on spine. Height: 7". (2)

1871 Boot. Laced on side. Brown glaze. (3) (#318) $90

1872 Coachman bottle. Bennington, 1849 mark). (1) (#2058) $375

1873C Coachman variant with tall hat. (1) (#591) $400

1874 Pig. Brown glaze. Length: 7". Not marked. (5) (#1479) $110

1875 Fish. (W. Northen Potter) (Vauxhall Lambeth) (Brighton Fish) (R. Cooper Railway Terminus Brighton). Length. 6½". (5) (#2430) $85

1876 Mermaid, breasts exposed. Brown glaze. (4) (#1544) $45

1876V Similar, variant. (4) (#1284) $90

1876V Similar. Face smaller, hooked nose. (4) (#366) $50

1877 Flintlock pistol. (Lambeth). Hammer broken. (5) (#574) $120

1878 Man in high hat on barrel. Brown glaze. (6) (#1155) $60

1879 Round doughnut. Dark brown glaze. (6) (#2400) $25

1880 Same. Gray glaze with brown spots. (6) (#2827) $95

1881 Flask shape. Brown glaze. (6) (#43) $75

1882 Flask shape. Brown glaze. (6) (#204) $90

1883 Same. (6) (#496) $90

1884 Brown pottery bust of Washington. Same as Simon's Centennial Bitters, but smaller. Height: 8½″. (3) (#2299) $70

1885 Book bottle. Height: 10½″. (Ladies Companion) on spine. (1)

1886 Book bottle. Height: 5½″. (2)

1887 Book bottle. (Bennington Battle) on spine. Height: 5¾″. (2)

1888 Pocketbook. Buff glaze. (6) (#2155) $50

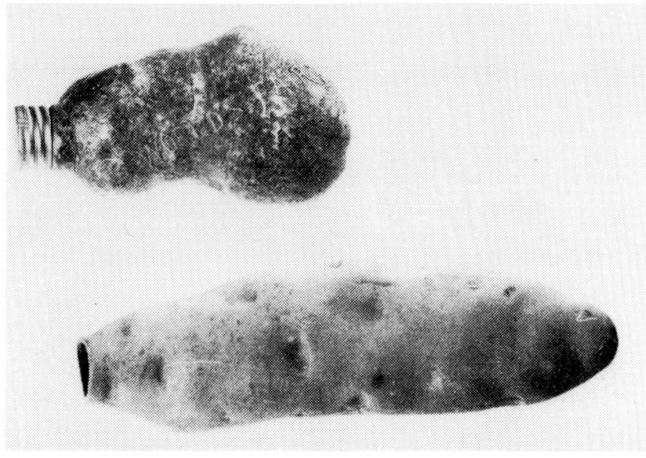

**Two potato bottles. Upper potato was souvenir of World's Fair and is marked. (1889, 1889A).**

1888A Barrel shape. Height: 2 5/8″. Deep brown glaze. (6)

1888B Same as above. Lighter glaze. Height: 4¾″. (6) (#677) $120

1889 Potato. Brown glaze but originally covered in silver luster. (5) (#2200) $65

1889A Same, but with gold luster. (5)

1890 Foot warmer. Jug shape. Flat on one side. (5)

1891 Pig. Brown glaze. No inscription. Length: 6½″. (4) (#109) $150

1892 Pig. Gray glaze. Length: 6 5/8″. (4) (#352) $300

1893 Handled jug. Mottled brown glaze. (B.F. & Co N.Y.) above game bag with game. Reverse: gun, dogs above (Buckley Fiske & Co New York). Height: 7 1/8″. (4) (#1255) $220

1894 Powder flask. Brown glaze. Dog on each side. (4)

1897 Foot warmer. Half-round with 7 panels. 2 depressions for feet. (3) (#143) $130

1898 Shaped like morning glory-eagle flask. Spread eagle to left on both sides. Pint. Mottled brown glaze. (2) (#2580) $925

1898A Bank, 6¼″ inches, brown glaze. (#347) $170

## Chapter Twenty-Eight

# Pickle and Peppersauce Bottles

Specialist-collectors of food storage bottles would be especially interested in this section of the Gardner catalog. The nineteenth century wide-mouthed pickle jars are particularly handsome. For some reason most of them are designed in a gothic shape and in their many shades of blue, aqua and green are especially handsome. Before the invention of the tin can there were few commercial food products that could be safely packaged and sold without spoilage. Pickles were probably the earliest product to be centrally prepared and packaged to be distributed to the general and grocery stores.

The cathedral-shaped pickle jars were produced from 1880 to 1920 and the Gardner collection included examples ranging from clear glass to dark amber and green. The darker colors were the most valuable of the group since the majority of the jars of this type were pale aqua. Specialists who appreciate the beauty of food jars and the history they represent will be especially envious of the quality and variety of the peppersauce and pickle jars listed on the following pages.

1895 Peppersauce. Hexagonal. Diagonal ribs. On base (S&P Pat App For). Height: 8". Blue green. (5) (#2089) $50

1896 Same as above. Emerald green. (5) (#1409) $15

Similar. No embossing, 8½". (#725) $35

1899 Same. 13 horizontal ribs. On base (Patented ERD & Co Feb '71). Height: 8". Blue green. (5) (#431) $20

Same. (#2554) $22.50

1899V Same. Horizontal ribbing. Around base (E.R.D. & Co Patd Feb 12 1874). On base (E.R. Durkee & Co N.Y.). Height: 8". Blue green. (5) (#989) $20

Similar. (Feb 17, 1874) (#1843) $45

1900 Square with scalloped corner. Two gothic sunken panels on each side. Height: 8½". (H.E. Swan) on one panel. Aqua. (5)

1901 Similar. 3 sunken panels on each side. Height: 8¾". Aqua. (5) (#1011) $40

1901A Same. 3 sunken panels on 3 sides. 1 plain. Height: 12". Aqua. (5)

1902 Similar. 3 sunken panels on each side. 2 panels plain and 2 paned. Height: 8½". Aqua. (5) (#2149) $27.50

**Three peppersauce bottles in variety of shapes.**

1903 Similar. Gothic panels. (WKL & Co) on panel. Height: 10". Aqua. (3) (#1523) $85

1904 Hexagon. Gothic panels. Height: 8½". Aqua. (5) (#2144) $27.50

1905 Same, but larger. Height: 8¾". (5) (#1714) $30

1906 Pickle. Cathedral arches. Height: 11". Dark amber. (2) (#1581) $1,550

1907 Peppersauce. Concentric rings tapering to neck. On base (E. R. Durkee & Co New York). Height: 7¾". Blue green. (4)

1908 Same. Round vertical ribs. 3 rings on neck. Height: 8". Aqua. (5) (#1632) $10

1908V Same. Height: 9½". Aqua. Original label. (4) (#1826) $30

Similar, partial label. (#623) $40

1909 Peppersauce. Round and ribbed. Marked (Wells Miller & Provost No 217 Front St. New York). Height: 8". Aqua. (5) (#345) $40

1910D **Square monument. Door and window on 1 side. Original stopper. Height: 14½″. Milk glass. (3)**

1910E Same as above, but green. (3) (#2224) $220

1910F Similar. Door on 1 side. 7 windows on 1 side and 1 each on other 3. Height: 8½″. Blue green. (4) (#446) $200

1911 Similar. Height: 12″. Aqua. (4)

1911A Similar. Height: 12″. Amethyst. (3) (#221) $280

1911B Similar. Height: 12″. Deep blue (3) (#1821) $120

1911X Similar. Height: 6½″. Clear. Label and tax stamp. (4)

1912 Similar. Height: 9¼″. Aqua. (5) (#1459) $180

1912B Similar. Height: 6½″. Milk glass. (4) (#622) $80

1912X Similar. Height: 6½″. Blue green. (4) (#569) $210

1913 Similar. Height: 6½″. Amethyst. Label. (4) (#1153) $250

1913A Similar. Height: 8″. Deep blue. (4) (#2665) $110

1913D Similar. Height: 9 5/8″. Clear. Door, but no windows. (5) (#1920) $20

1913E Similar. Height: 8″. Clear. (5) (#1026) $25

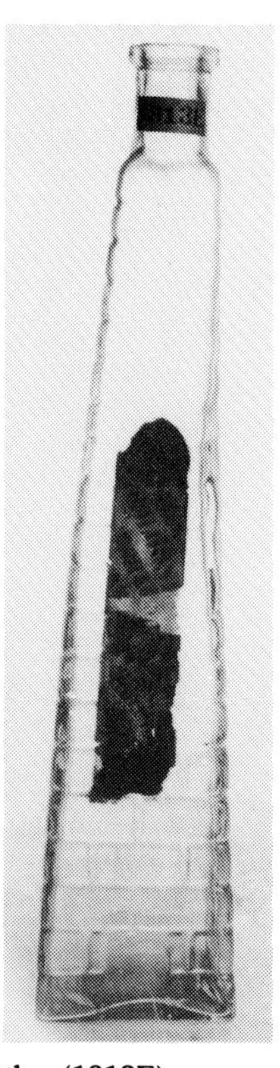

**Cologne monument bottle. (1913E).**

1913F Similar. Height: 6½″. Clear. (5) (#1637) $25

Similar. (#2414) $10

1913V Similar. Height: 8″. Opalescent. (4) (#77) $150

1913G Similar. Height: 8″. Opalescent. (4) (#2543) $75

1914 Barrel-shaped mustard jar. (H. J. Neuhauser) over eagle over (New York). Height: 5 1/8″. Aqua. (5) (#1330) $210

1915 Pickle. 2″ square. 3 panels decorated with diamond panes. Height: 5½″. Aqua. (4)

1916 Same as above. (4) (#463) $20

**Pickle bottle with diamond design on three panels. Aqua. (1916).**

1917 Pickle. Gothic panels. Height: 7 1/8″. Green. (6) (#2287) $150
Similar, (cracked). (#1125) $10

1918 Similar. Height: 7 1/8″. Aqua. (5) (#1125) $40

1919 Similar. Height: 9″. Green (4) (#923) $250

1920 Similar. Height: 11 3/8″. Aqua. (4) (#315) $50

1921 Mustard jar. Barrel-shaped. Eagle and shield. (Ciessmen's Union Mustard N.Y.). Height: 5″. Clear. (5) (#410) $45

1922 Pickle. Height: 11½″. Sea green. (4) (#1495) $160

1923 Similar. Height: 11¾″. Sea green. (4) (#1974) $150

1924 Similar. Height: 11¾″. Sea green. (4) (#2137) $160

1925 Similar. Hexagonal. Height: 13¼″. Blue aqua. (4) (#1583) $100

1926 Mustard jar. Barrel. Height: 5 1/8″. (5)

1927 Pickle. Height: 13½″. Aqua. Diamond panes. (4) (#2031) $70

1928 Similar. Height: 13 5/8″. Aqua. (4) (#1182) $350

1929 Similar. Height: 14″. Aqua. (3) (#1396) $675
Similar (reproduction). Green. (#1812) $55

1931 Similar. Height: 14″. Green. (4)

1932 Similar. Height: 14 1/8″. Aqua. (2)

1933 Similar. Height: 13¾″. Green. (1) (#400) $340

1933A Similar. Height: 14″. Dense amber. (1) (#541) $3,500

1934 Similar. Octagonal. Height: 8″. Aqua. (4) (#1876) $70

1935 Similar. Square. Height: 9″. Aqua. (6)

1936 Similar. Vertical ribs. Cracked, height: 8″. Amber. (4) (#2825) $1,500

1936A Similar to below. Height: 5¾″. Aqua. (4) (#1765) $30

1936V Similar. (WM&PNY) on base. Vertical ribs. Height: 7¾″. Aqua. (4) (#601) $65

1937 Similar. Round with 8 panels on neck and shoulders. Height: 8¾″. Amber. (5)

1939 Similar. Square. Plain panels. Height: 11″. Aqua. (6)

1934 Square, shaped like milk bottle. Height: 9 1/8″. Aqua. (6)

1945 Round, tapering from shoulders. Off-hand blown. 2 applied rings on neck. Height: 11″. Aqua. (5)

1946 Pickle. Gothic arches on 4 sides. Diamond design at top of 3. Ring at base of neck. Height: 6½″. Aqua. (4)

1947 Hexagonal. 5 panels, each with different design. Height: 9¼″. Aqua. (4)

1948 Round lighthouse. (Skilton Foote & Co Bunker Hill Pickles). Height: 11″. Light green. (4) (#63) $300

1948V Same. Light amber. (4) (#2077) $360

1949 Round jar. (Skilton Foote & Co's Bunker Hill Pickles Trade Mark) around monument. Pint. Amber. (5) (#2039) $110

1949V Same. Pint. Aqua. (5) (#1954) $40

1950 Round. 10 panels on neck. Height: 11½″. Aqua. (5) (#288) $35

1951 Same. (5) (#1039) $35

1952 Same. Dark olive green. (5) (#861) $325

1953 Same. Golden amber. (5) (#1918) $325

1954 Same. Aqua. (#1954) $40

1954A Pickle. 3 gothic arches, 1 plain. Height: 8 3/8″. Aqua. (4) (#732) $15

1954B Square. Octagon depression. Height: 8″. Aqua. (2) (#1058) $80

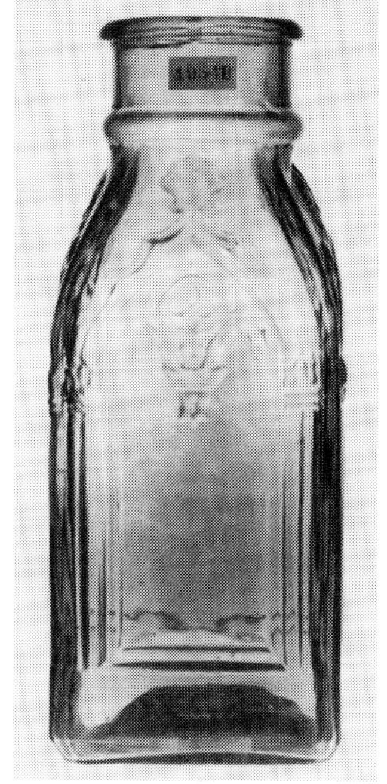

**Gothic style pickle jar. (1954B).**

1954C Same. Amber. (2) (#38) $130

1955 Similar. Gothic arches on 3 sides, other marked (SJG). Height: 9″. Aqua. (3) (#1736) $180

1956 Round, tapering from shoulders. Wide mouth with ground stopper. Height: 10½″. Clear. (4)

1957 Oval. Vertical ribs at base. Height: 11½″. Bright green. Tooled lip. (5) (#233) $40

1958 Round, paneled neck. (Wells Miller & Provost). Diamonds around base. 2 quarts. Aqua. (3) (#2459) $55

1959 Square. Gothic arches on 4 sides. Shells at top of 2 and clock faces set at 11:15 at top of other 2. Height: 11″. Brilliant olive green. (2) (#810) $825

1960 Same as above. Emerald green. (2) (#1327) $300

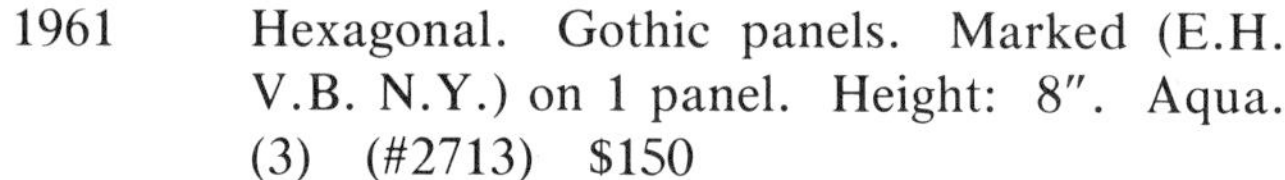

Round food jar marked "Wells Miller & Provost." (1958).

Pickle jar with scalloped design around panels. (1966).

1961 Hexagonal. Gothic panels. Marked (E.H. V.B. N.Y.) on 1 panel. Height: 8″. Aqua. (3) (#2713) $150

1962 Square. Gothic arches. Marked (Atmore's) on 2 panels. 3 sides ribbed, 1 plain. Height: 11¼″. Green aqua. (2) (#1604) $225

1963 Similar. 3 sides diamond panes. Height: 10 1/8″. Aqua. (3)

1965 Similar. Scalloped around panels. Height: 9″. Clear green. (3) (#572) $95

1966 Similar. Scalloped around panels. Height: 9″. Clear green. (2) $260

1967 Similar. Gothic panels with conventional cloverleaf design. Scallops around neck. Height: 11¼″. Deep green. (2) (#325) $600

1968 Peppersauce. Round with concentric rings. On base (C&D N.Y.). Height: 7¾″. Deep aqua. (5) $30

1969 Similar. Round. 10 panels on shoulders. Acorns below. Large (N) on side. Height: 7½″. Aqua. (6) (#2427) $25

Pickle jar in deep green color is rare type. (1967).

# Chapter Twenty-Nine

# Snuff and Blacking Bottles

Because both snuff and shoeblacking required small, wide-mouthed glass bottles, both products were packaged in the nineteenth century in the same kind of bottle and, unless an original label still exists on a bottle, it is impossible to tell which product was used in any sort of the small squat bottles made for both purposes. Fortunately, a few examples from the Gardner collection still had remnants of their original labels and some were embossed with the name of the firm that used the bottle for its product.

As any collector knows, there are hundreds of examples of snuff and blacking bottles, but those in the Gardner collection were mostly early and choice. Most of the bottles were small and averaged around five inches. The colors ranged from light green to dark olive amber. While a few of the bottles in this listing might have been used for products other than the two stipulated, all of them were of a shape that could have been used for shoe dressing or snuff.

1972 Blacking. Square with beveled corners. Height: 6 1/8″. Olive amber. (4) (#2528) $35

1973 Similar. Height: 5″. Amber. (4) (#432) $75

1974 Similar. Height: 4¾″. Green. (4) (#2774) $35

1975 Similar. Height: 4 3/8″. Olive green. (4) (#1855) $30

1976 Similar. Height: 4 3/8″. Dark amber. (4)

1977 Similar. Marked (Reakirt's) (Patent Japan) (Sponge) (Varnish). Height: 5 4/5″. Olive green. (3) (#1368) $500

1978 Similar. Height: 5″. Olive amber. (4)

1979 Oval. Marked (By A.A. Cooley Hartford). Height: 4½″. Olive amber. Original label. (3) (#2428) $110

1980 Snuff. Round, almost like an egg. Height: 3 7/16″. Olive amber. (3) (#714) $40

1981 Similar. Round, short neck. Height: 4½″. Olive amber. (3) (#518) $75

1982 Similar. Height: 4 9/16″. Light amber. (3) (#1814) $40

1983 Similar. Height: 5″. Dark amber. (3) (#1037) $55

1984 Octagonal. Height: 4½″. Olive amber. (3) (#2305) $80

1985 Rectangular. Height: 4½″. Olive amber. Original label. (3) (#604) $80

**Snuff bottle with remnants of original label. (1985).**

1987 Similar. Height: 4¾″. Amber. (3) (#475) $50

1988 Similar. Height: 5 3/16″. Dark amber. (3) (#379) $100

1989 Similar. Height: 4½″. Olive green. Heavy glass. (3) (#106) $50

1990 Similar. Height: 7″. Olive green. Bulge in neck. (3) (#327) $80

1991 Similar. Height: 6 1/8″. Olive green. Long neck. (3) (#1096) $130

1992 Similar. Height: 5 7/8″. Olive amber. Square. (3) (#2384) $75

1995 Similar. Height: 4″. Olive green. Lorillard label. (3)

1996 Similar. Height: 4¾″. Olive amber. (3) (#959) $35

1997 Snuff. Square. Height: 5¼″. Amber. (3) (#187) $50

1999 Snuff. Round. Height: 7¼″. Amber. Long neck. (3) (#2776) $425

2000 Snuff. Square. Height: 5¾″. Light green. (3) (#2399) $85

2001 Snuff. Square. Height: 5¼″. Olive amber. (1) (#1220) $20

**Snuff bottle with Lorillard label. (1995).**

2002 Snuff. Rectangle. Height: 5¾″. Light olive green. (3) (#2475) $70

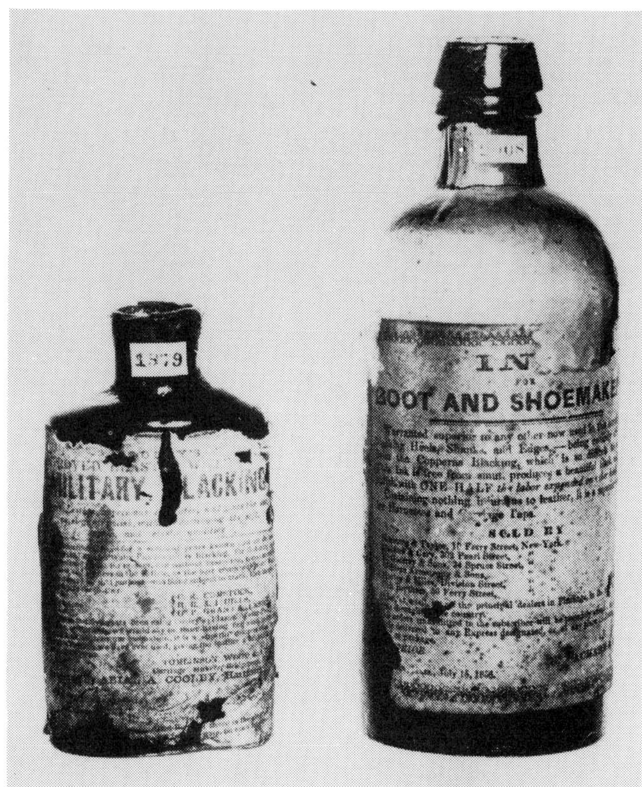


**Two blacking bottles, both with labels. (1979, 2008).**

2003 Snuff. Round. Height: 3 7/8″. Amber. (3) (#251) $55

2004 Snuff. Round. Height: 4 5/8″. Olive amber. (3) (#1186) $110

Same, cracked. (#2041) $20

2005 Snuff. Rectangle. Height: 6½″. Olive amber. (3) (#841) $40

2006 Snuff. Round. Height: 5½″. Dark green. (3) (#1553) $190

2007 Snuff. Rectangle. Height: 6 1/8″. Olive green. (3) (#1729) $140

Similar. (#1917) $140

2008 Blacking. Cylindrical. Original label. Pint. Olive amber. (5)

2009 Snuff. Height: 5¼″. Round. Green. (3) (#1912) $35

Similar, olive amber. 5¾″. (#1943) $140

2010 Shape of tall button shoe. Marked (Saratoga Dressing). Height: 4½″. Aqua. (5) (#399) $30

2011 Similar, only marked (Union Dressing). Height: 4 3/8″. Aqua. (5) (#331) $27.50

2012 Snuff. Rectangular. Height: 4¼″. Marked (E. Roome Troy N.Y.). Height: 4¼″. Olive green. (6) (#156) $60

2013 Similar. Height: 7¼″. Deep aqua. (3) (#1510) $70

2014 Similar. Square. Height: 4 5/8″. Cracked. Dark amber. (3) (#1623) $15

2015 Rectangular. (J.J. Mapes 461 Front St N-York). Height: 4¼″. Olive green. (3) (#2556) $275

2016 Square. Widely beveled corners. Height: 4″. Olive green. (2) (#2588) $60

2018 Rectangular. Height: 8¼″. Olive green. (1) (#2972) $110

Similar. Case-shaped. (#2062) $50

2019 Small bulbous flask, shaped like a Pitkin. Height: 4¾″. Dark olive green. Slightlv infolding collar. (3)

## Chapter Thirty

# Scent Bottles

No eighteenth or early nineteenth century lady or gentleman went anywhere without a tiny vial of perfume or scent that was used to cover less desirable odors. Every bottle firm produced small bottles to hold pungent liquid and that would fit easily into purse or pocket. These scent bottles were made in a great variety of shapes and colors and are the gems of any early bottle collection.

Because scent bottles did not have to stand, they could be blown or molded into a great variety of shapes and patterns that could not be used for larger bottles. Many were swirled and ribbed and, as is true of modern perfume bottles, more care was put into their design than usually goes into commercial bottles. Many figural designs were used to hold perfumes and colognes and there was a great variety of these in the Gardner collection.

Auction prices are given for those bottles that could definitely be identified. There were many discrepancies in colors and measurements.

2025 Globular. Height: 3 3/8″. Sea green. (2) (#2458) $190.

2026 Same. Height: 3 5/8″. Sea green. (2)

2027 Same. Height: 3 3/8″. Sea green. Squat. (2) (#1942) $95

2028 Same. Height: 4″. Sea green. Squat. (2) (2710) $210

2030 Same. Height: 5″. Sea green. (6) (#2047) $90

2031 Same. Height: 5 1/8″. Red amber. (2)

2033 Same. Height: 4″. Sea green. 2-mold. (5)

2034 Same. Height: 4″. Sea green. (2)

2035 Same. Height: 3″. Clear. Short neck. (6)

2036 Kidney-shaped. Basket design. Oval panel on side. Height: 2 7/8″. Aqua. (4) (#1783) $12.50

2037 Same, but handles higher on shoulders. Height: 3″. Aqua. (4) (#767) $35

2044 Vertical ribs. Corseted. Height: 3 1/4″. Clear. (4)

2045 Kidney-shaped. Height: 4 1/2″. Light yellow green. (2)

2046 Kidney. Height: 5″. Light yellow green. (5)

2047 Sea horse form with no tail. Rigaree on edges. White striations. Height: 2 5/16″. Clear. (3) (#412) $35

2048 Shape of small saddle flask. Height: 4 3/8″. Aqua. (5)

2049 Corseted with rigaree. Height: 2 1/2″. Aqua. (4)

2050 Round with rigaree. Height: 3 1/16″. Clear. (4)

2051 Flattened canteen shape. Gold and cotton twist on clear. Lutz glass. Height: 3 3/8″. (2) (#231) $100

2052 Same. Pink and cotton twist on clear. (2) (#1218) $65

2053 Sea horse. Milk stripes, blue rigaree. Height: 2 1/16″. Clear. (2) (#1922) 95

2054 Same. Height: 2 3/4″. (2) (#1621) $30

2055 Similar. Milk stripes. Clear applied. Height: 2 5/8″. (2) (#776) $22.50

2056 Similar. Clear, clear applied. Height: 2 3/4″. (2) (#992) $10

2057 Similar. Height: 2″. (2)

2058 Similar. Height: 3 1/4″. (2) (#2040) $40

2059 Similar. Height: 3″. Milk stripes on clear. (2) (#1892) $50

2060 Similar. Height: 2 1/2″. (2) (#726) $45

2061 Similar. Swirled to right. Height: 3 1/8″. Clear. (3)

2062 Similar. Height: 3 1/4″. Clear. (3) (#1576) $10

2063 Similar. Height: 3 3/8″. Wider ribbing. Clear. (3)

2064 Similar. Swirled to right. Height: 2 15/16″. Clear. (3) (#583) $15

2064V Similar. Height: 3 3/16″. Clear. (3) (#1331) $60

2065 Similar. Height: 2″. Light green. (2)

2066 Similar. Height: 3 3/16″. Brilliant green. (2) (#1171) $55

2067 Similar. Height: 3 1/8″. Light lavender. (2) (#2160) $40

2068 Similar. Vertical ribs. Height: 2 3/4″. Blue. (2) (#223) $80
Similar. (#1240) $55

2069 Stiegel-type. Swirled to right. Height: 2 9/16″. Clear olive green. (2)

2070 Similar. Swirled to right. Height: 3 5/16″. Blue. (2) (#543) $50

2071 Similar. Swirled to right. Height: 3 1/16″. Purple blue. (2) (#2598) $50

2072 Similar. Vertically ribbed. Height: 2 7/8″. Light amber. (2) (#2016) $80
Similar, citron. (#2527) $100

2073 Similar. Height: 3 1/8″. Purple blue. (2)

2074 Sea horse. Clear applied. Height: 2 7/8″. Clear. (2) (#1678) $30

2075 Sunburst on shield-shaped bottle. Corrugated edges. Height: 2″. Bright green. (2) (#893) $180

2076 Sunburst on round bottle. Corrugated edges. Height: 2″. Bright green. (2) (#750) $70

2077 Cut sunburst on round bottle. Height: 1 5/8″. Brilliant light blue. (6) (#380) $110

2078 Sunburst with beaded edge on shield-shaped bottle. Height: 2 5/8″. Shaded blue. (2) (#365) $130

2079 Cut, with pineapple design. Corrugated edges. Height: 2 13/16″. Honey amber. (6) (#636) $10

2080 Shape of sunflower. Height: 2 5/8″. Shaded amethyst. (2) (#2909) $275

2081 Sunburst on shield-shaped bottle. Height: 2 11/16″. Clear with beaded edges. (3) (#1446) $50

2082 Stiegel type. Swirled to right. Height: 2 7/8″. Deep blue. (2)

2083 Sunburst on flattened oval. Reverse: diamonds, beading and corrugations on edge. Height: 3 7/16″. Aqua. (2)

2084 Sea horse. Swirled right. Clear applied. Height: 3 1/16″. Aqua. (2) (#1235) $35

2085 Similar. Striped, white and blue. Clear applied. Height: 3″. Clear. (2) (#1492) $130
Similar. 12 1/2″. White specks, bright blue. (#282) $150

2086 Round sunburst on each side. Corrugated edges. Height: 2 3/16″. Clear. (4)

2087 Sandwich type. Octagonal. Pewter screw cap. Height: 2 1/2″. Blue lava. (4)

2088 Same. Hexagonal, corseted. Pewter screw cap. Height: 2 1/2″. Turquoise blue. (4)

2088A Same. Height: 2 1/2″. Deep amethyst. (4) (#254) $30

2089 Same. Height: 2 1/2″. Blue. Original label. (4) (#716) $45

2090 Same. Height: 2 9/16″. Opalescent. (4) (#1778) $20

2090 Same. Height: 2 1/2″. Milk glass. (4) (#1031) $30

2091 Same. Rectangular, widely beveled corners. Pewter cap. Height: 2 1/4″. Green. (4) (#303) $30
Similar. 3 1/4″. (#2624) $35

2091A Same. Opalescent. (4) (#430) $30
Similar. 2 1/2″. (#2485) $30

2091B Same. Deep purple. (4) (#1521) $30

2091C Same. Cobalt blue. (4) (#125) $25
Similar. (#2138) $20

2092 Same. Height: 2 1/2″. Blue. (4) (#1060) $45

2093 Same. Octagonal base, curved sides. Height: 3 1/4″. Sea green. (4)

2094 Same. Hexagonal base. Wide shoulders. Height: 3 1/4″. Purple. (4)

2094A Same. Height: 3 1/4″. Amethyst. (4) (#912) $40
Similar. Clear. (#700) $15

2095 Oval. 3 horizontal rinds. Height: 2 1/8″. Amethyst. (4)

2095A Same. Height: 2″. Opalescent. (4) (#1124) $40

2096 Same. Hexagonal, corseted. Height: 2 1/2″. Shaded amethystine. (4) (#2699) $90

2097 Same. Height: 2 9/16″. Blue green. (4)

2098 Sandwich type. Rectangular, widely beveled corners. Height: 2 1/4″. Amethyst. (4) (#2677) $35

2099 Same. Milk glass. (4) (#671) $25

2100 Same. Shaped like inverted morning glory. Star design on base. Height: 2 3/4″. Sapphire. (4)

2102 Same. Octagonal, corseted. Height: 6″. Cobalt blue. (4) (#2667) $130

2102 Hexagonal. Decorated on all sides with label panel on 1 side. Height: 9 1/4″. Deep blue. (4) (#2393) $220

2103 Sea horse. Blue and white stripes. Blue applied. Height: 2 1/2″. Clear. (2)

2104 Sandwich. Octagon base. Height: 3 1/4″. Clear. Filled with red powder. (2)

2105 Same. Milk glass. (4) (#268) $20

2106 Conventional bunch of grapes and leaves. Height: 2 3/8". Clear. (5)

2107 Similar, but larger. Height: 3 1/8". Clear. (5)

2108 Sandwich. Rectangular base, corseted. Height: 2 1/2". Milk glass. (4)

2109 Stiegel type. Rectangular. Enamel decoration and inscription. Height: 5 5/8". Blue. (2)

2110 Similar. Enamelled flower decoration with lovebird. Pewter cap. Height: 5 3/4". Clear. (2)

2111 Dresser bottle. Ball stopper. Round. Height: 5 3/8". Clear. (4) (#956) $60

2111A Same. Milk glass. (4) (#938) $65
Similar. (#1335) $70

2112 Hand-shaped with ring on finger. Height: 5 3/8". Clear. (4) (#304) $15

2113 Boot. Height: 5". Clear. (5)

2114 Boot. Height: 4 1/16". Clear. (5) (#1831) $10

2114V Boot. Height: 4 1/4". Clear. (5) (#814) $15
Same. 3 1/4". (#1815) $10

2115 Slipper. Height: 4 3/4". Clear. (5) (#1027) $30

2115A Slipper. Height: 6". Clear. (5) (#336) $10

2116 Slipper. Height: 5 3/8". Clear. (5) (#2479) $85

2117 Hessian soldier. Height: 7 1/8". Clear. (4) (#2922) $20

2118 Jester. Height: 7". Aqua. (4)

2119 Turtle. Head is stopper. Length: 4 7/8". Amber. (4) (#2382) $25

2120 Flat, elongated and pointed. Marked (EC). Length: 5 1/8". Clear. Waterford. (6) (#1279) $35

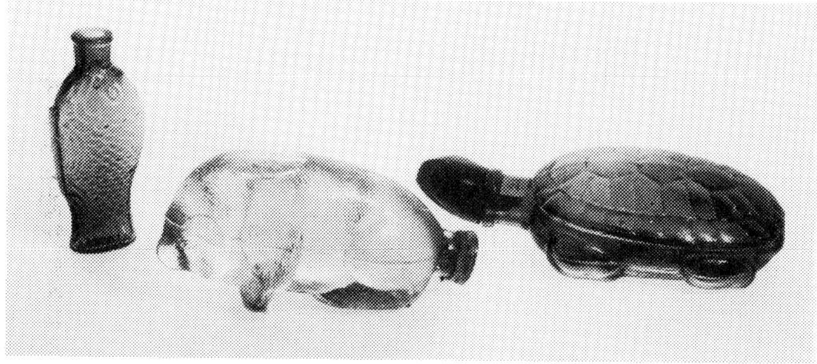

**Group of miniature figural bottles. Fish on left probably held cod liver oil. Turtle is #2119 in catalog. Groundhog is unlisted.**

2121 Rectangular. Etched on 4 sides. Height: 4 3/8". Deep plum, almost black. (5)

2122 Tiny cruet with applied handle. Stopper. Height: 4 1/2". Clear. (5)

2123 Round, plain bottle. Height: 4 5/8". Green. (6) (#1571) $55

2124 Round, alternate vertical ribs, plain and quilted. Height: 5¾". Blue. (5) (#2300) $85

2125 Round. 12 vertical panels. Slightly larger at shoulder. Height: 4 9/16". Blue. (4) (#2576) $100

2125A Similar. Height: 4 9/16". Electric blue. (5)

2126 Shaped somewhat like a violin. Conventional decorations. Height: 5 7/8". Aqua. (5) (#2889) $150

2127 Conventional. Height: 7 7/8". Aqua. (5)

2128 Similar. Height: 5 7/8". Aqua. (5) (#2781) $45

2129 Similar. Height: 4 1/8". Aqua. (5) (#494) $30

2130 Similar. Height: 5 1/4". Aqua. (5)

2131 Similar. Height: 3 13/16". Aqua. (6) (#783) $30

2132 Conventional scent bottle. Height: 6 1/2". Aqua. (5)

2133 Same. Height: 2 5/16". (HLICS) on side. Aqua. (5) (#2510) $30

2134 Same. Height: 4". Aqua. (5) (#2313) $15

2135 Same. Height: 6 3/8". Aqua. (5) (#1128) $30

2136 Same. Height: 5 3/4". Aqua. (5) (#40) $45

2137 Same. Height: 8 1/8". Aqua. (5)

2138 Same. Height: 4 1/2". Aqua. (5)

2139 Same. Height: 4 1/8". (HW&Co). Aqua. (6) (#1111) $45

2140 Same. Height: 5 5/8". Aqua. (5) (#1108) $55

2141 Same. Height: 6 3/4". Aqua. (5)

2142 Same. Height: 3". Aqua. (5)

2143 Same. Height: 3 1/2". Aqua. (6)

2144 Same. Height: 3 1/4". Aqua. (6)

2145 Same. Height: 4 5/8". 12 sides. (6)

2146 Same. Height: 6". Aqua. (5)

2147 Same. Height: 4 1/2". Aqua. (6)

2148 Cucumber. Length: 4 3/8″. Green. (5) (#480) $80
Similar. 6″. Clear. (#632) $25

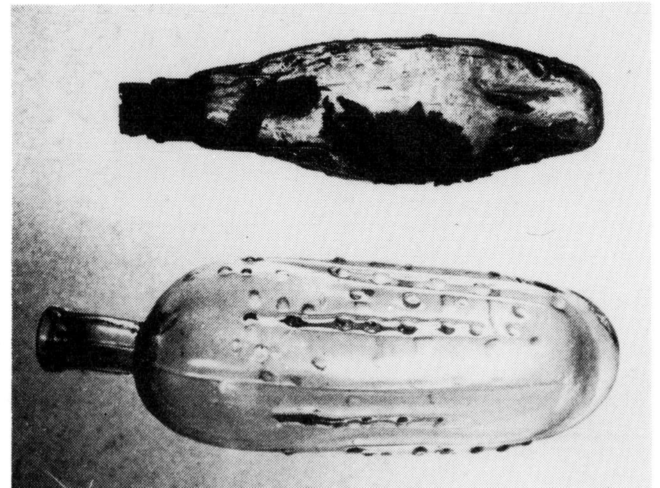

**Two small figurals in shape of cucumber. Bottle on bottom is #2148.**

2149 Conventional scent. Height: 3 3/7″. Aqua. (5) (#1751) $150

2150 Cannon. (Phalon & Son). Height: 7 3/8″. Aqua. (5) (#1123) $140

2150V Variant of above. Height: 7 3/8″. Aqua. (5) (#1751) $150

2151 Lady with bustle holding muff. Height: 6 1/4″. Aqua. (4) (#1317) $80

2152 Chinese figure. Height: 5 1/4″. Aqua. (4) (#328) $35

2153 Soldier. Height: 4 1/8″. (4) (#1797) $55

2154 Baby in shell. Length: 4¾″. Aqua. (Moses in basket in bushes.) (4) (#713) $45

2155 Crying baby. '(TPS&CONY) on base. Length: 6″. Clear. (4) (#2349) $70

**Baby in shell is unusual figural. (2154).**

2156 Bust, marked (Granger). On base (TPS&Co). Height: 6½″. Aqua. (2) (#1698) $50

2157 Bust of woman. Aqua. (2) (#141) $20

2158 Corseted bottle. (Charlie Ross). Height: 6″. Clear. (4) (#649) $170

2158V Variant of above. (4) (#1277) $75

2159 Variant of above. (4) (#2377) $200

2160 Conventional. Height: 5 5/8″. Aqua. (5) (#2348) $35

2161 Bust, marked (Beecher). Height: 6 5/8″. Clear. (2)

2162 Conventional. Height: 4¼″. Aqua. (5)

2163 Conventional. Height: 5½″. Aqua. (5) (#1653) $90

2164 Conventional. Height: 4″. Aqua. (5)

2165 Conventional. Height: 4″. Aqua. (5) (#2367) $20

2166 Conventional. Height: 5½″. Aqua. (6)

2167 Building. Marked (BF). Height: 4¾″. Milk glass. (5) (#2057) $310

2168 Octagonal. Corseted. Like #2101. Height: 4¾″. Transluscent blue. (2) (#1764) $450

2168A Same. Blue green. (2) (#2335) $230

2169 Bust, marked (Cleveland). Height: 10″. Frosted. (1) (#55) $85

2170 Baby in rocking chair. Height: 5¼″. Clear. (2) (#940) $70

**Baby in rocking chair. (2170).**

2171 Conventional. Height: 7″. Aqua. (5) (#237) $70

2172 Conventional. Height: 5½″. Aqua. (5)

2173 Conventional. Height: 6¼″. Aqua. (6) (#1847) $20

2174 Conventional. Height: 4″. Aqua. (6) (#250) $25

2175 Conventional. Height: 2 7/8″. Aqua. (6)

2176 Conventional. Height: 4″. Clear. (6) (#1040) $60
Similar, no embossing. (#573) $20

2177 Conventional barrel. Height: 2¾″. Aqua. (6) (#396) $15

2178 Conventional barrel. Height: 3″. Clear. (6)

2179 Conventional barrel. Height: 3″. Clear. (6)

2180 Tall, square. Decorated corners. Height: 7½″. Clear. (6) (#704) $250

2181 Lady's shoe. Height: 3¼″. Clear. (5) (#2425) $40

2182 Tiny oval pinchbottle. Height: 4 5/8″. Clear. (6)

2183 Bust of Garfield with turned wooden base. Height: 8″. Clear. (1) (#1382) $200

2184 Figure of Chinese woman. Height: 8¾″. Clear. (5) (#2333) $120

2185 Tower with figure ascending. Height: 9¼″. Clear. (4) (#2046) $50

2186 Octagonal, corseted. Height: 4 7/8″. Deep blue. (4) (#830) $95

2186A Same. Turquoise blue. (4) (#256) $140

2187 Same. Height: 4¾″. Amethyst. (4) (#1606) $60

2188 Square, thumbprints on 3 sides. Label panel on 4th. Decorated corners. Height: 5¾″. Deep amethyst. (4) (#112) $150

2189 12-sided. Height: 5¾″. Purple amethyst. (2) (#2076) $65
Similar. Teal blue, 4¾″. (#1975) $50

2190 Same. Squat. Short neck. Like Atwoods. Height: 4½″. Deep amethyst. (5) (#334) $60

2191 Same. Height: 11″. Deep purple blue. (2) (#735) $130

2192 Same. Height: 11¼″. Amethyst. (2) (#1713) $95

2193 Cylindrical. Height: 11″. Amethyst. (2)

2194 Cylindrical, 9¾″. Amethyst. (2) (#383) $160

2195 Monument. Height: 9 1/8″. Light green. (4)

2196 Pear-shaped with base. Yellow rose in stopper. Height: 7¼″. Clear. (1) (#655) $375

2197 12-sided. Height: 7¼″. Opalescent. (4) (#1182) $350
Similar. 8″. Olive-yellow. (#27) $210
Similar. 7½″. Amethyst. (#2152) $110

2198 Square. Rope corners and 5 stars on 3 sides. Height: 7 5/8″. Aqua. (5) (#1541) $40

2199 Conventional. Round, corseted near base. Height: 5¼″. Aqua. (4)

2200 Conventional. Height: 5¼″. Clear. (5)

2201 Monument. Marked (F.E. Martell & Co) (Cambrideport, Mass). Height: 6¼″. Clear. (5) (#2678) $30

2203 Stiegel scent swirled to right. Height: 2 13/16″. Brilliant green. (2)

2204 Same. Height: 3¼″. Globular, 24 ribs swirled to right. Deep blue. (2)

2205 Conventional. Bust of Grant in Wreath. Clear. (5) (#1599) $70

2206 Sandwich bear unguent. Removable head. Height: 3 7/8″. Black. (3) (#2143) $95

2207 Same. Marked on base (E.Z. & Co N.Y.). Height: 3¾″. Milk glass. (3) (#1853) $210

2208 Conventional. Round, 8 panels. 2 applied handles. Height: 6¾″. Clear. (5) (#1829) $20

2209 Small, globular bottle with paperweight stopper. In base: (K). (1) (#654) $500

2210 Shield-shaped with sunburst on either side. No dots on edge. Height: 2¾″. Clear. (2) (#2106) $35

2211 Conventional. Height: 6½″. Aqua. (5)

2212 Shield, similar to #2210. Height: 3″. Green. (2) (#1825) $90

2213 Stiegel. 20 vertical ribs. Height: 3″. Emerald green. (2) (#87) $40

2214 Sunburst in oval above (Peace). Diamond quilting in oval above (Plenty). Beaded edges. Height: 3¼″. Sapphire blue. (2) (#2232) $450

2215 Cylindrical, 6 ribbed panels and 6 plain. Height: 5¾″. Blue. (5)

2216 Cylindrical, 10 vertically beaded panels. Height: 5¾″. Milk glass. (5)

2217 Cylindrical. Tall, blown in 12-rib mold like French cologne. Height: 8¾″. Pale green. (5) (#234) $10

Figure of Chinese woman holding fan. (2184).

2218 Stiegel, 12 ribs swirled to right. Height: 3¼″. Amethyst. (2) (#1878) $40

2219 Bust of W. S. Hancock on turned wooden base. Height: 7¾″. Clear. (1) (#1061) $320

2220 Shape of a bear. Marked (G. F. Knapp Philada) on base. Label reads, "Bears Oil." 1-cent stamp attached. Contents intact. Height: 4″. Aqua. (5) (#1191) $35

2221 Round, tapering. Diagonal bands with 11 stars. Ring at base. Height: 5¾″. Milk glass. (4)

2222 Square, conventional design. Original cologne label intact. Paneled. Height: 7¾″. Aqua. (6)

2223 Shape of shell. Reverse label panel. Height: 3 5/8″. Clear. (6) (#2841) $35

2224 Canteen-shaped, cased glass. Stripes of white and turquoise on clear. Height: 3½″. (3)

## Chapter Thirty-One

# Early Wine Bottles

It was customary as far back as the early 1600s for British gentlemen to have special bottles made for their wine with their initials placed on a wafer-type glass seal. The seal would be applied in a blob after the bottle was finished and stamped with a stamp similar to that used for impressing sealing wax. The initials and numbers were often backwards because of this. The custom of personal identification of wine bottles spread from private individuals of the upper class to tavern keepers, merchants, bottlers and distillers.

Seal bottles were used for liquids other than wine, but generally they are placed in this category because this was the purpose for which most of them were used. The bottles that were thus personally identified were often also dated which makes them especially interesting to collectors of antique glass bottles. Most were free-blown bottles of very dark glass.

As this country became settled, the wealthier citizens continued the custom of having personalized bottles made with their intitials and the year date. It is difficult to judge whether these bottles were made in this country or ordered from abroad, but a bottle such as one in this group marked "Jon a Mason Boston" is a rare example of a seal bottle made for an American. Even though the use of seal bottles goes back to ancient times, most of those in private and museum collections are from the eighteenth and early nineteenth centuries. This was true of most of the wine bottles to be found in the Gardner collection.

3500 Cylindrical. On seal (ND 1790). Height: 10¾". Dark olive green. (2) (#2864) $260

3501 Same. On seal (John Pugh 1794). Height: 11¼". Dark olive green. (2) (#2981) $280

3502 Same. On seal (J. Whitwell 1805). Height: 11 1/8". Dark olive green. (2) (#2927) $200

3503 Same. On seal (Greenhill). Height: 8". (4) (#2656) $70

3504 Chestnut. On seal: man holding arrows in right hand. On seal (I. S. 1716). This was **Dean Swift's bottle. The man who wrote *Gulliver's Travels*. Height: 8 3/8". Dark** olive green. (1) (#2589) $1,400

3505 Cylindrical. On seal (Danl Jones 1760). Height: 9¼". Olive green. (2) (#3004) $250

**Chestnut bottle with seal. Originally owned by Jonathan Swift and dated 1716. Seal bottles are especially valuable when original owner was man of note. (3504).**

3506 Cylindrical. On seal (R. Green 1765). Height: 9". Olive green. (2) (#2505) $850

3507 Same. On seal (R.P.A. 1779). Height: 10¾". Olive green. (2) (#2958) $425

3508 Rectangular with widely beveled corners. On seal (Jno-Jackson 1751). Height: 9". Applied collar. Bottle green. (2) (#2629) $525

3509 Cylindrical. Oval seal marked (Madiera 1810). Height: 10 5/8". Bottle green. (3) (#2572) $150

3510 Globular. On seal (J:W 1824). "J" is reversed. Height: 10". Dark olive green. (2) (#2941) $250

3511 Cylindrical. On shoulder (Patent), on seal (Jno Furse 1823). On base (H. Ricketts & Co Glass Works Bristol). Height: 10¼". Dark olive green. (2) (#2507) $210

3512 Similar. Seal marked (H. Ellis 1780). Height: 9¾". Dark olive green. (2) (#2524) $425

3513 Globular with long neck. Seal marked (The White Bear at the Bridge Foot) over initials (TCD) over a bear. Height: 8¾". Wide ring at neck. Dark olive green. (1) (#2717) $2,000

3514 Globular with long neck. Height: 5½". Applied ring around neck. **Extremely rare in**

**this size.** Dark olive green. (1) (#2590) $800
Similar. (#2829) $1,050

3515 Same as above. Height: 5 7/8″. (2)

3516 Square, squat. Shoulders taper to mouth. Height: 8¾″. Dark olive green. (4) (#2569) $600

3517 Cylindrical. Seal marked (Leeds 1827). Quart. Dark olive green. (2) (#2918) $225

3518 Similar. Marked (Sir W. Strickland Bart Boynton). Quart. Dark olive green. (2) (#2862) $180

3519 Similar. Neck long, bottle squat. Deep push-up. Height: 6¼″. Olive green. (3) (#2920) $65

3520 Similar. Seal marked (Jos: Risdon 1818). Height: 9″. Olive green. (2) (#2902) $325

3521 Cylindrical. Seal marked (JAs Hole 1823). Height: 11½″. Olive green. (2) (#2943) $220

3522 Same. Seal marked (William Pomerow Northhill). On base (H. Ricketts & Co Glass Works Bristol). Height: 10¼″. Olive green. (3) (#2917) $65

3523 Same. Seal marked (Recd J. B. Melhuish). On base (H. Ricketts & Co Glass Works Bristol). Height: 11″. Olive green. (3) (#2631) $190

3524 Same. Seal marked (lin Coll). Height: 8 3/8″. Olive green. (3) (#2843) $160

3525 Inverted cone. 6 strips of rigaree. Seal marked (D. Mcl 1834). Height: 10½″. Deep olive green. (2) (#2959) $500

3526 Small, cylindrical bottle with long neck. Seal marked (Constantin Wyn). Height: 9″. Olive green. Applied ring. (4) (#2570) $60

3527 Globular. Seal marked (W. M. 1733). Light in weight and color for this type. Height: 9¼″. Light olive green. (3) (#2812) $550

3528 Cylindrical. Seal marked (John Andrew 1822). Height: 10¾″. Olive green. (2) (#2901) $200

3529 Same. Seal marked (P.B.) over square and compasses. Height: 7″. Olive amber. (3) (#2861) $400

3530 Same. Seal marked (T. Drufey 1772). Height; 8¼″. Olive green. (2) (#2685) $600

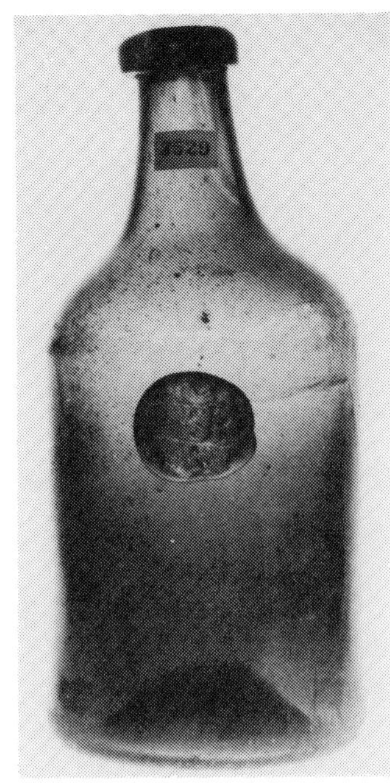

**Cylindrical seal bottle with mark "P.B." over square and compasses. (3529).**

3531 Squat, unusual shape tapering from base to shoulder. Bell-shaped. Height: 8½″. Applied ring. Deep olive green. (4) (#2523) $300

3532 Flattened, chest-type with thread of glass around neck. Found in Persia. Height: 9½″. Bright green. Tooled. (4)

3533 Inverted cone, 5 stripes of vertical rigaree. Seal marked (J&C McG 1820). Height: 10½″. Deep olive green. (2) (#2777) $250

3534 Cylindrical. Seal marked (Jon a Mason Boston). Height: 12½″. Dark olive green. (2) (#2686) $400

3535 Squat. Seal marked (R. Greene 1728). Height: 5 5/8″. Olive green. (2) (#2809) $675

3536 Cylindrical. Seal marked (Thos H. Jacobs & Co). Height: 12″. Blue green. (5) (#3002) $60

3537 Same as above. Seal marked (G.W. Huntington). Height: 12″. Blue green. (5) (#2879) $200

3538 Cylindrical. On seal (ASCR). Tag reads "Handcrafted in 1795 for All Souls College Common Room." Height: 10½″. Dense olive green. Applied ring. (4) (#2591) $60

3539 Kidney-shaped. Seal on one end marked (DI Wells 1764). Unusual shape. Height: 11″. Olive green. (1) (#2533) $450

# Chapter Thirty-Two

# Larson's Bottles (Reproductions)

Because one of the most outstanding listings in the Gardner collection is that of the blown-in-mold and expanded pocket flasks that were made in brilliant colors and pleasing shapes by most of America's early glass houses, the reproduction of this type of flask in this century might confuse the neophyte collector. Charley owned many reproductions of early American bottles and used them as a study collection. He was always quick to point out the subtle differences between the original and the new and this knowledge was frequently a help to collectors who might otherwise have paid high prices for new glass.

Most of the reproductions in the Gardner collection were not cataloged, with the exception of the following listing of small flasks. He felt they were so much like the originals that they might confuse any collector. Also, he did not want to discourage any new glass-maker from continuing to make bottles in the old tradition.

As long as the new bottles were not sold as old, but were genuine reproductions rather than fakes, he was happy to purchase them and to put them on his shelves. The Larson's bottles listed here are so much like the old bottles that he listed them to avoid confusion.

4300 Chestnut type. 12 expanded diamonds. Height: 5″. Emerald green. (3) (#2274) $175

4301 Similar. 18 ribs swirled to right. Height: 5″. Royal purple. (3) (#658) $220

4302 Similar. 18 ribs swirled to right. Height: 4¾″. Amethyst. (4) (#718) $65

**Unlike other reproduction bottles in the Gardner collection these Larson's bottles are listed to avoid confusion with earlier blown and expanded flasks. (4300, 4301). The quality is good enough so that the bottles could be taken as earlier examples.**

4303 Similar. Height: 5½″. Amethyst. (4) (#1376) $120 (#1622) $110

4304 Similar. 10 ribs swirled to right. Height: 5¼″. Deep amethyst. (4) (#252) $170

4305 Miniature chestnut type. Ribs indicated on base, but so expanded they disappear. Height: 2½″. Amethyst. (4) (#2432) $140

4306 Same as above, but plain. 2½″. Amethyst. (#3008) $220

4307 Same, 12 faint ribs. Height: 3½″. Amethyst. (4) (#1169) $80

## Chapter Thirty-Three

# Miscellaneous — Mostly Medicines and Cures

During the nineteenth century, when there were no restrictions on the products that could be sold under the name of "medicine," there were hundreds of concoctions that were advertised and sold to cure any physical problem a person might have. Many of the "cures" contained opiates or large quantities of alcohol, and it was not unusual for a user of many of the most popular products to become addicted to a favorite brand.

Today, there are thousands of collectors of the bottles that once held such popular products as "Roher's Wild Cherry Tonic," "Swaim's Panacea" or "Warner's Safe Remedy." The bottle manufacturers made hundreds of thousands of bottles that were embossed specifically for the noxious liquids and compounds. Some of the bottles were made in imaginative figural shapes such as an ear of corn or a bear. Because of the great variety of shapes, colors and embossments to be found on nineteenth century medicine bottles they have great appeal to collectors. Of special interest in the Gardner collection were the many bottles that still had their original labels which revealed the variety of illnesses the contents were supposed to cure. Included in this group were many early sarsaparilla bottles. This was a product that was supposed to have marvelous curative powers before it became a flavoring for a carbonated beverage.

**Many of the medicinal bottles in Gardner collection were never cataloged. These are two examples of gargling oil bottles. Medicine was advertised as being good "for man and beast."**

4000 Rectangular, beveled corners. (C. Brinkerhoffs Health Restorative Price $1.00 New York). Very heavy. ½ pint. Olive green. (3)

4001 Similar. (Chapman's Genuine No4 Salem St Boston). ½ pint. Olive amber. (3) (#2421) $250

Similar, oval. 6 5/8″. (Chapman's Cholera Syrup) (#2378) $160

4002 Square, beveled corners. (Doctor Asher Atkinson) (City of New York). ¾ quart. Green. (3) (#1799) $450

4003 Similar. (Lediard's Morning Call). ¾ quart. Clear green. (3) (#265) $150

4005 Barrel. (That's The Stuff). ¾ quart. Amber. (2)

4006 Rectangular, (gargling oil). Yellow green. Label. (#1926) $20

4007 Rectangular. (Dr. Gordack's Iceland Jelly). ½ pint. Aqua. (4) (#728) $100

4008 Rectangular. (I. D. Bull's HartfordCon). (Extract of Sarsaparilla). 6 oz. Aqua. (5) (#2038) $240

4009 Similar. (Bristol's) (Extract of Sarsaparilla) (Buffalo). 6 oz. Aqua. (5) (#1619) $60

4010 Cylindrical with 8 vertical panels. (Phelp's Arcanum Worcester Mass). Quart. Olive green. (3) (#2869) $300

4011 Melon-shaped. Ribbed. Marked on panel (H F & B N.Y.). ¾ quart. Oxblood amber. (2) (#140) $310

4012 Square with green quilling applied on bevels. (BM & EA) (Whitlock & Co New York). ¾ quart. Brown. (2)

4013 Flask. Marked (Lancaster Glass Works) (Full Pint). Pint. Aqua. (4)

4014 Oval flasks. (Henry Chapman & Co Sole Agents Montreal) in wreath. Stopper marked (Pat 1861). 4 oz. Amber. Inside threaded mouth. (4) (#2451) $250

4015 Similar. (M.F. Biern Magnolia Hotel 100 South St Phila) in wreath. 4 oz. Amber. (4) (#2411) $275

4016 Square with beveled corners. (Rockbridge Alum Water) (Alum Springs Virginia). Height; 13¼″. Clear olive green. (2) (#445) $850

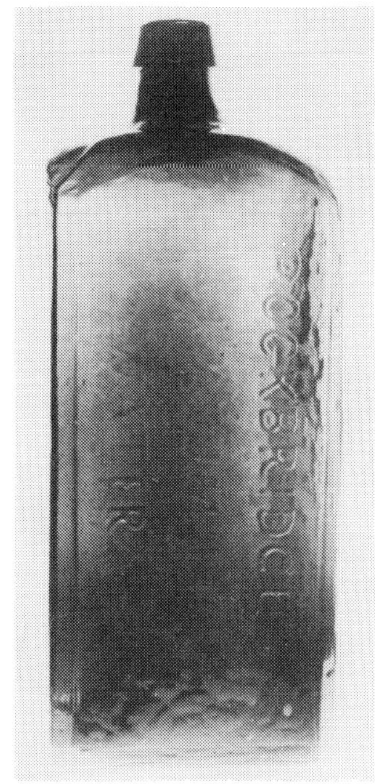

**Bottle for Rockbridge Alum Water. (4016).**

4017 Barber's bottle. Round, corseted. Height: 9″. Opalescent milk glass. (5) (#279) $35

4018 Flask with high central rib. On base (Ky G.W.) above (4). Pint. Aqua. Tooled lip. (5) (#418) $17.50

4019 Rectangular. (Rush's Sarsaparilla and Iron A. M. Flanders M. D. New York). Pint. Aqua. (5) (#1716) $20

4020 Rectangular. (A.H. Bull Hartford Conn Extract of Sarsaparilla). 6 oz. Aqua. (5) (#1525) $30

4021 Oval. (Dr. Guysott's Yellow Dock & Sarsaparilla John D. Park Cincinnati, O). ¾ quart. Aqua. (4) (#1133) $375

4022 Off-hand blown jug with heavy applied handle and collar. Around 2 gallons. Height: 13″. Deep aqua. (2) (#638) $175

4023 Shape marked (Quirye) over a dog's head in circle carrying small keg on collar, above (Dr. Kock Berlin). ¾ quart. Milk glass. (3) #1666) $130

4024 Rectangular. (Bush's Smilax Sarsaparilla). Quart. Aqua. (3) (#2969) $270

4025 Rectangular. (Dr. A. S. Hopkins Compound Ext Sarsaparilla). ½ pint. Aqua. (5) (#393) $7.50

4027 Oval. (Allen's Sarsaparilla). ½ pint. Aqua. (5) (#639) $10

4028 Oval. (J. L. Kelly & Co Chemists Portland Me), (Kelly & Co Sarsaparilla). ½ pint. Aqua. (#2896) $270

4029 Rectangular. (Jones American Chologogue New York). Height: 6½″. (5) (#782) $280

4030 Rectangular, beveled corners. (A. Morse Druggist Prov R. I.) Quart. Brilliant aqua. Triangular pontil. (5) (#873) $300

4031 Oval. (Dr. Morse's Celebrated Syrup). On base (1846). Label and contents intact. Quart. Aqua. (5)

4032 Rectangular. (Dalton's Sarsaparilla and Nerve Tonic) (Belfast) (Maine USA). Pint. Aqua. (6) (#1185) $7.50

4033 Cylindrical. On shoulder (Patent). On base (Brooklyn Glass Bottle Works). ¾ quart. Olive amber. (5) (#1584) $35

4034 Cylindrical. On base (Clyde Glass Works N.Y.) around (Clyde). Pint. Amber. (5) (#2032) $25

4035 Rectangular. (Ayer's Cherry Pectoral Lowell Mass). ½ pint. Aqua. (6) (#871) $4

4036 Octagonal. (Brandt's Indian Purifying Extract M.T. Wallace Proprietor). ½ pint. Aqua. (6) (#1687) $40

4037 Rectangular. (Constitutional) (Beverage). On edges (W. Olmsted & Co) (New York). Label intact. ¾ quart. Amber. (3) (#1333) $170

**Typical rectangular bottle for variety of cures for humans and horses.**

4038 Oval. (Connell's Brahminical Moon Plant East Indian Remedies). Reverse: 10 stars around print of 2 feet over (Reade Mark). Pint. Amber. (5)

4039 Small flat oval. (J.M. Kline & Cos Aromatic Cordial) in wreath. Less than ¼ pint. Amber. (3) (#1987) $90

4040 Log cabin. On roof (Perrine's Apple Ginger Phila). On sides (Perrine's) over an apple over (Ginger) (Depot No 27 No Front St Philada). Rope corners. ¾ quart. Amber. (2) (#538) $95

4041 Similar shape. Same lettering only address omitted. ¾ quart. Amber. (2) (#2142) $100

4042 Square, beveled corners. (Pine Tree Tar Cordial Phila) (L.Q.C. Wishart's) (Patent) above tree. (1859) below. Quart. Deep green. (3)

4042A Same. ¾ quart. Amber. (3)

4042B Same. Bright green. (3) (#812) $95

4042C Same. Blue green. (3) (#44) $60
**Similar, (#1287). $50**

4042D Similar. ½ pint. Green. Tree varies. (3) (#2201) $35

4042E Similar. Green. Tree varies. (3) (#1582) $90

4042F Similar. Green. Tree varies. (3) (#2045) $65

4042G Similar. Olive green. (3) (#1383) $75

4042H Similar. Emerald green. (3) (#892) $55

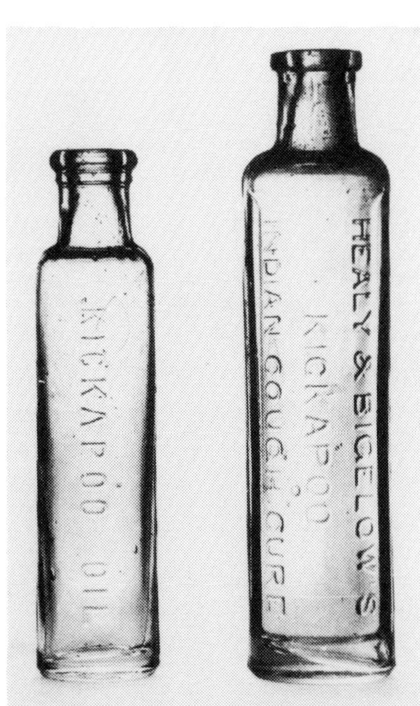


**Two small bottles for "Kickapoo Oil." Both are uncataloged.**

4043 Rectangular. (Roher's) (Lancaster Pa) Reverse (Expectoral) (Wild Cherry Tonic). Tapering from base. Rope corners. ¾ quart. Amber. (2) (#629) $150

4044 Round. 12 panels upright. (Swaim's) (Panacea) (Philada). ¾ quart. Aqua. (3) (#2297) $150

4045 Rectangular. (Genuine) (Swaim's Panacea) **(Philadelphia). ¾ quart. Aqua. (3) (#2158)** $450

4046 Cylindrical. Shape of log with canoe on side. Marked (Tippecanoe) (H.H. Warner & Co). On base (Pat Nov 20 83 Rochester N.Y.) (1). ¾ quart. Dark amber. Heavy glass. (2) (#550) $70

**Two figurals and hexagonal shape medicine bottle. (4046C, 4069, 3002).**

4046A Same, but (2) on base. Amber. (2) (#1070) $100

4046B Same, but dark olive green. (1) (#2933) $800

4046C Same, but marked (Rochester 3) on base. (2) (#2168) $80

4046D Same, but (4) on base. (2) (#968) $130

4046E Same, but (5) on base. (2) (#2472) $50

4046F Same, but (6) on base. (2) (#2662) $55

4047 Square. Squat. (Vaughn's) (Vegetable Lithontripic Mixture) (Buffalo). ¾ quart. Aqua. (6) (#101) $50

4048 Oval. (Warner's Safe Nervine) over safe. (Trade Mark) (Rochester N.Y.). Pint. Amber. (6) (#236) $25

4048A Same. ½ pint. Amber. (6) (#2206) $45

4048B Similar. (Warner's Safe Kidney & Liver Cure). Pint. Amber. (6) (#825) $15

4048C Similar, only safe has hinges on left. (3) (#1328) $55

4048D Similar. (Warner's Safe Remedies). ½ pint. (6) (#1636) $27.50
Similar. Amber. (#2541) $30

4048E Similar. 12½ oz. Clear. (6)

4049 Oval. (Dr. S.A. Weaver's Canker & Salt Rheum Syrup Providence R.I.). Quart. Aqua. (4) (#229) $35

4050 Square. Rope corners. (Wormwood Cordial) (Dunbar & Co) (Boston). ¾ quart. Aqua. (5) (#1701) $150

4051 Octagonal. (Dr. Wistar's Balsam of Wild Cherry Philada I. B). ½ pint. Aqua. (5) (#2715) $25

4052 Rectangular. (Smiths Green Mountain Renevator) (Renavator Co) (StAlbens Vt). Pint. Amber. (5) (#1923) $20

4052V Rectangular. Widely beveled corners. (Smith's Green Mountain Renevator, East Georgia, Vt). ½ pint. Olive amber. (3) (#1973) $350

4053 Rectangular. Indian head. (Healy & Bigelow) (Indian Sagwa). ½ pint. Aqua. (6) (#1318) $5
2 round 6¼". Indian Cough Cure. (#1192) $10

4054 Oval. (Clements) above standing Indian. (Tonic) (Prepared) (Geo A House). Label. ¼ pint. Aqua. (3) (#1028) $250

4055 Square. (Celery Compound). Reverse (Compound) in center of bunch of celery. Pint. Amber. (6) (#987) $2
Similar. (#2223) $50

4055A Similar, but marked (Paine's) (Celery Compound). No celery plant. ¾ quart. Amber. (6)

4056 Rectangular. Pawpaw tree with (Munyon's Pawpaw) across trunk. On edges (Munyon's) (Pawpaw). Pint. Golden amber. (4) (#827) $5

4057 Square, beveled corners. (Myers) (Rock Rose) (New Haven). Like early Townsend's bottle. ¾ quart. Aqua. (3) (#773) $325

4057A Rectangular. Same markings. Short neck. ¾ quart. Aqua. (3) (#1085) $55

4057B Rectangular. (A.B.L. Myersam) (Rock Rose) (New Haven). ¾ quart. Green. (3) (#2148) $300

4057C Rectangular. Marked (Myer's Rock Rose) (John F. Henry) (New York). Pint. Aqua. (5) (#2012) $25

4058 Rectangular. (H. Lake's Indian Specific). Bulge in neck. Very fancy bottle. ½ pint. Deep aqua. (2) (#1781) $320

4059 Oval. (Dr. Wood's) (Aromatic Spirit). Reverse (Bellows Falls Vt). Pint. Aqua. (6) (#32) $70

4060 Rectangular. Flat. (Dr. J.S. Wood's Elixer Albany N.Y.). Pint. Deep emerald green. (2)

4061 Barrel. (Turner Brothers New York). 10 rings or hoops. ¾ quart. Amber. (2) (#2415) $70

4061A Same, deep red. (2) (#1761) $125

4061V Same, only 9 rings. Green. (2) (#2357) $325

4062 Barrel. Marked (W.Wolf) (Pittsburgh). Quart. Blue. (1) (#2269) $2,600

4063 Barrel. (Mist of the Morning S.M. Barnett & Company). ¾ quart. Amber. (1)

4064 Barrel. (Bennett & Carrol 120 Wood St Pittsburgh). ¾ quart. Olive green. (1) (#1352) $120

4065 Barrel. (Hesperedina M.S. Bagley Un Barril). On base (Rio De Laplata Brazil). ¾ quart. Amber. (4) (#2716) $40

4066 Bear. Paws crossed on stomach. ¾ quart. Deep purple. (3) (#1624) $45

4067 Bear. 1 paw on stomach, 1 on chest. Claws, teeth and eyes vary from above. ¾ quart. Milk glass. (3) (#2559) $100

4068 Bear. Same as above. Olive green. (3) (#45) $40

4069 Ear corn. Thick, with panel extending from neck. No lettering. ¾ quart. Amber. (2) (#158) $170

4070 Ear corn. Plain panel surrounded by twigs running about halfway around bottle. ¾ quart. Clear. (2) (#652) $35

4071 Dutchman in high hat, holding a pipe. Marked on reverse (Van Dunck's Genever Trade Mark Ware & Schmitz). ¾ quart. Dense amber. (1)

4071V Same, but Ware and Schmitz is omitted. (1)

4072 Figure of rotund man in dress suit with high hat. Called "The Irish Squire." ¾ quart. Amber. (2)

4073 Fish. No lettering on sides. Marked on base (A Cod Liver Oil Bottle) ½ pint. Amber

(6) (#2298) $10
Similar. 3″. (Original) (#1272) $210

4074 Square. Column corners. No lettering. ¾ quart. Amber. (3)

4075 Square. Jockey on horse lengthwise. Marked (Ondon Jockey) (Club House Gin). ¾ quart. Light amber. (2) (#1677) $306

4075A Same. Emerald green. (2) (#862) $225

4075B Similar, but different mold. Green. (2) (#1569) $120

4075C Same. Clear green. (2) (#76) $55

4075D Similar, but different mold. Dark olive green. (2) (#2345) $250

4076 Triangular. (Wake Up) on 2 sides only. ¾ quart. Olive green. (2) (#1845) $500

4077 Square. (Udolpho Wolfe's) (Scheidam) (Aromatic Schnapps). Pint. Golden amber. (5) (#2967) $35

4078 Similar. Small "s" in "Wolfe's" and reverse "s" in Schnapps. Olive green. (4) (#1222) $35

4079 Similar. ¾ quart. Olive green. (5) (#349) $15

4080 Square, beveled corners. (T.J.Dunbar & Co Cordial Schnapps Scheidam). ¾ quart. Deep olive green. (5) (#37) $30

4081 Cylindrical, 7 rings around base and top. Broad band in center with fan-shaped panel for label. ¾ quart. Light amber. (6)

4082 Square with beveled corners. (C.A. Richards & Co) (99.Washington St) (Boston). All n's reversed. Paper label "Plantation Bourbon." Same as Sonoma Wine Bitters. ¾ quart. Amber. (5) (#1106) $20

4083 Square, beveled corners. (Monk's Old Bourbon Whiskey) (For Medicinal Purposes) (Wilson, Fairbank & Co Sole Agents). ¾ quart. Olive green. (4) (#747) $190

4084 Log cabin shape. Monogram (R&S) above (Roehling & Schultz Inc Chicago). Shingled roof. ¾ quart. Amber. (2) (#2845) $70

4085 Square, beveled corners. (Reed's Gilt Edge Tonic). ¾ quart. Amber. (6) (#1919) $20

4086 Cylindrical. (Moxie Nerve Food Co Lowell Mass Patented). Heavy glass. ¾ quart. Light blue. Funnel mouth. (4) (#1907) $15

4087 Cylindrical. (Carter's Spanish Mixture). ¾ quart. Deep olive green. (3)

4088 Triangular shape of tower with windows and door. Height: 11¼″. ¾ quart. Aqua. (6) (#1591) $5

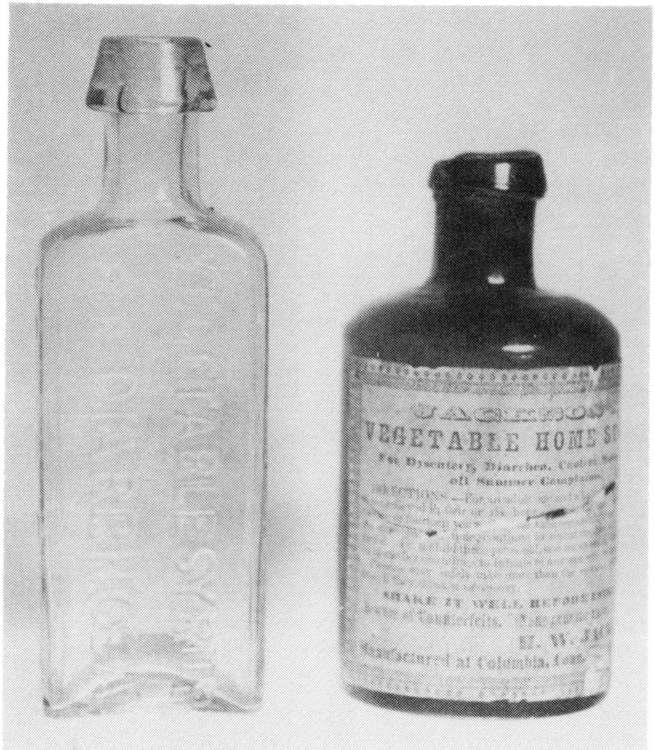


**Two products made from vegetables were considered cures for stomach disorders.**

4089 Rectangular. (Brown's Sarsaparilla) (For The Kidneys Liver and Blood). Pint. Aqua. (6) (#479) $10

4090 Oval. (Dr. Denison's Sarsaparilla). Pint. Green. (2) (#2477) $270

4091 Rectangular, beveled corners. On bevel and face (Sand's) (Sarsaparilla) (New York). Height: 6″. Aqua. (4) (#1144) $40

4092D Square, beveled corners. (Dr. Townsend's) Sarsaparilla) (Albany N.Y. No1). ¾ quart. Olive green. (1) (#111) $120

4092 Square, beveled corners. (Dr. Townsend's) (Sarsaparilla) (Albany N.Y.). Label intact. ¾ quart. Emerald green. (2) (#2314) $100

4092A Same. Olive green. (2) (#1601) $85

4092V Same. Green. No Albany, just (New York). (2) (#960) $60

4092B Same. Red amber. (2)

4092C Same. Clear green. Variant. (2) (#1491) $140

4093 Similar in shape, but marked (Old Dr. Townsend's) (Sarsaparilla) (New York). ¾ quart. Clear green. (2) (#2976) $150

4094 Similar in shape, but marked (Old Dr. J. Townsend's) (Sarsaparilla) (New York). ¾ quart. Yellow green. (2) (#362) $50

4095 Square, beveled corners. Shaped like Townsends. (Dr. Wilcox's) "s" reversed, (Compound Extract of Sarsaparilla). ¾ quart. Light green. (2)

4096 Rectangular, beveled corners. (Dr. Woodworth's Sarsaparilla) (Birmingham Ct). ¾ quart. Aqua. (2) (#381) $110

4097 Rectangular. (Dr. Wynkoop's Katharismic Honduras Sarsaparilla) (New York). Quart Blue. (1) (#1361) $1,650

4098 Rectangular. (John Bull) (Extract of) (Sarsaparilla) (Louisville Ky). Quart. Aqua. (3) (#2447) $85

4099 Rectangular. (Dana's Sarsaparilla) (Belfast) (Maine). Pint. Aqua. (6) (#2024) $5

4100 Shaped like Indian club. Marked (St Helen's) (25th Jany 1859). On base (K). Pint. Dense olive green. (5)

4101 Square with beveled corners. (Jones & Banks) (Importers) (58 Broad St N.Y.) ¾ quart. Amber. Inside thread. (6) (#1944) $65

4102 Grenade. (Harden's Hand Fire Extinguisher (Grenade) (Patented). Ring at base of neck. Height: 5″. Blue. (5) (#1656) $45
Similar. 4 7/8″. Sapphire blue. (#1256) $390

4103 Cylindrical. In circle around base (Willington Glass Works) "s" 's in "Glass" reversed. Dot in center of base. Quart. Olive amber. (5)

4104 Rectangular. (J.V.Babcock) (Gold Medal) (Sarsaparilla). ½ pint. Deep amber. (4) (#1400) $30

Figural bottle. (4106).

4105 Cylindrical. Typical beer bottle. On base (Rochester Glass Works N.Y.). Pint. Amber. (5) (#1135) $10

4106 Figure of draped woman. Different from usual madonna. Height: 1¼″. Bright amber. (3) (#2732) $30

4107 Cylindrical base, pear-shaped body. In ring around body (Healy's Hand Fire Extinguisher). Quart. Amber. (5) (#2074) $100

4108 Globular with long neck. Marked (Stout Dyer & Wicks) in arch above (X). Pint. Aqua. (4) (#2315) $25

4109 Bottom half of grenade (Harden's Improved Grenade Fire Extinguisher Pat Oct. 7th 1884). On base (No 2). Blue. Looks more like an ashtray or lamp. (4) (#1890) $160

4110 Globular. Marked (John W. Stout & Co) (X) (New York). ½ pint. Aqua. (6) (#54) $15

4111 Cylindrical. On base (Ky G.W.) and (66). ¾ quart. Dark amber. (6) (#2461) $20

4112 Rectangular. On bevel (Dr. B. Ober's). On front (Compound Extract of Mountain Ash). ½ pint. Aqua. (4) (#702) $200

Six-sided bottle for "Gibb's Bone Liniment." (4113).

4113 6-sided. (Gibb's Bone Linament). Height: 6¼″. Olive green. (2)

4114 Cylindrical. (JSP) (Registered 1889) Paper label. "Joseph H. Peterson." ½ pint. Blue green. (6) (#631) $22.50
(#831) $10

4115 Cylindrical. 3-mold. Unusual collar. Deep depression running around collar near base. On base (Lyon Bros Maker). Quart. Olive green. (6) (#462) $15

4116 Rectangular. (Bristol's) (Genuine) (Sarsaparilla) (New York). Quart. Aqua. (5) (#1270) $22.50

4117 Rectangular. (Dr. Greene's) (Sarsaparilla). ½ pint. Aqua. (5) (#393) $7.50

4118 Figure of J.L. Sullivan in 2 parts. Height; 14½". (1) (#1990) $375

# Chapter Thirty-Four

# Bitters Bottles

"Bitters" was a nineteenth century drink claimed by many to have great curative powers. The ingredients used in making the drink were mainly herbal extracts and pure grain alcohol. They created an alcoholic euphoria that would convince their users that their restorative powers were unique. Since there were no laws against private enterprise in the nineteenth century, many wild claims were made by the pitchmen who peddled bitters and other medicinal products. There was little anyone could do to cure most illnesses, anyway, in those days, but thousands of satisfied customers of bitters attested to the miraculous powers of their favorite brands.

Bitters bottles are an area for specialized collecting for many, and of special interest are the figural bottles. There are almost a thousand varieties of bitters bottles known to today's collectors and the field has been made less complicated by two collectors and writers. The earliest important book on the subject was written by James H. Thompson in 1947. A more recent publication, *Bitters Bottles,* by Richard Watson categorized all known examples up to 1965. For this exhaustive study the Gardner collection was carefully examined and listed by the author. Following the publication of the book Charles Gardner added Watson numbers to his bitters collection listing for easier identification in the catalog. These numbers have been included in the following list to enable the many bitters collectors to find more information concerning the bottles than will appear in the Gardner catalog.

Bitters bottles are an especially fascinating segment of the story of American bottle manufacture and collectors will be interested in the large amount of bottles in this section of the Gardner collection that still have their original labels. Many of the Gardner bitters bottles established record prices at auction and this placed new importance on this collecting category.

1019 Square. (BIG BILL BITTERS). ¾ quart. Amber. (W-41) (3) (#1341) $80

1020 Rectangular, flat. (ANDREWS JAUNDICE BITTERS PROVIDENCE R.I.) (W-10) (3) (#967) $350

1022 Square, rope corners. (BAKERS ORANGE GROVE BITTERS). Original label. ¾ quart. Amber. (W-23) (3) (#1247) $225

1022A Same. Dark brown amber. (3) (#982) $190

Group of three bitters bottles. (5218, 1022, 3379).

1024 Round, with sunken panels. (DR. BIRMINGHAMS ANTIBILLIOUS BLOOD PURIFYING BITTERS THIS BOTTLE NOT TO BE SOLD). ¾ quart. Green. (W-42) (2) (#2695) $600

1025 Pig. (BERKSHIRE BITTERS A MANN & CO CINCINNATI, O). ¾ quart. Deep amber. (1) (#2651) $1,100

1026 Barrel. (BOURBON WHISKEY BITTERS). ¾ quart. Deep amber. (W-52) (2)

1026A Same. Tobacco brown. (2) (#853) $200

**Two pig bottles used for bitters. (1025).**

1026V Same. Puce. (2) (#1213) $250

Same. Gray green. FM. (#7) $160

1028 Triangular. 3 indented panels. (THE GREAT TONIC CALDWELLS HERB BITTERS). 1 panel latticed. 1 plain. ¾ quart. Amber. (W-65). (2) (#837) $180

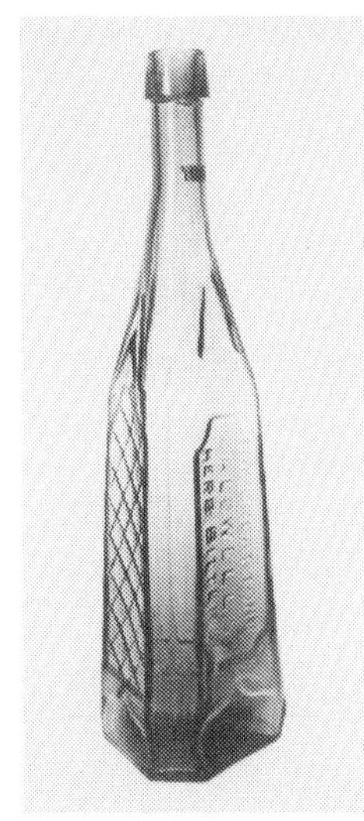

**Triangular tapering bottle. (1028).**

1028A Same. Quart. Amber. Variant. (2) (#1645) $100

1028V Same. Red amber. (2) (#2757) $225

1030 Rectangular, beveled corners. (ONLY 70 CTS CLARKS VEGETABLE SHERRY WINE BITTERS SHARON MASS). ½ gallon. Aqua. (W-88, Var. G). (2) (#2552) $40

1030V Similar. Inscription on 6 lines, no ONLY 70 CTS. ½ gallon. Aqua. (2) (#199) $35

1030B Similar. Gallon. Aqua. (2) (#743) $95

1030C Similar. Quart. Aqua. (3) (#2070) $85

1030D Similar. (ONLY 25¢) added. Label. (3) (#1663) $85

1030E Similar. (ONLY 25¢) omitted. (3) (#2838) $50

1031 Ear of corn. (NATIONAL BITTERS). On base (PATENTED 1867). ¾ quart. Clear amber. (W-236). (1) (#1949)$375

1031D Same. Clear light amber. (1) (#901) $225

1032 Same. Aqua. (1) (#1197) $1600

1032V Same. Deep wine. Original label. (1) (#2613) $1,000

1034 Square. (CRIMEAN BITTERS ROMAINES CRIMEAN BITTERS PATENTED 1863). ¾ quart. Golden amber. (W-282). (3) (#2391) $160

1034V Same, with (W. CHILTON & CO) added. ¾ quart. Amber. (3) (#2648) $140

1037 Cylindrical. (CURTIS & PERKINS WILD CHERRY BITTERS). Original label. Pint. Aqua. (W-102). (3) (#807) $150

1038 Cylindrical, 12 panels on neck. (CURTIS CORDIAL CALISAYA THE GREAT STOMACH BITTERS 1866 CCC 1900). ¾ quart. Amber. (W-101). (3) (#1309) $575

1040 Square. (DOYLES HOP BITTERS 1872) and hop branch. ¾ quart. Dark amber. (W-110). (5) (#360) $25

1040C Similar, with variations. (5) (#648) $35

1040D Similar, with variations. (5) (#1644) $20

1041 Similar, with variations. (5) (#1712) $20

1041E Similar, with variations. (5) (#2136) $25

1041F Similar, with variations. (5)

1042 Barrel. (B.T. 1865 S.C) (SMITHS) (DRUID BITTERS) on 3 lines. ¾ quart. Amber. (W-120). (1) (#1101) $525

1043 Rectangular. (EXCELSIOR AROMATIC BITTERS DR. D.S. PERRY & CO NEW YORK) (1800). ¾ quart. Smoky amber. (W-119). (2) (#2455) $250

1044 Rectangular. (EXCELSIOR AROMATIC BITTERS DR. D.S. PERRY & CO NEW YORK) (1800). ¾ quart. Smoky amber. (W-119) (2) (#839) $400

1050 Square. (ELECTRIC BITTERS H. E. BUCKLEN & CO CHICAGO ILL). Pint. Amber. (W-114). (6) (#2376) $10

1050E Same, letters heavier. Original label. (6) (#984) $15

1050G Same. Quart. (6) (#456) $25

1050F Similar, but (ELECTRIC BITTERS) only on both sides. Pint. Amber. Cracked. (6) (#1968) $8

1050B Similar, but (ELECTRIC BRAND) only on both sides. Quart. Amber. (6) (#1408) $15

1050V Similar, but 1050 inscription added. Pint. Amber. (6) (#1936) $7.50

1050C Similar. Quart. Amber. (6) (#1294) $10
Similar. Yellow amber. (#2694) $25

1051 Square. (DR. F. FLESCHUT'S) (CELEBRATED STOMACH BITTERS) (LAPORTE PA). ¾ quart. Aqua. (W-451). (3) (#1214) $70

1052 Form of fish. (DOCTOR FISCH'S BITTERS W. H. WARE PATENTED 1866). ¾ quart. Golden amber. (W-124). (2)

1053 Similar, but marked (THE FISH BITTERS), etc. Original label. ¾ quart. Golden amber. (2) (#2839) $380

1054 Similar. Lime green. (W-125). (#2117) $6,300

1055 Similar. Different scales on fish. Marked on base (W.H. Ware patented). ¾ quart. Light greenish amber. (1) (#1437) $200

1055A Same. Green. (1) (#1709) $1,050

1055B Same. Clear. (1) (#693) $800

1055E Same. Dark amber. (2) (#453) $150

1056 Square. (FOX & CO HYGEIA BITTERS). (L&W) on base. ¾ quart. Amber. (3) (#2390) $20

1057 Barrel. Spiral ribbing with 2 panels. (FAVORITE BITTERS POWELL & STUTENROTH). Around shoulder (PAT APPLIED FOR). Pint. Amber. (1) (#1405) $1,000

1058 Cylindrical, tapering from base. On shoulder (GLOBE) (BITTERS BYRNE BROS & CO NEW YORK). On side, vertically (GLOBE BITTERS MANUFACTURED ONLY BY BYRNE BROS. & CO NEW YORK). ¾ quart. Amber. Square collar. (1) (#455) $300

1060 Barrel. (GREELEY'S BOURBON BITTERS). Original label and tax stamp. ¾ quart. Puce. (W-144). (2) (#1933) $250

1060B Same. Greenish amber. (2) (#2133) $325

1060C Same. Different shade of greenish amber. (2) (#981) $310

1061 Barrel. (BOURBON WHISKEY BITTERS) (GREELEY'S) vertically, right and left. ¾ quart. Aqua. (W-145). (2) (#1549) $1,000

1061B Same. Puce. (2) (#1021) $190

1062 Same. Barrel, but no inscription. ¾ quart. Amber. (3)

1062A Same. Blue. (2) (#69) $950

1063 Square. (GREAT WESTERN TONIC BITTERS PATENTED JANY 21, 1868) (O.P. BISSELL & CO PEORIA ILL). On base (L&W). ¾ quart. Dense amber. (2) (#167) $80

1064 Rectangular. (DR. HOOFLAND'S GERMAN BITTERS) (LIVER COMPLAINT) (DYSPEPSIA &c) (C.M. JACKSON PHILADELPHIA). ½ pint. Aqua. (W-174). (4) (#887) $55

1064E Same. Height: 9″. Aqua. (Variant A). (4) (#118) $45

1065 Triangular. (HAGEN'S BITTERS). ¾ quart. Smoky amber. (W-149). (3) (#1215) $110

1066 Barrel. (HALLS BITTERS E.E. HALL NEW HAVEN ESTABLISHED 1842). Original label. ¾ quart. Light amber. (2) (#2085) $120

1066V Barrel. (HALLS BITTERS) only. ¾ quart. Amber. (W-152) (1) (#597) $725

1067 Square, beveled corners. (DR. A.S. HOPKINS UNION STOMACH BITTERS). Original label. ¾ quart. Amber. (W-177). (3) (#2840) $45

1067A Same, with (HARTFORD CONN) added. (Variant A). (4) (#1520) $45

1067F Same, with (F.S. AMIDON SOLE PROP HARTFORD CONN) added. (Variant B). (4) (#854) $20

1068 Log cabin. Square. (HOLZTERMANNS PATENT STOMACH BITTERS). Original label. ¾ quart. Smoky amber. (W-172). (2) (#469) $175

1068A Similar, with rectangular 2-sided roof. No bark on logs. Amber. (Variant A). (1) (#549) $550

1069 Square. (DR. J. HOSTETTERS STOMACH BITTERS). On base (A&DHC). ¾ quart. Amber. (W-179). (6) (#2344) $20

1069A Same, on base (S MCKEE & CO). (W-179). (6) (#1167) $50

1069B Same, with (18 FLUID OUNCES) added. (6) (#1264) $22.50

1069C Same as #1069. On base (L&W). (6) (#1264) $22.50

1069D Same. Olive green. (1) on base. (5) (#1263) $60

1069V Same, but with different arrangement of letters. (S. MCKEE & CO) on base. Amber. (6) (#2344) $20

1070 Rectangular. (DR. RIVENBURG'S INDIAN VEGETABLE BITTERS N.Y.). ¾ quart. Aqua. (W-279). (3) (#2616)$700

1071 Retangular. (DR. STEPHEN JEWETTS CELEBRATED HEALTH RESTORING BITTERS RINDGE N.H.) Pint. Rich amber. (W-193). (2) (#1117) $350

1071C Same. Pale green. (2) (#613) $410

1071V Same shape. (JEWETT) and (RINDGE) on bevels. Pint. Golden amber. (Variant A.) (1) (#293) $425

1072 Rectangular. (DR. GEO. PIERCES INDIAN RESTORATIVE BITTERS). ½ pint. Aqua. (W-258). (3)

1072V Same. Pint. Aqua. (4) (#1759) $55
Same. ¾ quart. Aqua. (#136) $15

1073 Indian queen (BROWN'S CELEBRATED INDIAN HERB BITTERS PATENTED 1867). ¾ quart. Amber. (W-57, Variant A). (1) (#357) $350

1074 Indian queen. Similar, but shielded on shoulder. Marked (H. PHARAZYN PHILA RIGHT SECURED). ¾ quart. Amber. (1) (#1173) $950

1075 Same as #1073 except marked (PATENTED FEB 11, 1868). ¾ quart. Amber. (W-57, Variant B). (1) (#2453) $400

1075A Same. Aqua. (1) (#485) $2,000

1075B Same. Light amber. (1) (#1869) $300

1076 Log cabin like Booz bottle. (JACOBS CABIN TONIC BITTERS) (JACOBS CABIN BITTERS) (LABORATORY, PHILADELPHIA). ¾ quart. Aqua. (W-191). (1) (#2181) $4,000

**Figural bottles of Indians. (2951, 1075B)**

1077 Rectangular. (DR. JACOBS BITTERS S.A. SPENCER NEW HAVEN). ½ pint. Aqua. (W-190, Variant A.) (3) (#647) $110

**"Dr. Jacobs Bitters" and bottle for "Soloroso" bitters with pineapple trademark.**

1077V Same. ¾ quart. Aqua. Original label. (3) (#1567) $110

1078 Log cabin. 2-sided roof. (KELLY'S OLD CABIN BITTERS) (PATENTED 1863). ¾ quart. Dense amber. (W-199). (1) (#1469) $525

1078V Similar, different neck. Green. (1) (#2853) $1,600

1078X Same as above, but (KELLY'S) omitted. ¾ quart. Amber. (W-239). (1) (#421) $900

1079 Barrel. (KEYSTONE BITTERS). Original label. ¾ quart. Amber. (W-201). (2) (#165) $350

1080 Cylindrical. (DR. LANGLEY'S ROOT & HERB BITTERS 76 UNION ST BOSTON). Pint. Green. (W-206). (5) (#2614) $45

1080A ¾ quart. Green. (99 UNION ST). (Variant B.) (5) (#1359) $50

1080B Same, only (76 UNION ST). (Variant C.) (5) (#1504) $30

1080C Pint. Deep aqua. (99 UNION). (Variant E.) (5) (#2278) $45

**Two bottles for "Old Cabin Bitters." (1078V).**

1080E ¾ quart. Aqua. Same. (Variant C.) (5) (#391) $70

1080V Cylindrical. (DR. LANGLEY'S ROOT & HERB BITTERS) on sunken panel. Paper label intact. height: 6″. Amber. (5) (#1152) $50

1080D Same. Aqua. (99 UNION ST). (Variant D.) (5) (#1934) $20

1084 Square. (E. DEXTER LOVERIDGE WAHOO BITTERS XXX PATD DWD 1863). Original labels. ¾ quart. Dense amber. (W-348). (3) (#471) $200

1084V Same, but different eagle on panel. (3) (#1071) $75

1085 12-sided. (DR. BAXTER'S MANDRAKE BITTERS LORD BROS. PROPRIETORS BURLINGTON VT). ½ pint. Deep aqua. Original label. (W-29). (5) (#2374) $15

1086 Square. (JOHN STEELE'S NIAGARA STAR BITTERS 1864) and 3 stars. ¾ quart. Deep amber. (W-316). (3) (#1023) $160

1086A Same, different eagle. (W-316). (3) (#791) $150

1086V Same. Eagle flying left. (Variant A). (3) (#71) $180

1087 Square. (MISCHLER'S HERB BITTERS). Gradations on sides. ¾ quart. Amber. (W-229). (3) (#792) $40

1087G Same. Reverse (DR. S.B. HARTMAN & CO). ¾ quart. Deep amber. (Variant B.) (3) (#408) $20

1087E Same. Light amber. (3) (#2104) $35

1088B Log cabin. (OLD HOMESTEAD WILD CHERRY BITTERS PATENT). ¾ quart. Blue. (W-242). (1) (#1053) $16,500

1088A Same. Greenish amber. (2) (#2341) $550

1088E Same. Dark amber. (2) (#2261) $250

1088V Similar, with smaller shingles and doorstep. ¾ quart. Dark yellow amber. (2) (#2565) $195

1089 Triangular. (MORNING * BITTERS INCEPTUM 5869 PATENT 5869). Diagonal ribbing. ¾ quart. Amber. (W-244). (2) (#1731) $160

1090 Barrel. (OLD SACHEM BITTERS AND WIGWAM TONIC). ¾ quart. Amber. (W-244). (2) (#391) $375

1090B Same. Light green. (2)

1090D Same. Light amber. (2) (#21) $110

1091 Same. Clear olive green. (2) (#2229) $950

1091E Same. Medium amber. (2) (#1757) $175

1091C Similar, but 10″ high. Aqua. (Variant A.) (2) (#2725) $800

1092 Rectangular. (OXYGENATED BITTERS FOR DYSPEPSIA, ASTHMA & GENERAL DEBILITY). ½ pint. Aqua. (W-249). (3) (#487) $40

1092V Same, only 6″ high. Aqua. (3) (#2759) $55

1095 Oval. (DR. PETZOLDS GENUINE GERMAN BITTERS INCPT. 1862). Corrugated edges. ¾ quart. Amber. (W-256). (3) (#2343) $120

1095V Same. Pint. Amber. (Variant A.) (3) (#966) $100

1096 Rectangular, with widely beveled corners. (PHOENIX BITTERS) (JOHN MOFFAT) PRICE 1 DOLLAR) (NEW YORK). 6 oz. Olive green. (W-257). (3) (#965) $200

1096A Similar. (PRICE $1.00). Aqua. (Variant C.) (3) (#311) $60

1096B Same. Olive green. (3) (#2006) $140

1096D Same as #1096. Clear. Folded lip. (3) (#1615) $180

1096E Same. (PRICE $1). Deep amber. (Variant A.) (3) (#1311) $275

1096V Same. (JNo MOFFAT) (PRICE $1). (Variant B.) (3) (#2936) $110

1098 Log cabin. (S.T. DRAKE 1860 PLANTATION BITTERS PATENTED 1862). 4 logs. (X) on roof. ¾ quart. Amber. (W-111, Variant B.) (4) (#2469) $160

**Bottle for "Drake's Plantation Bitters" is in shape of log cabin. (1098).**

1098A Similar. Brown. 6 logs. (W-111, Variant A.) (4) (#1293) $450

1098B Same. Clear green. (W-111). (1) (#1005) $850

1098V Similar. Puce. (W-111, Variant A.) (4) (#2647) $1,250

1099 Similar, but (X) omitted. Amber. (4) (#1861) $50

1099A Similar to #1098B. Greenish amber. (4) (#5) $1,200

1099B Same. Deep red. (4) (#501) $900

1099V Same. Honey amber. (4) (#2101) $350

1100 Similar, with arabesques. Amber. (Variant C.) (3) (#689) $150

1100A Similar, with variations. 5 logs. (Variant D.) (3) (#117) $160

1100B Drakes with 4 label panels. 6 log variant. ¾ quart. Amber. (2) (#1805) $125

1100V Similar to a 6 log Drakes, except no lettering. 2 corners beveled. ¾ quart. Amber. (3) (#619) $250

1101 Rectangular. (DR. FLINT'S QUAKER BITTERS PROVIDENCE R. I.). ¾ quart. Aqua. (W-126). (4) (#1168) $50

**Two examples of bitters bottles with Quaker labels. "Dr. Flint's Celebrated Quaker Bitters."**

1101A Similar, but different labels. (4) (#2294) $25

1101B Similar. (PROVIDENCE) omitted. (4) (#2726) $25

1101C Similar, different labels. (4) (#2566) $50

1101V (OLD DR. WARREN'S QUAKER BITTERS FLINT & CO PROV R. I.). Original label. ¾ quart. Aqua. (W-357). (4) (#198) $40

1102 Rectangular, beveled corners. (S.O. RICHARDSON BITTERS SOUTH READING MASS). ½ pint. Aqua. (W-275). (4) (#2327) $30

1102V Similar, but marked (W.L. RICHARDSON). ½ pint. Aqua. (W-276). (4) (#2615) $220

1103E Barrel. (DR. G.W. ROBACKS STOMACH BITTERS CINCINNATI, 0). Pint. Amber. (W-280, Variant A.) (2) (#2805) $200

1105 Same. Quart. Copper amber. (W-280). (2) (#709) $325

1105A Same. Emerald green. (1) (#645) $850

1106 Square. (RUSH'S BITTERS) (A.H. FLANDERS M.D. NEW YORK). ¾ quart. Amber. (W-289). (3) (#424) $20

1111 Square, rounded corners. (REX KIDNEY & LIVER BITTERS REX BITTERS NOTHING ELSE). ¾ quart. Amber. (W-274). (4) (#166) $30

1111V Same. (THE FINEST LAXATIVE AND BLOOD PURIFIER). Amber. (Variant A.) (5) (#134) $5

1113 Bust of Washington. (SIMONS CENTENNIAL BITTERS TRADE MARK). ¾ quart. Aqua. (W-304). (1) (#503) $650

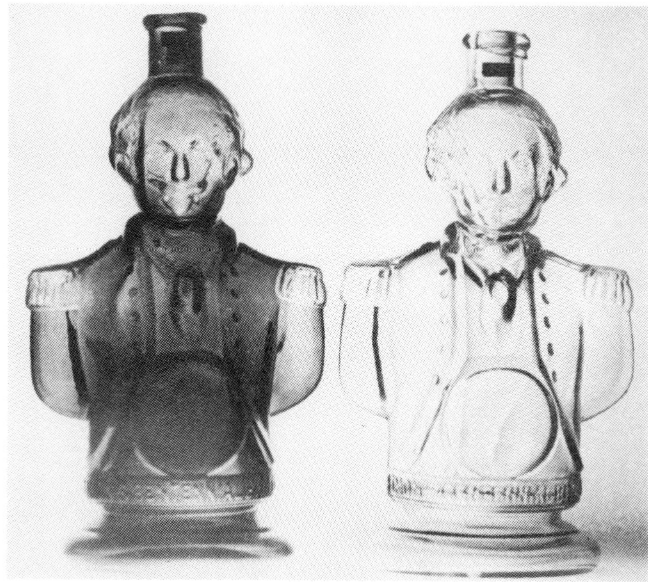

**Bottles for "Simons Centennial Bitters" are in shape of bust of Washington. (1113, 1113B)**

1113B Same. Amber. (1) (#1837) $1,200

1114 Square. (RUSS ST DOMINGO BITTERS NEW YORK). ¾ quart. Amber. (W-290). (3) (#1870) $15

1115 Rectangular, beveled corners. (DR. SKINNERS CELEBRATED 25 CENT BITTERS SO READING MASS). Long neck. ½ pint. Aqua. (W-306). (3) (#2007) $15

1116 Pig. (SUFFOLK BITTERS PHILBROOK & TUCKER BOSTON). ¾ quart. Amber. (1) (#1453) $525

1124 Flattened, chestnut type, with applied nadle. (OLD DR. TOWNSEND'S CELEBRATED STOMACH BITTERS). ¾ quart. Light amber. (W-333). (1) (#2549) $3,200

1128 Square. (IMOK Y "Y" WAHOO & CALISAYS BITTERS JACOB PINKERTON). ¾ quart. Dark amber. (W-349). (3) (#1518) $170

1130 Barrel. (BROBST & RENTSCHLER, READING PA W.C. BITTERS). ¾ quart. Amber. (W-347). (2) (#2855) $375

1133A Oval. (WARNERS SAFE BITTERS) On base (A&DHC). (W-336, Variant A.) (1)

1133D Same. Pint. Amber. (W-336). (1) (#2503) $350

1133V Similar. Marked (WARNERS SAFE TONIC). Paper label reads "WARNERS SAFE TONIC BITTERS." Pint. Amber. (1) (#1693) $200

1136 Square, 5-story building. (WILDER'S STOMACH BITTERS EDW WILDERS & CO WHOLESALE DRUGGISTS LOUISVILLE KY). ¾ quart. Aqua. (W-366). (3) (#2856) $130

1140 Ben Franklin bitters. Round with irregular depressed panel. Paper label. ¾ quart. Clear olive green. (W-L 52). (3) (#1149) $400

1140A Same, with original labels. (3) (#2277) $225

1144 Square. (C.A. RICHARDS & CO 99 WASHINGTON ST BOSTON). Label reads "Sonoma Wine Bitters." ¾ quart. Amber. (W-L 120). (4) (#152) $15

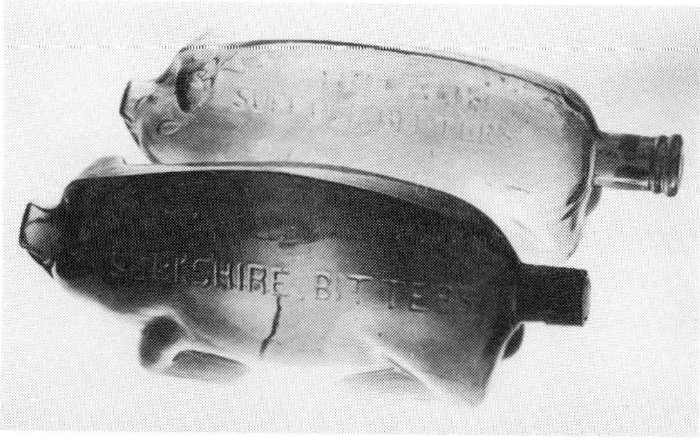

**"Suffolk" and "Berkshire" bitters were both sold in pig-shaped bottles. (1116).**

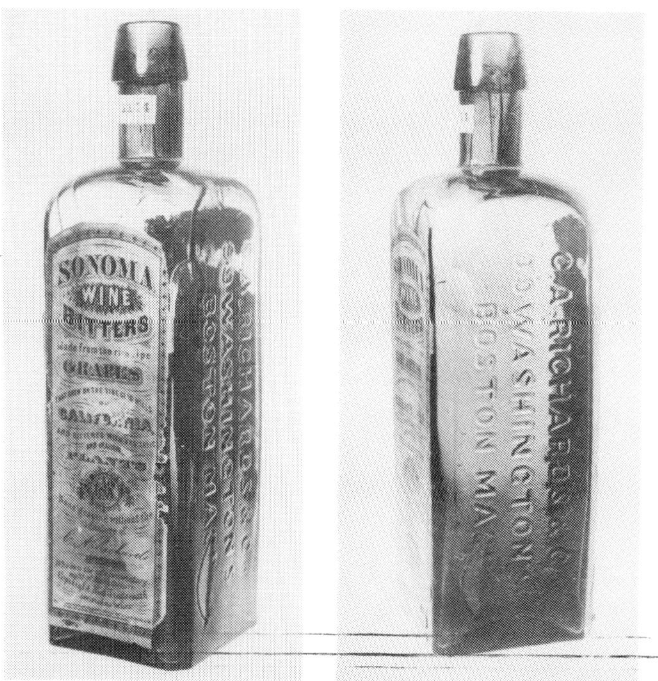


**Front and side of rectangular embossed bottle for "Sonoma Wine Bitters." (1144).**

1147 Square. (TYLER'S STANDARD AMERICAN BITTERS). ¾ quart. Amber. (W-337). (3) (#615) $75

1149 Rectangular, with beveled corners. (WHITWELL'S TEMPERENCE BITTERS BOSTON). ½ pint. Aqua. (W-364). (3) (#567) $110

2801 Rectangular, widely beveled corners. (C) eye (O) over (BITTERS). Reverse (ISAACSON SEISAX & CO 66 & 68 COMMON STREET). ¾ quart. Amber. (W-187). (1) (#1503) $475

2808 Rectangular. (VONHUMBOLDT'S DYSPEPSIA & c). Original label. ½ pint. Aqua. (W-345). (3) (#1455) $130

2809 Rectangular. (ROYAL PEPSIN STOMACH BITTERS L & A SCHARFF SOLE AGENTS ST LOUIS US & CANADA). ¾ quart. Amber. (W-287). (3) (#1022) $55

2809V Same. Pint. (Variant A.) (3) (#2646) $65

2810 Rectangular, beveled corners. (KIMBALLS JAUNDICE BITTERS TROY N.H.). ½-pint. Olive amber. (W-202). (3) (#2279) $170

2811 Barrel. (HIGHLAND BITTERS AND SCOTCH TONIC). ¾ quart. Olive green. (W-170). (1) (#1613) $1,075

2812 Oval. (F. BROWN BOSTON SARSAPARILLA & TOMATO BITTERS). Pint. Aqua. (W-58). (3) (#2103) $60

2814 Square. (OLD HOME BITTERS LAUGHLIN SMITH & CO WHEELING W. Va). ¾ quart. Amber. (W-241). (3) (#1903) $160 $160

2816 Flattened barrel. (CHAS NICHOLS JR. & CO PROPS LOWELL MASS DR. CHANDLER'S JAMAICA GINGER ROOT BITTERS). Original label. ¾ quart. Amber. (W-82). (2) (405) $1,950

2817 Square. (DR. X.X. LOVEGOOD'S FAMILY BITTERS). Quart. Amber. (W-220). (2) (#2837) $1,250

2818 Oval on sunken panel. (DR. HARTSHORN'S FAMILY MEDICINES). Label, "Jaundice Bitters." Pint. Aqua. (6) (#1952) $10

2820 Square, beveled corners. (DR. J. SWEET'S STRENGTHENING BITTERS). Pint. Aqua. (W-328). (4) (#8) $20

2821 Flat, with wide rib on sides. (XXX DANDELION BITTERS). Reverse: plain. ½ pint. Aqua. (W-104). (3) (#248) $10

2823 Oval, marked (1834) on shoulder. Man in derby, short beard and cane. On sides (TRAVELLERS) (BITTERS). ¾ quart. Amber. (W-334). (1) (#2405) $2,600

2824 Square, beveled corners. (SHARPS) (MOUNTAIN) (BITTERS) (HERB). ¾ quart. Dark amber. (3) (W-301). (#1407) $40

2825 Rectangular. On edges (DR. RUSSELL MED CO) (PEPSIN CALISAYS BITTERS). ¾ quart. Emerald green. (W-253). (4) (#2328) $45

2826 Triangular, beveled corners. (NIGHT CAP BITTERS SCHMIDLAPP & CO DISTILLERS CINCINNATI, O A GOOD BEVERAGE). ¾ quart. Clear. (W-238). (3) (#695) $100

2828 Rectangular, rope corners. (CAREY'S GRECIAN BEND BITTERS). Tapering. ¾ quart. Puce. (W-70). (1) (#885) $3,700

**Bitters were bottled in a variety of molded shapes.**

2830 Oval. Flask shape. (DEWITTS STOMACH BITTERS). Original label. (½-pint. Amber. (W-107). (4) (#1456) $40

2831 Square. (DR. GILBERT'S ROCK & RYE STOMACH BITTERS). Pint. Blue green. (W-132). (3) (#119) $190

2832 Cylindrical. On base (J. WALKER'S VB) in circle. Pint. Yellow green. Heavy glass. Flanged lip. (W-L 140). (5) (#1838) $20

2833 Cylindrical, bulging neck. (REEDS BITTERS) 2 lines lengthwise. ¾ quart. Amber. (W-272). (1) (#1093) $175

2833V Same, with earlier label. Amber. (4) (#1472) $30

2834 Square. On shoulders (HOPS & MALT) (BITTERS). On sides (HOPS & MALT). Above sheaf (TRADE MARK). Above

(BITTERS). ¾ quart. Amber. (W-176). (3) (#359) $50

2835 Rectangular with vertical ribbing. On edges (AUGAUER BITTERS) and (AUGAUER BITTERS CO CHICAGO). ¾ quart. Green. (W-21). (4) (#1614) $50

2836 Pillar or column shape. (LACOURS BITTERS). On other side (SARSAPARIPHERE). ¾ quart. Dark amber. Flanged. (W-204). (4) (#197) $125

2837 Shaped like square face gin. (LITTHAUER STOMACH BITTERS INVENTED 1864 BY JOSEF LOWENTHAL). ¾ quart. Clear. (W-216). (4) (#1872) $45

2837A Same. Milk glass. (3) (#983) $50

2838 Square. (DR. LOEW'S CELEBRATED STOMACH BITTERS & NERVE TONIC) (THE LOEW & SONS CLEVELAND O). Very fancy bottle. ¾ quart. Bright green. (W-296, Variant A.) (3) (#1551) $95

2841 Cylindrical with bulging neck. On shoulder (P.H.D. & CO). On base (SAZARAC AROMATIC BITTERS). Pint. Milk glass. (W-296, Variant A.) (2) (#1821) $450

2841A Same, greenish amber. (2) (#2693) $600

2841B Same. Quart. Milk glass. (W-296). (1) (#1389) $325

2841V Same, deep blue. (1) (#149) $7,000

2842 Rectangular, beveled corners. (DR. BLAKES AROMATIC BITTERS NEW YORK). ½-pint. Aqua. (W-45). (3) (#1863) $95

2843 Rectangular, beveled corners. (DR. SKINNERS SHERRY WINE BITTERS SO READING MASS). Pint. Aqua. (W-307). (3) (#1119) $60

2845 Triangular, beveled corners. (O.H.P. ROSE E.G.R.I. GREAT PERUVIAN KING BITTERS). ¾ quart. Amber. (W-L 110). (3) (#1648) $60

2846 Square, beveled corners. (SARASINA STOMACH BITTERS). ¾ quart. Amber. (W-294). (3) (#1310) $25

2851 Square, beveled corners. (DR. STOEVER'S BITTERS) (ESTABLISHED 1837) (KRYDER & CO PHILADELPHIA). Original label. ¾ quart. Amber. (W-320). (3) (#1566) $55

2852 Square, beveled corners. Paper label only, "The Life Preserver or Dr. Richard's Renown Bitters". ¾ quart. Amber. (W-107). (4) (#1662) $25

2853 Square, beveled corners. (HUNKIDORY STOMACH BITTERS). Reverse: (H.B. MATTHEWS CHICAGO ILL). ¾ quart. Amber. (W-181). (3) (#1647) $60

2854 Rectangular. (WHEAT). Reverse: (BITTERS). ¾ quart. Amber. (W-360). (3) (#1104) $45

2856 Rectangular. (HIERAPICRA BITTERS EXTRACT FIGS) (BOTANICAL SOCIETY) CALIFORNIA). On base (FIG). Pint. Aqua. (W-169). (3) (#1864) $85

2857 Square, beveled corners. (LORIMER'S) JUNIPER TAR) (BITTERS) (ELMIRA N.Y.) Pint. Blue green. (W-219). (3) (#1743) $325

2858 Square, beveled corners. (HOP AND IRON BITTERS) (UTICA N.Y.). Original label. Pint. Amber. (W-175). (3) (#568) $45

2859 Rectangular, with rounded corners. (DR. VONHOPFS) (CURACOA BITTERS) (CHAMBERLAIN & CO DES MOINES IOWA). ½-pint. Golden amber. (W-343). (3) (#1198) $130

2861 Rectangular, widely beveled corners. (DR. E.P. EASTMAN'S) (YELLOW DOCK BITTERS) (LYNN, MASS). Pint. Aqua. (W-112). (3) (#1391) $130

2863 Rectangular, beveled corners. (JACKSON'S AROMATIC LIFE BITTERS). ¾ quart. Dark olive green. (W-188). (2) (#1935) $325

2864 Square, beveled corners. (HOFFHEIMER BROTHERS) (BAVARIAN BITTERS). ¾ quart. Dark amber. (W-28). (3) (#2664) $140

2865 Rectangular, beveled corners. (WILLIAM ALLEN'S CONGRESS BITTERS). Original label. ¾ quart. Deep emerald green. (W-5). (2) (#933) $250

2865A Same. Puce. (2) (#2053) $625

2865V Similar to above, but (CONGRESS BITTERS) on both edges. ¾ quart. Aqua. (W-94). (3) (#2471) $80
Reproduction from Gardner mold. Pint. Amethyst. (#2934) $250 (#3000) $60

2867 Rectangular, beveled corners. (GOLDEN SEAL BITTERS) (G.C.SEGURS) (SPRINGFIELD MASS). Pint. Aqua. (W-300). (3) (#2807) $80

2868 Square, beveled corners. (WEST INDIA STOMACH BITTERS) (ST. LOUIS MO). On base (WIMCo). Original label. ¾ quart. Amber. (W-359). (3) (#2456) $30

2869 Square, beveled corners. (HOME BITTERS) (SAINT LOUIS MO). ¾ quart. Amber. (W-173). (3) (#1453) $35

2870 Cylindrical, covered with wicker except over glass label (TILTON'S DANDELION BITTERS). ¾ quart. Golden amber. (W-L 131). (3) (#2165) $275

2873 Blown, ribbed, globular with applied handle. Marked (ALPINE BITTERS). ¾ quart. Clear. (#934) $40

2874 Drum-shaped. (DINGENS NAPOLEAN BITTERS). Original label. ¾ quart. Clear. (W-109). (3) (#261) $1,650

2875 Square, with rounded corners. (BEN HUR BITTERS). 2 lines. ¾ quart. Amber. (W-36). (3) (#1967) $40

**Bottles for three different types of bitters.**

**Original label on "Toneco Stomach Bitters." (2877).**

2876 Square, beveled corners. (YOCHIM BROS CELEBRATED STOMACH BITTERS). Original label. ¾ quart. Amber. (W-376). (3) (#696) $35

2877 Square, rounded corners. (TONECO STOMACH BITTERS) (APPETIZER & TONIC). Original label. (W-330). ¾ quart. Clear. (4) (#1966) $6

2878 Square, beveled corners. (COLUMBO PEPTIC BITTERS) (L.E. JUNG NEW ORLEANS LA). (A.B.Co) on base. ¾ quart. Amber. (W-93). (4) (#808) $30

2879 Shape of horseshoe. (HORSE SHOE MEDICINE Co) (COLLINSVILLE, ILLa). Reverse (HORSE SHOE BITTERS). On base (PATENT APPLIED FOR). ¾ quart. Amber. (W-178). (2) (#1773) $850

2880 Square, beveled corners. (WAMPOO BITTERS) (SIEGEL & BRO NEW YORK). ¾ quart. Amber. (W-354). (3) (#2263) $45

2881 Square, beveled corners. (W.F. SEVERA) (STOMACH BITTERS). Original label. ¾ quart. Amber. (W-321). (4) (#1862) $10

2882 Oval. (BROWN'S AROMATIC BITTERS HANNIBAL MO). 5 lines. Pint. Aqua. (W-55). (3)

2883 Square. (M.G. LANDSBERG CHICAGO) (1778) (1876). Stars, cannon balls, swords, axes and cannons. Diamond corners. Reverse plain with unmarked panel. ¾ quart. Amber. (W-205, Variant.) (2) (#2696) $70

2884 Flask. (YERBA BUENA) (BITTERS, S.F. CAL). Pint, Golden amber. (W-375). (3) (#1007) $40

2884A Similar, with (NO2) on shoulder. (Variant B.) (3) (#2375) $35

2885 Cylindrical. (AFRICAN STOMACH BITTERS). Quart. Amber. (W-2885). (3) (#120) $15

2885A Same, with (SPRUANCE STANLEY & CO). (Variant B.) (3) (#1744) $20

2885V Same, with (SPRUANCE STANLEY & CO) on reverse. (Variant A.) (3) (#2214) $25

2886 Cylindrical. (DAMIANA BITTERS) (BAJA CALIFORNIA). ¾ quart. Aqua. (W-103). (3) (#566) $15

2886A Same. Aqua, with (LEWIS HESS MANUF'R). (3) (#1774) $25

Front and reverse views of three heavily embossed bitters bottles.

2887 Rectangular. (FAITH WHITCOMB'S A-GENCY) (BOSTON, MASS U S A) (FAITH WHITCOMB'S BITTERS). ½-pint. Aqua. (W-362). (3) (#1904) $20

2887V Similar, with paper label only. (5) (#1710) $20

2888 Rectangular. (ATWOOD'S) (VEGETABLE DYSPEPTIC) (BITTERS). ½ pint. Aqua. (W-19). (3) (#2183) $100

2889 Oval. Paper label. Picture of invalid on bed. "This Will Cure You" "Vegetable Cathartic Bitters" "F.D. Hamilton, Middlefield, Mass." 6 oz. Aqua. (W-L 22). (5) (#936) $5

2890 Rectangular, flat. Paper label. On one side (DR. BULL'S MEDICINE BOTTLE) On label "Dr. Bull's Stomach Bitters" (W-L 22). (5) (#504) $7.50

2891 12-sided. (ATWOOD'S JAUNDICE BITTERS MOSES ATWOOD GEORGETOWN
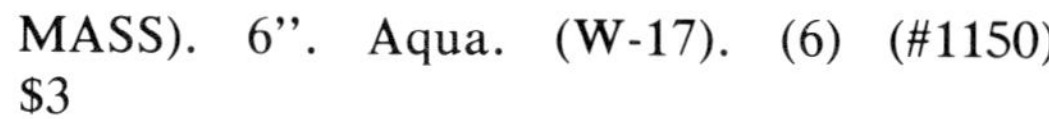
MASS). 6". Aqua. (W-17). (6) (#1150) $3

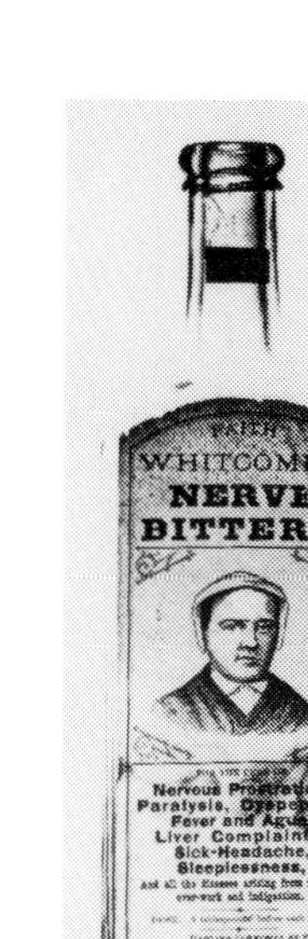


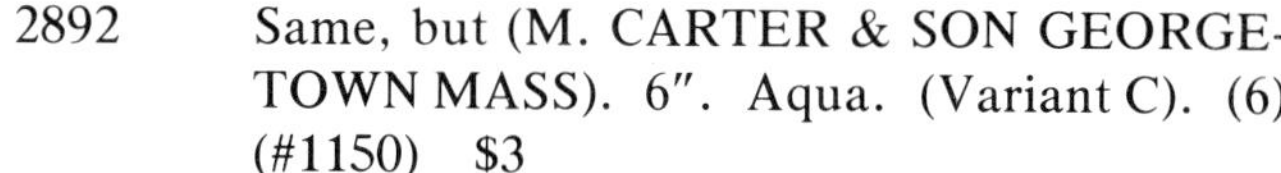
**Nerve medicine made by Harvard (Massachusetts) Community of Shakers. (2887).**

2892 Same, but (M. CARTER & SON GEORGETOWN MASS). 6". Aqua. (Variant C). (6) (#1150) $3

2893 Square, beveled corners. (ROCKY MOUNTAIN) (TONIC BITTERS) (1840 TRY ME 1870). ¾ quart. Amber. (W-281). (2) (#599) $75

2894 Rectangular, beveled corners. (DR. BALL'S VEGETABLE STOMACHIC BITTERS NORTHBORO MASS). Pint. Aqua. (W-25). (3) (#2806) $100

2895 Rectangular. (JOHN ROOT'S BITTERS 1834 BUFFALO 1834). ¾ quart. Dark amber. (W-284). (3) (#215) $175

2896 Flat flask shape with rib on edge. Paper label only. "Hill's Mountain Bitters Indiana Specialty Co. Indianapolis, IND." ½ pint. Amber. (W-L 62). (5) (#600) $25

2898 Cylindrical, decanter type. Engraved in wreath (ST JACOBS BITTERS). Quart. Clear. (2) (#168) $50
Square. (Saint Jacob's Bitters). Amber. ¾ quart. W-453. (#2232) $20

2899 Round, handled jug. Paper label only. "Old Jamaica Stomach Bitters." ¾ quart. Amber. (W-L 72). (4) (#1519) $25

2900 Globular, like grenade. Flat panels on 2 sides. Marked (HERKULES BITTER) (1 QUART CA). Quart. Vivid green. (W-166). (3) (#1965) $1,050

**Globular-shaped bottle is unusual for bitters. (2900).**

2901 Square. (JACKSON'S STONEWALL BITTERS QUINLAN BROS & CO ST. LOUIS MO). Covered with stone wall design on 3 sides. ¾ quart. Amber. (W-189). (2) (#2789) $1,400

2902 Square, beveled corners. (POLO CLUB STOMACH BITTERS TRADE MARK F&M). ¾ quart. Amber. (W-260). (3) (#342) $30

2903 Similar to #2883 but marked (LANDSBERGS CENTURY BITTERS A HELLER & BRO, NEW YORK). ¾ quart. Amber. (W-205). (3) (#551) $750

2904 Rectangular, beveled corners. (CLARKE'S SHERRY WINE BITTERS ROCKLAND ME). ¾ quart. Aqua. (W-99, Variant E.) (3) (#694) $25

2905 Square, beveled corners. (WAIT'S KIDNEY AND LIVER BITTERS). Reverse (CALIFORNIA'S OWN TRUE LAXATIVE AND BLOOD PURIFIER). ¾ quart. Amber. (W-350). (4) (#1246) $50

2906 Square, beveled corners. (PERUVIAN BITTERS) in arch above sunken panel. Reverse (H&K) in shield. ¾ quart. Amber. (W-254 Variant.) (4) (#742) $25

2906V Same, with PBCO) on shield. (4) (#2408) $25

2907 Square, beveled corners. On 2 sides (WAMPOO BITTERS) (BLUM SIEGEL & BRO NEW YORK). ¾ quart. Amber. (W-354, Variant A.) (3) (#664) $50

2908 Square. (BROWN'S IRON BITTERS) (BROWN CHEMICAL CO). On base (X). Pint. Amber. (W-399). (4) (#2086) $30

2909 Cylindrical. (LASH'S BITTERS CO SAN FRANCISCO CALIF). Quart. Amber. (6) (See 2909V)

2909A Square. (LASH'S LIVER BITTERS). Reverse (NATURES TONIC LAXATIVE). On base (3). ¾ quart. Amber. (W-209). (6) (#2470) $50

2909V Square. (LASH'S BITTERS). Paper label and contents intact. On base (3). Reverse (NATURES TONIC LAXATIVE). ¾ quart. Dark amber. (5) (#1360) (#1694) (#1760) Sold in lot for $30

2910 Cylindrical. (LASH'S BITTERS CO N.Y. CHICAGO S.F.) Label for "Homers Ginger & Brandy." Quart. Amber. (6) (See 2909V)

2911 Rectangular, beveled corners. (ENGLISH FEMALE BITTERS) (DROMGOOLE) (LOUISVILLE KY). Pint. Clear. (W-116). (4) (#2296) $90

2912 Rectangular, beveled corners. (ATWOOD'S QUININE TONIC BITTERS). Original label. ¾ quart. Aqua. (W-18). (4) (#502) $20

2913 Rectangular. (BURDOCK BLOOD BITTERS) (FOSTER MILBURN & CO) (BUFFALO N.Y.). ½ pint. Aqua. (5) (#1966) $6
Similar. Clear. Machine mouth. Labels. (#2280) $6

2914 Cylindrical, bulging neck. Paper label only. "Imperial Boonkamp Bitters." ¾ quart. Amber. (4) (#1392) $20

2914A Similar, different label. Red amber. (4) (#470) $30

2914V Similar, but different label. (4) (#1392) $20

2915 Square. (J.T. HIGBY) (TONIC BITTERS) (MILFORD CT). ¾ quart. Amber. (W-331). (4) (#392) $35

2916 Cylindrical. (DR. HENLEY'S WILD GRAPE ROOT IXL BITTERS). Quart. Aqua. (W-164). (3) (#1502) $55

2916V Similar, different mold. Light blue. (#2056) $80

2917 Oval. (HARTSHORN'S JAUNDICE BITTERS NO 42). Pint. Aqua. (W-L 59). (5) (#1952) $10

2918 Square, beveled corners. Paper label only "Skandinavian Tonic Bitters Campello, Mass." ¾ quart. Amber. (W-L 118). (5) (#552) $55

2919 Rectangular, beveled corners. (OLD DR SOLOMON'S) (GREAT INDIAN BITTERS). ½ pint. Aqua. (W-311). (3) (#806) $45

2919V Rectangular. Mark similar but (INDIAN WINE BITTERS). ½ pint. Aqua. (W-312). (3) (#2326) $55

2920 Oval. (DR. COPP'S WHITE MOUNTAIN BITTERS) over (JC) above (JCOPP & CO MANCHESTER N.H.). On base (W.T. & CO). Pint. Aqua. (W-98). (3) (#1440) $30

2921 Square, rope corners. Very elaborate decorations. (PROFESSOR GEO. J. BYRNE NEW YORK) (THE GREAT UNIVERSAL COMPOUND STOMACH BITTERS) (PATENTED 1870) (U S A) (DC) (CC) (LK) (XM). ¾ quart. Amber. (W-63). (3) (#1741) $750

2921V Same, clear. (3) (#133) $510

2922 Cylindrical, bulging neck. (ZINGARI BITTERS) (F. RAHTHER). ¾ quart. Amber. (W-377). (3) (#1565) $140

2923 Rectangular, rounded corners. (DR. HARTER'S WILD CHERRY BITTERS ST. LOUIS). On base (DESIGN 24 PATENTED). ¾ quart. Amber. (W-158). (4) (#2120) $5

2923V Trial size, 4″ x 2¼″ x 1¼″, with label. (Variant 8). Amber. (5) (#2392) $40
Pint. Aqua, oval. Same as 2923, no base marks. W-157. (#1262) $310

2924 Square, beveled corners. (CLIMAX BITTERS) (SAN FRANCISCO CAL). ¾ quart. Amber. (W-89). (4) (#1775) $70

2925 Cylindrical. Shield marked. (MK) below (CALIFORNIA WINE BITTERS M. KELLER LOS ANGELES). Quart. Olive green. (W-68). (3) (#1120) $700

2926 Square, beveled corners. (MARSHALL'S BITTERS) (THE BEST LAXATIVE AND BLOOD PURIFIER). ¾ quart. Amber. (W-227). (4) (#200) $30

2927 Square, beveled corners. (MALARION BITTERS) (SNYDER GUE & CONDELL) (ST LOUIS MO). On base (Mc Co). ¾ quart. Amber. (W-223). (3) (#2295) $25

2928 Rectangular. (PERUVIAN TONIC) (BITTERS). Crosses on corners. Original labels. ¾ quart. Amber. (W-255). (3) (#1151) $60

2929 Square, beveled corners. (Dr. HUNTINGTON'S GOLDEN TONIC BITTERS) PORTLAND MAINE). ¾ quart. Amber. (W-182). (3) (#407) $80

2933 Rectangular, widely beveled corners. (DR. MANLY HARDY'S) (GENUINE) (JAUNDICE BITTERS) (BANGOR ME). Pint. Aqua. (W-155). (4) (#1711) $85

2935 Rectangular, beveled corners. (DR. BISHOP'S WAHOO BITTERS) (WAHOO BITTERS CO) (NEW HAVEN CONN). ¾ quart. Amber. (W-43). (3) (#2215) $290

2937 Square, beveled corners. (GERMAN BALSAM BITTERS W.M. WATSON & CO SOLE AGENTS FOR U.S.A.). ¾ quart. Milk glass. (W-129) (3) (#423) $300

2938 Square, beveled corners. (KENNEDY'S EAST INDIA BITTERS) (ILER & CO, OMAHA NEB). ¾ quart. Clear. (W-200). (4) (#856) $15

2939 Rectangular, beveled corners. (HUTCHING'S DYSPEPSIA BITTERS NEW YORK). Pint. Aqua. (W-184). (3) (#2231) $55

2940 Cylindrical. On shoulder (LEWIS' RED JACKET BITTERS). On base (NEW HAVEN, CONN). ¾ quart. Amber. (W-213). (3) (#1072) $30

2941 Square. On shoulders (GERMAN HOP BITTERS 1872). On side (READING MICH). ¾ quart. Amber. (W-130). (3) (#1824) $40

2942 Rectangular. (GOLDEN BITTERS) (GEO C. HUBBELL & CO). ¾ quart. Aqua. (W-138). (3) (#951) $180

2943 Rectangular. (SWILL STOMACH BITTERS) (THE ZOELLER MEDICINE CO PITTSBURGH, PA). ¾ quart. Amber. (W-329). (3) (#1295) $70

2944 Barrel. (ORIGINAL POCOHONTAS BITTERS). ¾ quart. Clear. (W-259). (2) (#2293) $1,400

2945 Rectangular. (A.M.S. 2 1864 CONSTITUTION BITTERS SEWARD & BENTLEY BUFFALO, N.Y.) ¾ quart. Olive green. (W-95). (3) (#1901) $650

2946 Square. (THE GLOBE TONIC BITTERS). ¾ quart. Amber. (W-134). (4) (#663) $30

2947 Round, form of lighthouse. (PANACEA BITTERS SOLFRANK'S FRANK HAYMAN & RHINE NEW YORK). ¾ quart. Dark amber. (W-310). (3) (#309) $500

2948 Round. Lighthouse. (SEAWORTH BITTERS CO CAPE MAY, N.J. USA). ¾ quart. Amber. (W-299). (1) (#1661) $2,450

2949 Square. (1880 W.R. TYREE'S CHAMOMILE BITTERS). Pint. Amber. (W-338). (3) (#2119) $120

2950 Square, beveled corners. Roof like cabin, grapes and vines on corners. (STEINFELD'S FRENCH COGNAC BITTERS) (FIRST

PRIZE PARIS EXHIBITION 1867). ¾ quart. Amber. (W-317). (3) (#1695) $900

Lighthouse is appropriate shape for "Seaworth Bitters." (2948).

Indian queen. Marked (MOHAWK WHISKEY PURE RYE) (PATENTED FEB 11 1868). ¾ quart. Amber. (1) (Not a bitters bottle) (#2601) $850

2953 Square, beveled corners. (COCAMOKE) (COCAMOKE BITTERS CO, HARTFORD, CONN). ¾ quart. Amber. (W-90). (3) (#1616) $65

2954 Rectangular, beveled corners. (LIPPMAN'S GREAT GERMAN BITTERS SAVANNAH GEORGIA). ¾ quart. Amber. (W-215). (3) (#903) $150

2956 Square. (REGISTERED IN U.S. PATENT OFFICE) (U.S. GOLD BITTERS) (U.S. GOLD) and (U.S. 1877). ¾ quart. Aqua. (W-340). (3) (#2389) $325

2957 Globular with long neck. (EAGLE ANGOSTURA BARK BITTERS EAGLE LIQUEUR DISTILLERIES). On base (PATENT FEB 4 1902). (W-11). (4) (#245) $55

2957V Similar, but paper label marked "Eagle Aromatic Bitters." On shoulder (EAGLE LIQUOR DISTILLERIES). ½ pint. Amber. (W-L 46) (6) (#2262) $50

2958 12 vertical panels. (DR. BOYCE'S TONIC BITTERS). Pint. Aqua. (W-53). (5) (#358) $10

Similar. Unembossed. Label. Sample, aqua. (W-620). (#2854) $20

2961 Rectangular, beveled corners. (E. R. CLARKE'S SARSAPARILLA BITTERS SHARON MASS). ½ pint. Aqua. (W-86). (3) (#2407) $260

2962 Square. (HAVIS' IRON BITTERS) (THE WILLIAMSBURG DRUG CO WILLIAMSBURG, KY). ¾ quart. Amber. (W-160). (3) (#294) $45

2963 Square, rounded corners. (POND'S BITTERS) (AN UNEXCELLED LAXATIVE). Original labels. ¾ quart. Amber. (W-261). (4) (#1694) $10

2964 Square. (LOWELL'S) (INVIGORATING BITTERS) (BOSTON, MASS). Pint. Aqua. (W-221). (3) (#1118) $75

2966 Flask-shaped. Flat rib. (BEGG'S DANDELION BITTERS). ½ pint. Amber. (W-30). (4) (#6) $30

2967 Square. (JOHNSON'S CALISAYA BITTERS BURLINGTON VT). ¾ quart. Amber. (W-194). (3) (#1344) $70

2968 Cylindrical. Panels on base and neck. (MOULTON'S OLOROSO BITTERS TRADE (Pineapple) (MARK). ¾ quart. Aqua. (W-233). (3) (#1517) $90

2971 Decanter type. Engraved (STOUGHTON) in wreath. ½ pint. Clear. (4)

2972 Square. (GREER'S ECLIPSE BITTERS). Pint. Amber. (W-147). (3) (#1822) $35

2973 Square. (FERRO QUINA STOMACH BITTERS BLOOD MAKER DOGLIANA ITSLIA D.P. ROSSI 1400 DUPONT STR S.F. SOLE AGENT USA AND CANADA). Quart. Amber. (W-123). (4) (#711) $40

2974 Square. (DR. F. WOODBRIDGE) (HEADACHE) (BITTERS). ¾ quart. Dark amber. (W-161). (3) (#488) $130

2975 Oval. (WILLARD'S GOLDEN SEAL BITTERS). ½ pint. Aqua. (W-367). (3) (#2264) $30

Same (#902) $8.75

2976 Cylindrical, bulging neck. (SCHROEDER'S BITTERS LOUISVILLE KY). On base (KYGWC). ¾ quart. Brown amber. (W-297). (3) (#389) $225

2977 Square. Paper label only. "HVS Asparagus Bitters Channell & Co Sacramento, Cal." On a Hostetter's bottle. ¾ quart. Amber. (W-L 68). (4) (#1552) $25

2978 Square. (BERLINER MAGEN BITTERS CO). ¾ quart. Amber. (W-39). (4) (#790) $25

2979 Oval. Paper label only. "Dr. Charles Sweet's Celebrated Restorative Wine Bitters Lebanon Conn." ½ pint. Aqua. (W-L 127). (4) (#422) $12

**Elongated, bulbous-necked bottle. (2976).**

**Paper label remains intact on "H.V.S. Asparagus Bitters." (2977).**

2980 Square. Flags and cannon balls on corners. Cannons on 3 sides, tent and flag on 1. Crossed swords and cannons on roof. ¾ quart. Dark amber. (3) (#2501) $525

2981 Rectangular, rounded corners. Paper label only, "C.K. Wilson's Original Compound Wa-Hoo Bitters." 11½ oz. Clear. (W-L 147). (5) (#1102) $6.25

2982 Square. Tapering like a gin bottle. (HART-WIG KNTOROWICZ) (POSENHAMBURG GERMANY). Paper label marked "Lithuanian Bitters." ¾ quart. Milk glass. (W-216V). (3) (#2568) $100

2983 Square. Tapering like gin bottle. Paper label, "Danziger Magenbitter Rheinstrom Bros. Cincinnati, O. Sole Agents." On back (R.B.). ¾ quart. Milk glass. (W-L 39). (3) (#263) $100

2984 Square. CARMELITER BITTERS) (FOR ALL KIDNEY & LIVER COMPLAINTS). Reverse (CARMELITER) (FRANK R. LEONORL & CO PROPRIETORS) (NEW YORK). ¾ quart. Amber. (W-71). (3) (#622) $15
Similar. ¾ quart. Olive green. (W-71 Variant A.) (#2791) $65

2985 Square. (C.P. SWAIN'S). Reverse (BOUR-BON BITTERS). ¾ quart. Amber. (W-326). (3) (#1806) $65

2986 Rectangular. (GOFF'S BITTERS). Label intact. 4 oz. Clear. (W-137). (6) (#2280) $6

2987 Rectangular. (POOR MAN'S FAMILY BIT-TERS). Paper label intact. ½ pint. Aqua. (W-262). (4) (#2342) $30

2988 Shape of cannon. (GENL SCOTTS NEW YORK ARTILLERY BITTERS). Height: 12½". Amber. Ground lip. (W-298). (1) (#1261) $11,000

2989 Cylindrical. On shoulder (ORRURO BIT-TERS). ¾ quart. Olive green. (W-248). (4) (#1406) $10

**Cannon-shaped bottle for "Genl. Scott's Artillery Bitters." Other bottle is for "Travellers Bitters." Both of these figurals are rare.**

2990 Cylindrical. On shoulder (DR. J.G.B. SEIGERT). On base (ANGOSTURA BITTERS 4). ½ pint. Green. (5) (#1760) $5

2991 Square. (DR. WALKINSHAW'S CURATIVE BITTERS BATAVIA N.Y.). Pint. Amber. (W-352). (3) (#1998) $145

**Group of three bitters bottles. Bottle on right is in shape of drum and cannon balls.**

2992 Cylindrical. (CHAS A. BAKER DRUGGIST). On paper label "Whipples Stomatic Bitters or Bitterized Cider." Pint. Aqua. (W-L 145). (4) (#952) $3

2993 Rectangular. Paper label only "Billings Mandrake Tonic Bitters." On base (214). 8 oz. Aqua. (W-L 14). (5) (#710) $15

2994 Rectangular. Paper label only "Tuft's Tonic Bitters." Pint. Aqua. (W-L 133). (5) (#936) $5

2995 Cylindrical, like small beer bottle. On shoulder (CARONI). On base (CARONI BITTERS) (4). (W-72). (5) (#2134) $5

2995A Miniature. Olive amber. (6) (#2792) $10

2995V Same. Olive green. (Variant.) (6) (#2790) $5

2996 Unusual shape, expanded around middle. (HART'S STAR BITTERS). Skeleton star enclosing (1868) and (O B L P C) (PHILADELPHIA) below. ¾ quart. Clear. (W-156). (3) (#1951) $250

2997 Square. (DR. GOODINS COMP GENTIAN BITTERS). 5 ribs on 2 sides. ¾ quart. Aqua. (W-135). (3) (#2167) $260

2998 Rectangular. (JONE'S INDIAN SPECIFIC) (HERB BITTERS). Above figure of Indian (S.W. JONES PROPRIETOR PHILADA). (PATENT 1863). ¾ quart. Amber. (W-196). (4) (#2728) $75

2999 Rectangular. (CAPITOL BITTERS) (DR. M.M. FENNER'S) (FREEDONIA N.Y.). (W-122). (4) (#1808) $30

3000 Cylindrical, bulging neck. On shoulder (CANTON * BITTERS). ¾ quart. Amber. (W-69). (3) (#2551) $250

3001 Rectangular, widely beveled corners. On edges (COLLETON) (BITTERS). 6 oz. Aqua. (W-91). (3) (#151) $110

3002 Hexagonal, depressed panels. (WHEELER'S) (BERLIN) (BITTERS) (BALTIMORE). Quart. Brilliant olive green. (W-361). (3) (#805) $4,000

3003 Square. (STEKETEE'S BLOOD PURIFYING BITTERS). Label intact. ½ pint. Amber. (W-318). (3) (#2808) $50

3004 Cylindrical, with long bulging neck. On base monogram (JFT). Paper label "Bonekamp Maagen Bitters." (W-L 17). (4) (#1472) $30

3005 Square, beveled corners. (DEMUTH'S) (STOMACH BITTERS) (PHILADA). ¾ quart. Amber. (W-106). (3) (#2727) $40

3006 Shape of drum, shoulders covered with cannon balls. Marked (MCKEEVER'S ARMY BITTERS). ¾ quart. Amber. (W-228). (1) (#741) $1,500

3007 Square, barrels on corners. (HARVEY'S) (PRAIRIE) (BITTERS). Shoulders in form of globe. On shoulder (PATENTED). ¾ quart. Amber. (W-159). (2) (#1357) $1,100

3008 Oval. Paper label only. "Dr. Kaufmann's Sulphur Bitters." Pint. Aqua. (W-L 77). (4) (#950) $25

3309 Square. (CATAWBA WINE BITTERS). Bunches of grapes on 2 sides. ¾ quart. Amber. (W-408). (3) (#855) $420

3310 Square. (CARMELITER STOMACH BITTERS CO NEW YORK). On base (WB). Reverse: Monogram (JS) over (REGISTERED). ¾ quart. Olive green. (W-71, Variant A.) (4)

3311 Oval. (OSWEGO BITTERS *25c*). ½ pint. (W-477). (3) (#2758) $75

3311V Same. Paper label only. (5) (#24) $30

3312 Rectangular. (DR. MARCUS' UNIVERSAL BITTERS PHILADA). Pint. Aqua. (W-465). (3) (#1439) $150

3313 Rectangular. (LYMAN'S DANDELION BITTERS) (C. SWEET & BRO. BANGOR ME). ¾ quart. Aqua. (W-460). (3) (#70) $20

3314 Rectangular. (DR. M.C. AYER RESTORATIVE BITTERS, BOSTON, MASS). Pint. Aqua. (W-460) (3) (#406) $25

3315 Rectangular. (N.K. BROWN IRON & QUININE BITTERS BURLINGTON VT). Height: 7¼". Aqua. (4) (#246) $45

3316 Triangular. (O.K. PLANTATION PATENTED 1869) ¾ quart. Amber. (2) (#2005) $1,800

3317 Square. Paper label on an Hostetter's bottle. "Star Kidney and Liver Bitters." ¾ quart. Amber. (W-L 123). (4) (#1950) $15

3318 Oval. (DR. WILSON'S HERBINE BITTERS THE BRALEY DRUG CO ST JOHNS N.B. LIMITED). Height: 6". Aqua. (W-368). (W-368). (4) (#2182) $10

3318V Same, with paper label intact. (4) (#2166) $15

3319 Round. (GREEN MOUNTAIN CIDER BITTERS). Original label. Quart. Aqua. (W-146). (2) (#1056) $40

3320 Square. Roof like Drakes. Rope corners. (THE BEST BITTERS IN AMERICA B. DESENBERG & CO KALAMAZOO MICH). (W-40). (1) (#2663) $1,500

3321 Square. (WEBB'S IMPROVED STOMACH BITTERS) (C.E. WEBB & BRO JACKSON, MICH). ¾ quart. Amber. (W-358). (3) (#1758) $45

3322 Rectangular, 2" mouth. (GENUINE BULL WILD CHERRY BITTERS). ¾ quart. Clear. (W-59). (2) (#1358) $30

3323 Square. (ST. GOTTHARD HERB BITTERS METTE & KANNE PROS ST LOUIS MO). ¾ quart. Amber. (W-141). (2) (#1488) $20

3324 Cylindrical. Paper label only "Sonny Medicinal Stomach Bitters Sonny Bitters Co Chicago Ill." ¾ quart. Amber. (W-L 119). (4) (#1470) $5

3325 Square. (HIGHLAND STOMACH BITTERS SCOTCH TONIC MEMPHIS TENN MANSFIELDS NEW STYLE). On base (A&DHC). ¾ quart. Amber. (W-464). (3)

3326 Square. (LIPPMAN'S GREAT GERMAN BITTERS NEW YORK AND SAVANNAH GEO. ¾ quart. Amber. (W-215, Variant.) (3) (#1342) $60

3327 Cylindrical. On shoulder (S.S. ABBOTT & CO BALTIMORE). On base (ABBOTTS BITTERS). ½ pint. Dark amber. (W-1). (4) (#2134) $5

3328 Cylindrical. On base (MALT BITTERS COMPANY BOSTON U.S.A.). ¾ quart. Deep green. (W-224). (4) (#2072) $20

3329 Square. (W. RITTMIER'S CALIFORNIA WINE BITTERS). On base (T.W. & CO). ¾ quart. Amber. (W-492). (3) (#2054) $50

3330 Square. (ISHAM'S STOMACH BITTERS). ¾ quart. Amber. (W-452). (3) (#1487) $35

3331 Oval. (CLARKE'S COMPOUND MANDRAKE BITTERS) ½ pint. Aqua. (W-85). (3)

3332 Square. (O'LEARY'S 20TH CENTURY BITTERS). ¾ quart. Amber. (W-245). (3) (#1696) $45

3333 Rectangular. (CLARK'S GIANT BITTERS PHILADA PA). Original label. Height: 6¾". Aqua. (W-412). (4) (#72) $20

3334 Rectangular. (C. GATES & CO) (LIFE OF MAN) (BITTERS). ½ pint. Aqua. (W-214). (3) (#1166) $25

3335 Oval. (COMPOUND HEPATICA) (HFS) (BITTERS) (PREPARED BY H.F. SHAW MT VERNON ME). Pint. Aqua. (W-416). (3) (#390) $35

3336 Rectangular. (DR. PORTER NEW YORK). Label reads "Zadock Porter Medicated Stomach Bitters. Hall & Bruckel Manufacturers." Height: 7 5/8". Aqua. (W-L 101). (4) (#2280) $6

3337 Cylindrical. (N. WOOD SOLE PROPRIETOR) (ATWOODS GENUINE BITTERS). Label intact. Height: 6 ¾". Aqua. (W-15). (4) (#1966) $6

3338 Cylindrical. Paper label only "Bourbon Whiskey Bitters." Columbia and shield. ½ pint. Dense olive green. (W-L 19). (6) (#1519) $25

3339 Square. (SUNNY CASTLE STOMACH BITTERS JOS. DUDENHOEFER MILWAUKEE). ¾ quart. Amber. (W-325) (3) (#2055) $20

3340 Rectangular. On edges (OLD CONTINENTAL) (BITTERS). ¾ quart. Amber. (W-240). (3) (#295) $150

3341 Rectangular. Paper label only "Dr. Burnhams Timber Bitters." Pint. Amber. (5) (#710) $15

3342 Oval. Paper label only. "American Stomach Bitters." Pint. Clear. (5) (#1102) $6.25

3343 Square. (BROPHY'S BITTERS) (TRADE MARK) around star. Height: 7½". Clear. (W-397). (4) (#2230) $25

3344 Rectangular. (DR. CARSON'S STOMACH BITTERS). Height: 7½". Deep aqua. (W-74). (3) (#840) $223

3345 Typical gin shape. (GEO. P. CLAPP SOLE PROPRIETOR) (BOSTON MASS) (EAST INDIA ROOT BITTERS) (ESTABLISHED 1858). Height: 9½". Brilliant amber. (2) (#712) $95

3346 Rectangular. (EDWARDS BITTERS PREPARED BY STEVENS & CO) (73 MERRIMAC ST BOSTON). Height: 8½". Aqua. Heavy glass. (2) (#23) $280

3347 Gin shape. (GENTIANA ROOT AND HERB BITTERS) (SETH E. CLAPP & CO SOLE PROPRIETORS) (BOSTON MASS). Height; 9 7/8". Deep Aqua. (1) (#1999) $55

3348 Rectangular. (JOHNSON'S) (INDIAN) (DYSPEPTIC) (BITTERS). Height: 6½". Aqua. (W-195). (3) (#1055) $120

3349 Cylindrical. (RAMSEY'S TRINIDAD BITTERS). Height: 8½". Green. (W-268). (3) (#2454) $25

3350 Square. (WONSER'S BITTERS) (U.S.A.). ¾ quart. Blue green. (W-519). (3) (#1103) $80

3351 Square. (CALIFORNIA FIG BITTERS) (CALIFORNIA EXTRACT OF FIG CO SAN FRANCISCO, CAL). On base (3138). ¾ quart. Amber. (W-66). (3) #1776) $35

3352 Square. (CALIFORNIA FIG & HERB BITTERS) (CALIFORNIA FIG PRODUCTS CO SAN FRANCISCO CAL). On base (313H). ¾ quart. Amber. (W-67). (3) (#262) $35

3353 Rectangular. (MACK'S SARSAPARILLA BITTERS) (MACK & CO PROP'RS SAN FRANCISCO) ¾ quart. Amber. (W-462). (2) (#247) $80

3354 Rectangular. (DR. MOWE'S) (VEGETABLE BITTERS) (LOWELL MASS). Quart. Aqua. (W-235). (2) (#1807) $110

3355 Oval. (JOHN A. PERRY DR. WARREN'S BILIOUS BITTERS BOSTON MASS). Height: 6½". Aqua. (W-513). (3) (#454) $10

3355V Similar. (Variant B.) (4) (#472) $25

3356 Cylindrical. Paper label only. "Windsor Pale Orange Bitters Hanley-Hoye Co Providence R.I." ¾ quart. Aqua. (4) (#1470) $5

3357 Square, rope corners. (RUSSIAN) (IMPERIAL) (TONIC BITTERS). ¾ quart. Aqua. (W-450). (1) (#2550) $525

**Square bottle with roped corners was used for "Russian Imperial Tonic Bitters." (3357).**

3358 Cylindrical. (BYRNE & CASTREE). On base (SALUTARIS BITTERS). Pint. Puce. Tooled collar. (W-292). (1) (#2213) $410

3359 Square. Paper label only. "Spring Bitters." ¾ quart. Amber. (5) (#150) $50

3360 Rectangular. (DR. W.B. BANCROFT) (MARSHFIELD VT) (BANCROFT BITTERS). Pint. Aqua. (W-387). (3) (#2184) $40

3361 Rectangular. (ATWOOD'S) (VEGETABLE JAUNDICE BITTERS) (GEORGETOWN MA). Height: 6½". Aqua. (W-20). (3) (#1343) $55

3362 Cylindrical. (BELL'S COCKTAIL BITTERS JAS M. BELL & CO NEW YORK). Pint. Light amber. (W-32). (2) (#1069) $350

3363 Gin shape. (LOHNGRIN BITTERS ADOLF MARCUS VON BUTON GERMANY). ¾ quart. Milk glass. (W-218). (2) (#2373) $120

3364 Rectangular. (OLD DR. GOODHUE'S ROOT & HERB BITTERS) (J.H. RUSSELL & CO) (Salem Mass). ½ pint. Aqua. (W-437). (3) (#214) $25

3365 Square. (VERMO STOMACH BITTERS) (TONIC AND APPETIZER). ¾ quart. Clear. (W-342). (4) (#1968) $8

3366 Oval. Paper label only. "Native Celebrated American Tonic Bitters." ½ pint. Aqua. (5) (W-L 90). (#950) $25

3367 Oval. Paper label only. "McNeill's Indian Vegetable Bitters." Height: 6¾". Aqua. (W-L 204). (5) (#902) $8.75

3368 Cylindrical. (H.H. HAY SON-LF) (ATWOOD LF) (ATWOODS IMPROVED PHYSICAL BILIOUS JAUNDICE BITTERS). Label intact. Height: 6¾". (6) (#952) $3

3369 Cylindrical. (TO-NI-TA TRADE MARK LORENTZ MED CO). Paper label reads "D'Artigan To Ni Ta Bitters." ¾ quart. Amber. (5) (#744) $10

3370 Rectangular. Paper label only. "Dr. Kraft's Celebrated Aromatic Herb Bitters." ¾ quart. Amber. (5) (#1568) $32.50

3371 Cylindrical. On base (LEIPZINGER BURGUNDER WEIN BITTERS THE HOCHSTADER CO). Quart. Green. (W-212). (4) (#1054) $60

3372 Square. (HENTZ'S) (CURATIVE BITTERS) (PHILADELPHIA). ¾ quart. Clear. (W-165). (5) (#1486) $5

3373 Rectangular. (COLE BROS VEGETABLE BITTERS) (C.L. COLE PROP'P.) (BINGHAMPTON N.Y.). Height: 8". Aqua. (W-413). (4) (#2102) $10

3374 Cylindrical. Pottery. (HANSARD'S SWANSEA AND LLANELLY GENUINE HOP BITTERS). Pint. Two-tone brown. (5) (#2071) $100

3375 Rectangular. (WOODCOCK PEPSIN BITTERS). ¾ quart. Amber. (W-374). (3) (#2088) $20

3376 Rectangular. Label only. "Todd's Bitters Athens Ga." ½ pint. Aqua. Threaded mouth. (6) (#866) $10

3377 Rectangular. Paper label only. "Nobles Hop & Buchu." ½ pint. Aqua. (6) (#1710) $20

3378 Square. (DR. SIMS' ANTI-CONSTIPATION BITTERS). ¾ quart. Clear deep amber. (3) (#310) $45

3379 Cylindrical. Paper label. "Tomato, Sarsaparilla, Blackberry, etc." Marked (S.D. DUNBAR TAUNTON MASS). Pint. Aqua. Pour spout. (4) (#1871) $160

3380 Oval. (DR. BEARD'S ALTERNATIVE TONIC & LAXATIVE BITTERS NATICK MASS). Pint. Aqua. Flanged Mouth. (3) (#598) $25

3381 Square. (DR. L.C. BERTRAM'S LONG LIFE AROMATIC STOMACH BITTERS). ¾ quart. Amber. (2) (#2760) $220

3382 Square. (J.W. COLTON'S NERVINE STRENGTHENING BITTERS). On base (W.T. & CO). Pint. Amber. (4) (#1296) $35

3383 Rectangular, tapering from shoulder to base. (DIDIER'S) (BITTERS). Height: 7¾". Amber. (3) (#1742) $110

3384 Oval. (WHEELER'S GENUINE BITTERS). ¾ quart. Aqua. (4) (#1024) $45

3385 Square. (ARABIAN BITTERS) (LAWRENCE & WEICHSELBAUM SAVANNAH GA). ¾ quart. Amber. (4) (#838) $60

3386 Rectangular. Paper label "Indian Root Bitters put up by Kimball, White & Co Chicago, Ill. Price $1.00." Height: 8½". Deep aqua. (6) (#1710) $20

**Group of bitters bottles, all were given names or labels that denoted products were made by Indians.**

3387 Oval, with flat rib. Label. "Emerson's Excelsior Botanic Bitters, Prepared and sold by E. H. Burnes Augusta Maine. Price 50 cents." Height: 8½". Clear. (6) (#504) $7.50

3388 Cylindrical. (DR. HIBBARD'S WILD CHERRY BITTERS C.N. CRITTENTON PROPRIETOR N.Y.). ½ pint. Aqua. Height: 6¾". (5) (#1968) $8

3388V Same. Height: 8¼". (3) (#312) $50

3389 Rectangular. (WAKEFIELD'S STRENGTHENING BITTERS). Height: 7 7/8". Aqua. (4) (#22) $15

3390 Square. (E.J. ROSE'S MAGADOR BITTERS FOR KIDNEY STOMACH & LIVER) (SUPERIOR TONIC, CATHARTIC AND BLOOD PURIFIER). ¾ quart. Amber. (3) (#2087) $65

3391 Round. Sides paneled. (WOODBURY'S BITTERS). On base (STEINHARDT & CO N.Y.) Height: 8½". Brilliant amber. (W-373). (3) (#216) $40

3391V Round. Similar to above only (S BITTERS) on shoulder. (WOODBURY) omitted. Same embossment on base. Amber. (4) (#2216) $25

3392 Square. Label: "Traudt's Alternative Bitters Manufactured by Francis J. Traudt, Ph. B. St Louis Mo." On a Hostetter's bottle. ¾ quart. Amber. (5) (#1950) $15

3393 Oval. (DR. LYFORD'S BITTERS C. P. HERRICK TILTON N.H.). On base (W.T. & CO). Height: 8½". Aqua. (W-222). (4) (#344) $20

3394 Rectangular. On base (DR. STEWART'S TONIC BITTERS COLUMBUS O). Label intact. ¾ quart. Amber. (W-500A). (3) (#1568) $32.50

3395 Square. (ROSE HILL) (STOMACH BITTERS) (H.M. MOSHER & CO NEW YORK). ¾ quart. Amber. (1) (#1216) $120

3396 Rectangular. (CHEW'S LAXATIVE BITTERS BARNEGAT, N.J.). Height: 7". Amber. (3) (#646) $85

3397 Cylindrical. Ribbing on shoulder. (BOYER'S STOMACH BITTERS) (CINCINNATI). ¾ quart. Clear. (3) (#1312) $30

3399 Triangular. (HI-HI BITTERS) (HI-HI BITTERS CO ROCK ISLAND ILL). ¼ quart. Amber. (W-167). (2) (#1839) $110

3399V Same, but (SANITARIUM BITTERS) added. Yellow green. (3) (#1390) $60

5200 Square, tapering from shoulder to base. Label only. "Capuziner Stomach Bitters." Quart. Dark amber. (3) (#1245) $260

5201 Square. (CARPATIAN HERB BITTERS) (HOLLANDER DRUG CO BRADDOCK PA). On base (RG&BCO 98). ¾ quart. Amber. (4) (#1008) $30

5202 Rectangular. Sloping shoulders. (DR TOMPKINS' VEGETABLE BITTERS). ¾ quart. Blue green. (W-504). (4) (#2135) $65

5203 Cylindrical with bulging neck. (KAISER WILHELM) (BITTERS CO) (SANDUSKY, O). Quart. Dark amber. (W-197). (3) (#904) $80

**Uniquely shaped bottle for "Capuziner Stomach Bitters" has all original labels. (5200).**

5204 Square. Paper label only. "Dr. Parola's Hungarian Bitters A.J. Perry." ¾ quart. Amber. (5) (#1662) $25

5205 Round. Paper label only. "American Deobstructent Bitters." ½ pint. Aqua. (6) (#952) $3

5206 Flask. Paper label only. "B&L Invigorating Bitters." ½ pint. Aqua. (6) (#886) $10

5207 Same. Quart. Aqua. (5)

5208 Oval. (EDWARD'S O.F. NIMS APOTHECARY BITTERS). Height: 7½". Aqua. (4) (#2406) $25

5209 Cylindrical lady's leg. (WALKER'S COCKTAIL BITTERS). Height: 11". Deep amber. (2) (#565) $325

5210 12-sided. (BARBER'S) (INDIAN VEGETABLE) (JAUNDICE BITTERS) (OLIVER JOHNSON & CO) (PROVIDENCE R.I.). Height: 6". Aqua. (W-26). (3) (#616) $100

5211 Rectangular. (DR. SPERRY'S) (FEMALE STRENGTHENING BITTERS) (WATERBURY C). Label intact. ¾ quart. Aqua. (3) (#1471) $55

5212 Square. (DR. W.L. WILBUR'S) (AROMATIC BITTERS) (FREEDONIA N.Y.). Label intact. ¾ quart. Amber. (W-365). (3) (#1438) $55

5213 Square. Paper label only. "Donnell's Indian Root Stomach Bitters." ¾ quart. Amber. (W-L 44). (4) (#1552) $25

5215 Square. (German Hop Bitters) (Dr. C.D. Warner Reading, Mich) (Warner) at top on two sides. ¾ quart. Amber. (W-355). (#2325) $140

# Chapter Thirty-Five

# "Go-Withs"

Although they were uncataloged, the most fascinating objects in the Charles B. Gardner collection of bottles are the materials he gathered over the years that reflected the history of glassmaking in America. His illustrations of the nineteenth century glassworks were unique and gave one a clear picture of how and where nineteenth century American glass bottles and other glass products were made. Some of these engravings appear on old billheads and stationery of the glass firms and the written record gives us an idea of how the glass business was conducted in the early days.

Advertising handbills for the glass firms are also revealing in that they tell us of the enormous variety of products some of the firms produced. An advertisement for the glassware manufactory at Stoddard, New Hampshire offers "demi johns, flasks, wine bottles, soda bottles, mineral water bottles, ale bottles, ink and blacking bottles, bay water bottles, cologne and hair oil bottles, bottles for patent medicine 'and all other kinds of bottles &c., &c.'." All were offered in black, green and amber.

Stock certificates of early glasshouses are also fascinating and the artistic scrip issued instead of hard cash to pay workers in the glasshouses are indicative of the manner in which nineteenth century industrialists paid their workers. The scrip was used in factory-owned stores and the workers paid rent to landlords who were also their employers. The scrip was printed in all denominations and all business within the glassmaking communities was conducted with this paper money.

Of great historical interest is a photograph of the employees of the Dyottville Glass Works. The photo was taken in 1869 and shows the workers lined up with some of their tools. The man who is obviously the master glassblower of the firm is holding his blowpipe and he is seated prominently in the front center of the group.

Other less unique, but more decorative, "go-withs" are the many temperance pictures that Charley collected over the years. Some of these are Currier and Ives color lithographs that were especially popular during the nineteenth century. An early Currier print, made before the famous lithographer went into partnership, illustrates the "Drunkard's Progress" from "A Glass With a Friend" to the inevitable "Death and Suicide." Another fascinating temperance picture has a tree being choked by a serpent marked "Alcohol" and the sickly tree bears such bitter fruit as "A bloated countenance," "Idiocy" and "Beggary." A pair of prints illustrate the handsomeness of the daughters and sons of temperance.

Although the Gardner collection did not include every known example of American bottle made before the invention of the automatic bottle machine at the beginning of this century, there were few categories that were missing. He did have many individual beer and soda bottles, but these were never entered in the catalog. There can be little argument that it would be almost impossible for a bottle collector starting out today to gather under one roof such a valuable and diversified collection of bottles. That Charles B. Gardner always wanted to share his knowledge and enthusiasm with as many collectors as possible has been the inspiration for the publication of this book.

**View of American Flint Glass Works, South Boston, from the harbor.**

**George W. Kearns & Co. Glass Works, Zanesville, Ohio.**

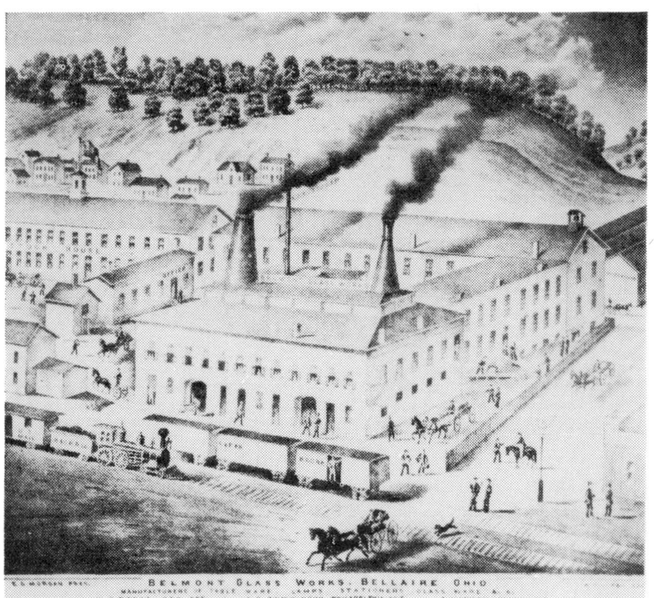


Belmont Glass Works, Bellaire, Ohio.

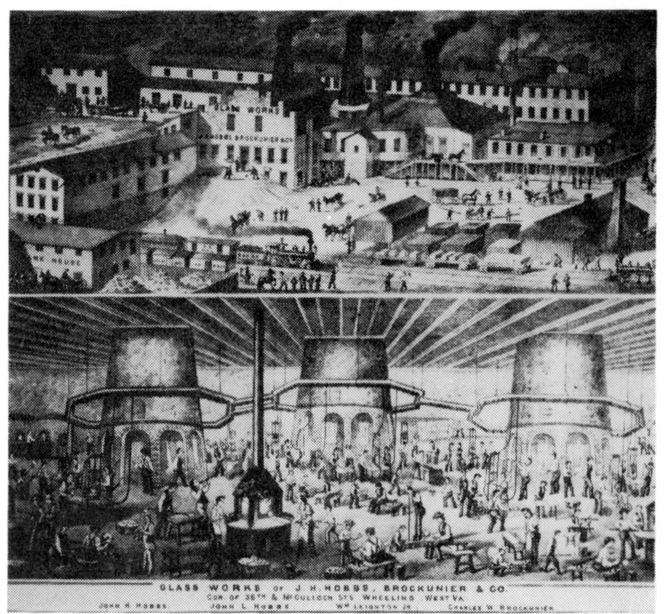


Engraving of glassworks in Wheeling, West Virginia.

Interior and exterior views of Illinois Glass Company.

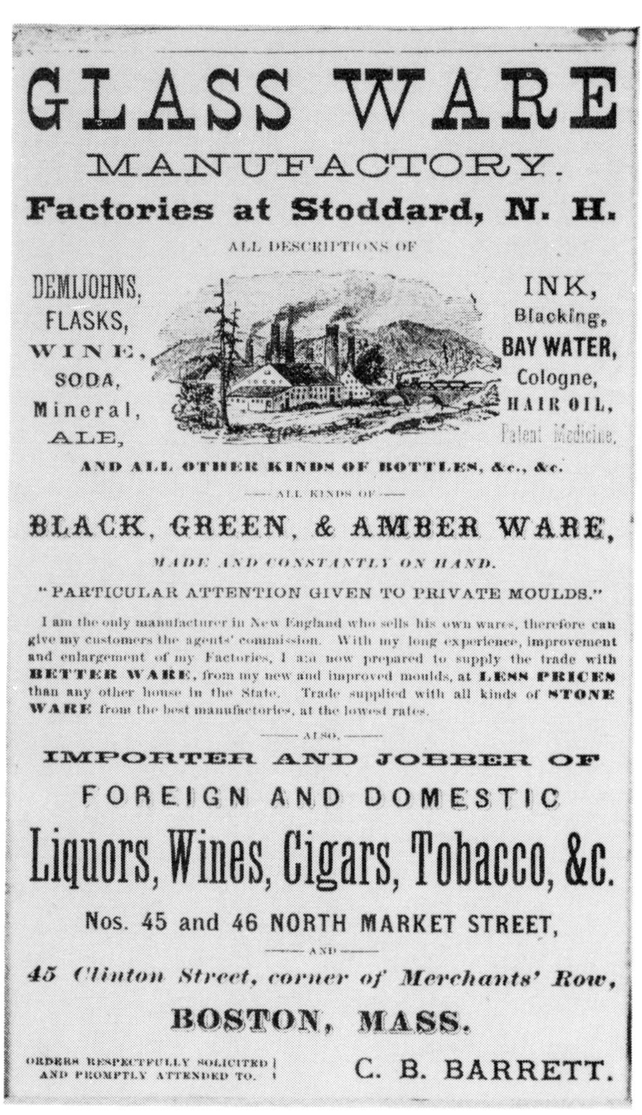


Advertisement for glassware made at Stoddard, New Hampshire.

Glass company in Oswego County, New York.

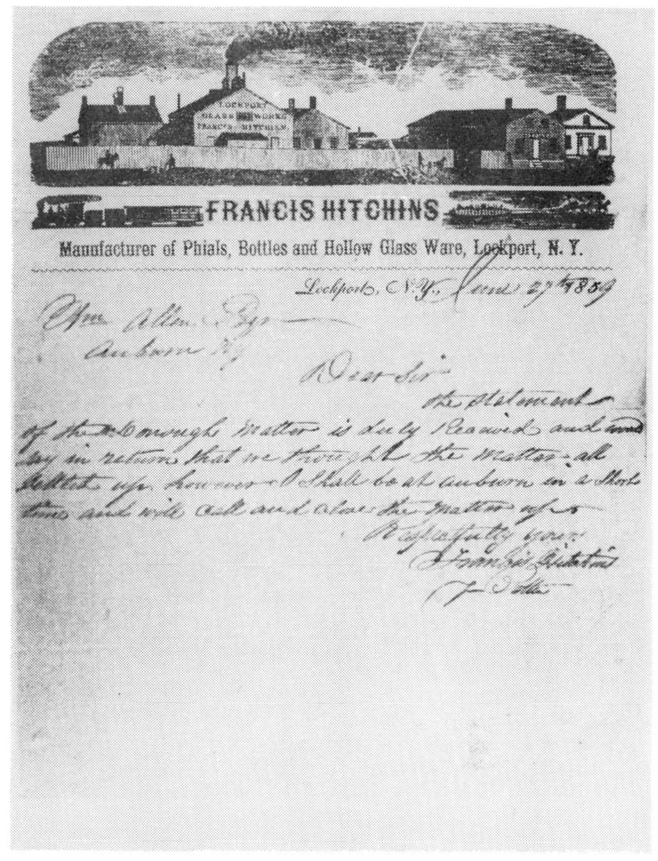
FRANCIS HITCHINS

Manufacturer of Phials, Bottles and Hollow Glass Ware, Lockport, N. Y.

Lockport, N.Y. June 27th 1859

Wm Allen Esqr
Auburn N.Y.

Dear Sir

the statement of the ... matter is duly Received and ... say in return that we thought the matter all settled up however I shall be at auburn in a short time and will call and close the matter up

Respectfully yours
Francis Hitchins

Letterhead for Lockport, New York, glassworks. Dated 1859.

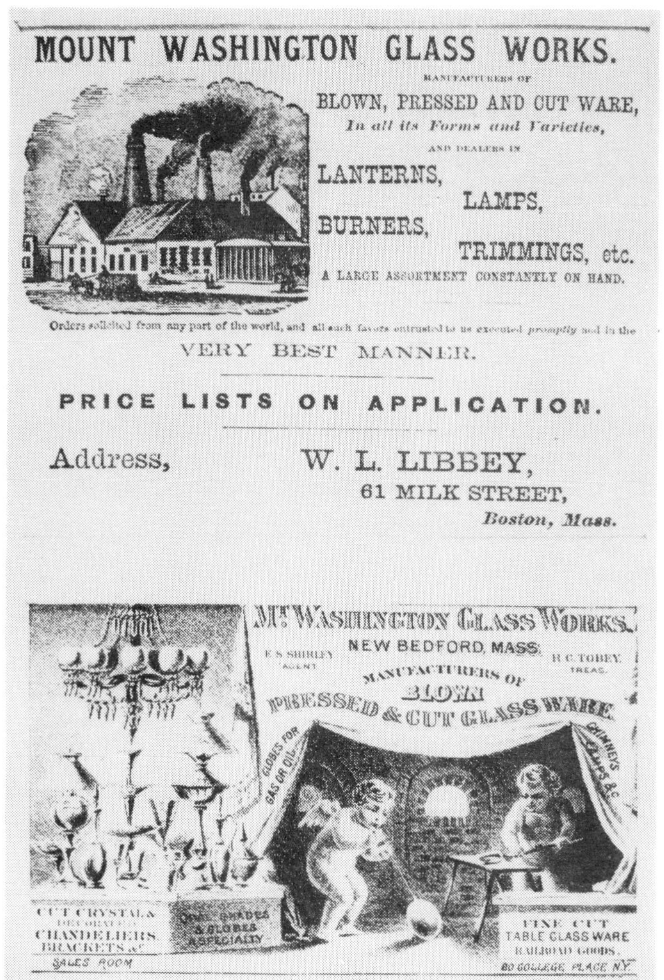


Advertisement for Mount Washington Glass Works of New Bedford, Massachusetts.

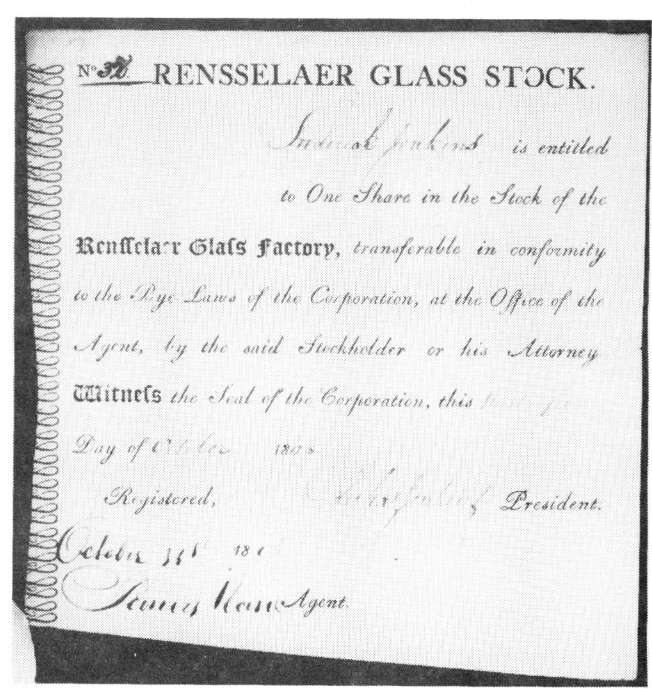
No 30 RENSSELAER GLASS STOCK.

... is entitled to One Share in the Stock of the Rensselaer Glass Factory, transferable in conformity to the Bye Laws of the Corporation, at the Office of the Agent, by the said Stockholder or his Attorney.

Witness the Seal of the Corporation, this ... Day of October 1808

Registered, ... President.

October ... 180...

... Agent.

Share of stock issued in 1808 for Van Rensselaer Glass Factory.

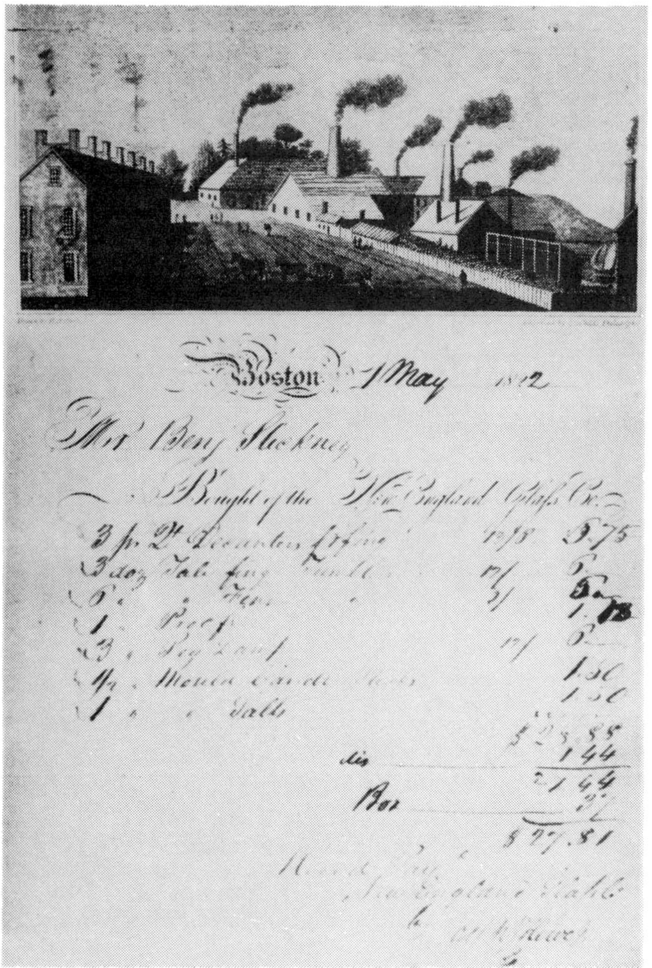
Boston 1 May 1822

Billhead for New England Glass Company, dated 1822.

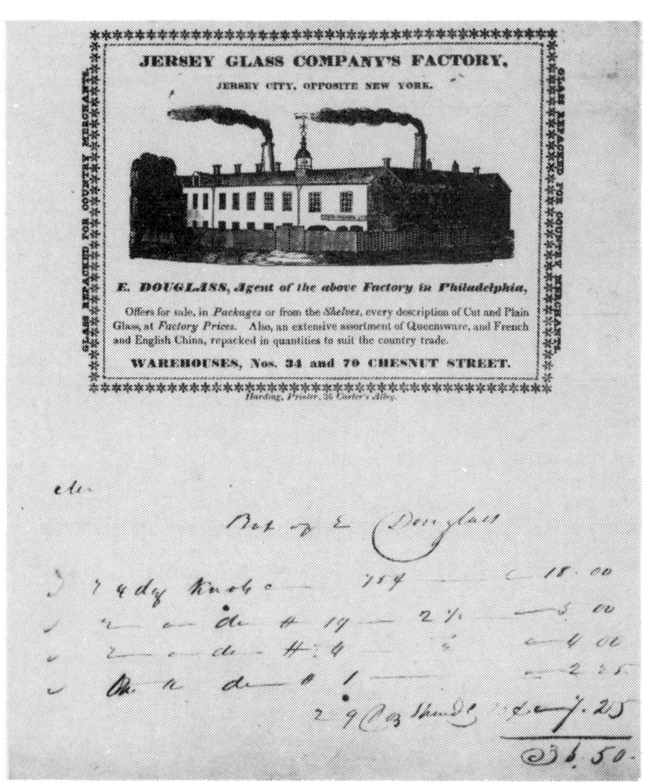
JERSEY GLASS COMPANY'S FACTORY,

JERSEY CITY, OPPOSITE NEW YORK.

GLASS REPACKED FOR COUNTRY MERCHANTS.

E. DOUGLASS, *Agent of the above Factory in Philadelphia,*

Offers for sale, in *Packages* or from the *Shelves*, every description of Cut and Plain Glass, at *Factory Prices*. Also, an extensive assortment of Queensware, and French and English China, repacked in quantities to suit the country trade.

WAREHOUSES, Nos. 34 and 70 CHESNUT STREET.

*Harding, Printer, 36 Carter's Alley.*

Billhead for Jersey Glass Company has view of factory.

Scrip for workers of Kensington Glass Works is signed by T. W. Dyott, owner. Dated 1837.

Photograph, dated December 4th, 1869, shows employees of the Dyotville Glass Works, Philadelphia.

Salary scrip used by Vermont Glass Factory. Dated 1814.

N. Currier lithograph, "The Drunkard's Progress."

Currier and Ives lithograph of "De Lime Kiln Club" is temperance item.

Temperance lithograph illustrates the evils of drink.

Lithograph, "Daughters of Temperance."

Lithograph, "Sons of Temperance."

Advertising poster for nineteenth century bitters.

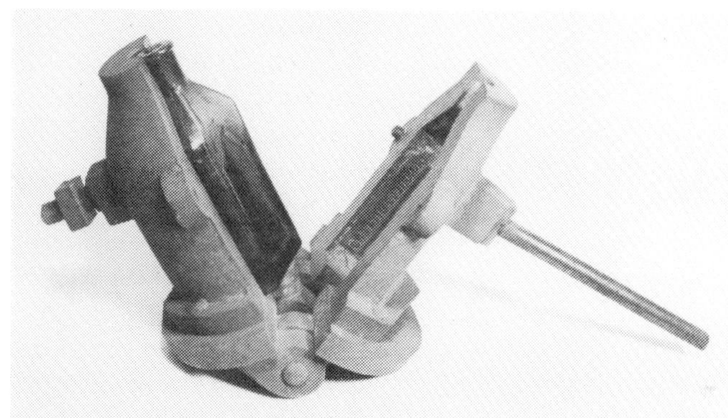

Two-part iron mold from Gardner collection exhibits how bitters and other bottles were made in second half of nineteenth century.

# Postscript: The Auction

During the first half of the 1970s, as Charles Gardner entered the ninth decade of his life, he began to explore the possibility of keeping his collection intact and on public display after his death. He wanted to arrange for this while he was still able to advise any museum that might be interested in purchasing the collection of its history and value. Certainly, there were few people in the country who had the expertise and knowledge of glassmaking history that he did. Although he felt he was not in a position to donate the collection to an institution, he was willing to sell it at a price far below its market value in order that it be kept together as a memorial.

Charley's first desire was that the collection, if kept intact, should remain in New England and most especially, in his home state of Connecticut. The collection was particularly strong in bottles from that state and the Connecticut bottles represented the early social and economic history of Connecticut. The Gardners knew it would be impossible for a similar collection to be gathered in the future.

Unfortunately, there were no takers. The museums that were interested had neither the funds nor the expertise to catalog and house the collection. Those museum directors and curators who understood the great value of the collection were unable to convince less knowledgeable boards of directors or trustees of the importance and value of the collection. To many, old bottles were not works of art and certainly not a purchase to consider at a time when many local museums and historical societies were having great difficulty making ends meet.

In 1973 a large Midwestern glass firm became interested in purchasing the collection. They had borrowed several bottles from the Gardner collection to use as models for new molds from which they made limited quantities of reproductions as collectors' items for the Bicentennial. The tentative plans were for the Gardner collection to be purchased and kept intact until such time as a new corporate building would be erected which would include the "Charles B. Gardner Museum of American Glass Bottles." There, the collection would be cataloged and displayed to the public in perpetuity.

Representatives from the firm were sent to arrange for a preliminary and, later, a final appraisal and it appeared that the purchase would be completed. All that remained was for the company's board of directors to approve the purchase which would have included the Gardner library of books on American glass and glassmaking as well as all of the valuable adjunctive material having to do with the history of American glassmaking. After many months of discussion and negotiations, the board of directors decided not to go ahead with the project. When the Gardners received word that the museum was not to become a reality, Charley called his friend, auctioneer and appraiser Robert W. Skinner of Bolton, Massachusetts, and told him that he had decided to put his entire collection up for public auction.

Word of the impending auction spread rapidly throughout the bottle-collecting world. Many collectors who had been trying to purchase certain bottles from Charley for years begged him to let them buy the bottles they coveted before the auction, but all offers were refused in order to give every collector an opportunity to bid. This seemed the only fair thing to do and the Gardners stood firm once the decision had been made.

The auction of American bottles in the Charles Gardner collection is now history. Over 3,000 bottles were sold in two three-day sessions. The first session was held on September 25, 26 and 27, 1975. Admission price was $100, a sum which could be applied to purchases, although as it turned out, less affluent collectors had a difficult time finding desirable bottles at that price and either faced the loss of the admission or spent much more than that sum. Even with the stiff admission price both sessions of the auction were heavily attended with collectors from all sections of this country and several from England.

The cobalt blue "Columbia" flask with Columbia faced to the left and with 13 stars and an eagle embossed, pontilled and with minor mouth flasks, established the high price record at the first session. It sold for $21,000. The Connecticut "Cornucopia" flask, pontilled and with an oversized mouth, brought $17,000 at the first session and a sapphire blue Cabin Bitters, embossed "Old Homestead Wild Cherry Bitters" sold for $16,500. "Genl Scotts New York Artillery Bitters" sold for $11,000. A Sunburst flask with Maltese cross in the center on both sides, corrugated edges, pint, sheared mouth and pontilled base sold for $9,900. Other prices were correspondingly high and, at 3 p.m. on Saturday afternoon of the first session, the auctioneer announced that the sale had reached the $500,000 mark. At this point it was clear that the Gardner collection would bring well over $1,000,000.

The second session of the auction was held on November 20, 21 and 22 and it was obvious from the attendance that the impetus had not been lost. As in the first session, three auctioneers alternated every 50 lots and momentum continued, never to be interrupted, until the afternoon of the last day when the audience, almost hypnotized after watching one glass gem after another being placed on the spotlighted showcase, saw that the runner had put up a recently emptied contemporary beer bottle. The comic relief was welcomed by an audience which had invested enormous energy, emotions and funds in six days of constant bidding. At 11:45 that morning the auctioneer had announced that a winning bid of $440 for a Pikes Peak Flask had pushed total sales over the $1,000,000 mark and collectors applauded themselves, the Gardners and the auctioneers.

Many record prices were set at the second session with the highest price ever paid for an American bottle at $26,500 for the embossed Jared Spencer flask with reverse reading "Manchester Con." The aqua pint Andrew Jackson flask with a reverse embossment of a Masonic arch and fleur-de-lis brought $25,000. An "American Systems" flask with "Use Me But Do Not Abuse Me" embossed, sold for $10,000. "Old Dr. Townsend's Celebrated Stomach Bitters," quart, light amber, with sheared mouth sold for $3,200 and an "Indian Queen Mohawk Whiskey Pure Rye" on shield, with patent date Feb 11, 1868, yellow amber, rolled mouth, smooth base, sold for $850. Most bottles, no matter in what category, brought comparably high prices.

Throughout the two three-day sessions, Charles Gardner sat in the front row of the audience and recorded bidding prices in his catalog. Before and after each session he autographed copies of the catalog and renewed acquaintances with old friends and collectors, many of whom had traveled across the country to attend both sessions. Some bottle collectors' clubs had sent representatives with instructions to bid on certain bottles and most collectors seemed to have come with no illusions that anything in the Gardner collection could have been purchased at bargain prices. Most bidders knew what bottles they wanted well before the auction, had inspected all bottles carefully before they bid and were prepared to pay high prices for what they wanted. They knew that any bottle in the collection, barring any mishap in the display room, would be exactly as represented in the catalog and that any bottle tagged "from the Charles B. Gardner collection" would probably have increased value in the future.

The lavish party held in honor of the Gardners immediately following the sale of the final lot was a suitable ending to a long career of the study, collecting and promoting of the hobby of American glass bottles. The Gardners appeared to have no regrets that half a lifetime spent in the pursuit of the finest examples of glass bottles was over. The Gardner bottle room had already been converted to a comfortable bed-sitting room and the valuable library and "go-withs" had been sold intact. The many collectors who for years had wanted certain bottles from the Gardner collection in order to help complete their own specialized collections and who had been able to afford the prices were happy that they had had the opportunity to purchase what they had wanted. What had been lost, the opportunity for one of the finest and most complete collections of American glass bottles to be kept intact for future collectors, scholars and historians to look at and study, was no longer mentioned.